Style Meister™

The Quick-Reference Custom Style Guide

by Lana R. Castle

Style Meister™: The Quick-Reference Custom Style Guide

Portions of this book have appeared previously under the author's byline in the *Austin Writer, OfficePRO,* and *The Secretary.*

Castle, Lana R.

Style Meister: The Quick-Reference Custom Style Guide

ISBN 0-9662926-1-8

Printed and bound in the United States of America. First edition.
First printing, March 1998.
Second printing, December 1998.

Library of Congress Catalog Number: 98-159723

Contact the publisher for information about the electronic version of *Style Meister™,* with interactive forms for multiple platforms.

Address all inquiries to:
Castle Communications, P.O. Box 200255-358,
Austin, Texas 78720, Fax: 512/346-0690
E-mail: lc@castlecommunications.com
Web: www.castlecommunications.com

Contents

3 But I Thought . . . ?: Common Problems & Outdated Rules

STYLE & MECHANICS

4 Does This Require a Comma?: Punctuation

5 *I Before E Except After C*?: Spelling

6 Should I Hyphenate *Anal Retentive*?: Compound Words & Word Division

7 The Ups & Downs of It All: Capitalization

8 S.O.S.!: Abbreviations, Acronyms & Initialisms

9 $E = mc^2$: Numbers, Signs & Symbols

STYLE & USAGE

10   PC, or Not PC?: Bias-Free Language & Word Preference

11   This, That & the Other: Special Cases, Odds & Ends

STYLE & FORMAT

12   Points & Picas: The Basics of Physical Format

13   Production Pointers: Specifying Type & Desktop Publishing

STYLE & TECHNOLOGY

14 Put That Computer to Work!: Automating Style Preferences

Appendix: Customizing Tools

Annotated Bibliography

Glossary

Index

Preface

Why Another Style Book?

This book is about publication style. It makes little sense to talk about style without defining its meaning, for the term means different things to different people. Some writers equate style with literary or personal flair, which this book addresses only to a limited degree. Other writers equate style with grammar—the system of rules that governs the structure of a language. But, on the whole, grammar has more permanency than style. This book includes minimal grammar information—just enough to help you find your way around.

Webster's Ninth New Collegiate Dictionary defines style as "a convention with respect to spelling, punctuation, capitalization, and typographic arrangement and display followed in writing or printing." Webster's definition comes closer to my own, which encompasses both editorial and physical formatting conventions. I must emphasize this word, *conventions*, for publication style involves a multitude of widely accepted—but often conflicting—conventions. That's where confusion and indecision come from.

Now let me tell you where I'm coming from. . . .

Why I Wrote This Book

This book evolved out of my personal frustrations. The concept began to surface when I was working at a desktop publishing bureau. Our company served a large variety of clients: high-tech firms, retail stores, colleges, government agencies, nonprofits—all with different style preferences. Like many people, I mistakenly believed that the English language involves absolute "rights" and "wrongs" (though what those rights and wrongs were wasn't always clear). I'd placed my faith in a few well-known authorities, but I soon learned the inadequacy of a "one-size-fits-all" approach to publication style. It simply didn't meet our clients' needs. Everyone had their own style preferences. Exceptions popped up in every project. How could we ever keep on top of such diversity?

We needed tools for identifying preferences, recording decisions, and communicating standards. We needed tools to help us locate answers at a glance. We needed tools to help us organize production information: page layouts, type specifications, and special formats. And, because style tends to change—even during the life of a single project—we also needed tools we could update easily.

After moving on to other jobs, I learned just how prevalent such needs are. Every new organization, new client, and new project required a new approach. The most effective communications were therefore customized.

These experiences guided the direction of this book. While you should find *Style Meister* informative, even entertaining, you'll gain the greatest benefit through active application—using the forms in this book and applying its information time and time again.

THE Answer

Most people I've encountered view style the way I used to—as an either/or proposition. They want THE answer to whatever question they currently confront. They seek a rule they can apply to any situation, any time. They want an authority to back up their decisions. They want certainty where *certainty rarely exists.*

It's time we trotted the truth out of the closet: What's "right" is simply a matter of style. Period! Often, the most honest answer to a style question is, *It depends.* Exceptions can emerge for any rule because what's "right" depends on the situation—especially in this age of global communications and accelerated change. The truth is, THE answer varies with the audience, market, medium, organization, publication, product, personal taste, and the writer's intent. It also varies from country to country. Besides all that, style simply changes over time, adapting as our language changes. Just like the rest of life, publication style is a work in progress.

The Reality

Many style guides prescribe one option over another—not because that option is inherently "right," but because most style guides are written for *very specific markets*. Often, such guides don't acknowledge that, in other situations, a different guideline may be preferable. The following books are but a few examples of popular style guides tailored for specific needs:

- *Associated Press Stylebook and Libel Manual* and *United Press International Stylebook*—for print and broadcast media

- *Chicago Manual of Style* and *Words into Type*—for books

- GPO's *Manual of Style*—for government agencies

- *MLA Handbook*—for academic research

- *The Microsoft Manual of Style* and *Wired Style*—for high tech

- *Publication Manual of the American Psychological Association*—for scholarly journals

The rules in these books and similar style guides are not universal. The style that works for book publishers often counters that used for magazines and newspapers. Large organizations often scorn styles that work for smaller firms. U.S. style often differs from British. So, using one style guide for every situation rarely does the trick.

You may work in more than one medium. Or, you may use a primary style guide but need to make occasional exceptions. *Style Meister* fills the void that such needs present. This book—

- Helps writers write successfully for different audiences,

- Helps editors deal with subtle differences between projects or publishers,

- Helps production people manage physical formatting issues and individual preferences, and

- Helps office personnel deal with all of the above.

How This Book Is Organized

Style Meister provides a foundation to help you develop custom style guides. The first chapter introduces some customizing concepts that will help you make solid style decisions.

The heart of the book consists of five major sections:

1. Style & Grammar (Chapters 2–3)

2. Style & Mechanics (Chapters 4–9)

3. Style & Usage (Chapters 10–11)

4. Style & Format (Chapters 12–13)

5. Style & Technology (Chapter 14, Appendix)

An annotated bibliography, a glossary, and an index follow these major sections.

Acknowledgments

Few books are one-person productions. I owe a tremendous debt to so many people for their support and assistance in bringing *Style Meister* to fruition.

First, I must express my deepest appreciation to four colleagues who are the best editors I know: Jill Mason, Rebecca Sankey, Maria Veres Homic, and Dyanne Fry Cortez. Their meticulous attention to detail—as well as that of my able assistant, Pam Renwick—has added immeasurably to this book.

For their undying support and unlimited patience, I thank both past and present members of the Old Quarry Study Group for reviewing multiple drafts: Diane Barnet, Judy Woodard, Dayna Finet, Janis Russell, Jean Bonnen, Mark Juditz, Marge Harrington, Fred Fredman, Ana McDonald, Gretel Baacke, Sylvia James, Sivagami Natesan, and Susan Meredith.

I'm grateful to Suzanne Pustejovsky and Jan Adams for their input on the design of the "innards" of the book, and to David Mider and Joan Rivers for their roles in implementing the cover.

I'm also indebted to many teachers, mentors, and publishing professionals for their generous advice: Shirley Crook, Bill Korbus, Tom and Marilyn Ross, Dan Poynter, Michael Morgan, Ray Bard, Evelyn Palfrey, Gina Maria Jerome, Ed Tittel, Noreen Garrison, Donn LeVie, Pamela LaRocque, Linda Gail Christie, Larry Brill, Ray Bronk, Dana Lovvorn, Pat Saunders, Dottie Wood, and the helpful folks at Adobe and Morgan Printing.

I cannot overlook the contributions of my students and the readers of my columns. Their questions and insights have also shaped this book. I'm grateful for the support of Carmen Keltner and Judy Barrett, editors of the *Austin Writer*; and of Angela

Hickman Brady, Susan Fitzgerald, and Debra Stratton, the editors and publisher of *OfficePRO* and *The Secretary.*

My employers and clients also made invaluable contributions, particularly Carol Martin, Kristy Sprott, and Debra Schorn of the electronic publishing group at Holt, Rinehart, Winston, Oscar Mink of The University of Texas at Austin and The Mink Group, and Lori Brix of Silent Partners.

I cannot overlook the value added by the members and staff of three marvelous organizations: the Austin Writers' League—especially Angela Smith and Sally Baker—the Society for Technical Communication, and the First Tuesday networking group sponsored by Association for Women in Communications.

Last, but by no means least, I'm grateful to my entire family for their long-standing love and sacrifice. In particular, I'm deeply indebted to Ralph, Tom, and Joy Gohring for constantly cheering me on. I could never have completed this project without their steadfast support.

Dedication

I dedicate this book to—

- my mother, Carol Castle, who sparked my initial interest in reading and writing,

- my father, Carl Castle, who instilled my burning desire to communicate effectively, and

- my uncle, Emery Castle, who in 1960 helped me prepare my very first submission to a publisher.

1

A Matter of Style

An Overview

READ THIS CHAPTER CAREFULLY! I can't overstress its importance. It describes *Style Meister*'s unique approach to publication style and helps you apply it successfully. This chapter explains how to use the quick-reference charts in Chapters 2–11 and the customizing forms in the appendix. It also suggests a process and format for creating custom style guides.

Why You Need a Style Guide

Let me first clarify that this book addresses publication style, not literary style. *Literary style* is the unique way in which a writer conveys a message. *Publication style,* which includes editorial style and physical format, can enhance literary style but not replace it.

Style guides exist to help people produce consistent, effective communications—in whatever form they take. Such guides offer standards for abbreviation, capitalization, hyphenation, punctuation, and spelling. They also suggest ways to treat lists, numbers, tables, footnotes, and references.

Some style guides describe standards for physical style (page layouts and type specifications). Others concentrate purely on contents and mechanics.

In any case, regular use of a good style guide can simplify the writing process, streamline production, and improve the quality of your work.

How to Use This Book

Unlike most style guides, which serve the needs of very specific markets, this book shuns the prescriptive approach. Instead, it presents widely accepted—yet often conflicting—standards and steers you toward those options that best fit your situation. This approach makes *you* the authority. If a guideline doesn't feel right for your situation, feel free to ignore it. Few guidelines fit everyone's needs every time.

Style Meister's flexibility allows you to create your own custom style guides. You may create a single guide to use with all of your communications, or multiple guides tailored to individual clients, markets, products, or publications.

Style Meister favors flexible guidelines over rigid rules, and graphic presentations and quick-reference charts over lengthy explanations. To help you make informed decisions, it discusses considerations that underlie style conventions.

Now let's explore the quick-reference charts.

Style Meister's Quick-Reference Charts

A glance at the quick-reference charts for Chapters 2–11 will reveal that, for many style questions, two or more different standards may apply. The quick-reference charts illustrate such style guidelines in graphic form.

The layout of these charts varies from chapter to chapter. Instructions for using the charts therefore precede each set. All of the quick-reference charts read essentially from left to right. Figure 1 shows a sample segment from a Chapter 4 chart on punctuation. The text after the figure explains its contents.

END	Mark	Example	✔
Items in a **series**, when each requires special **emphasis** • Some writers capitalize the words right after each question mark.	**?** *question mark*	Do you write novels? Short stories? Poetry? [INITIAL CAPS]	___
• Others leave them lowercase.		Do you write novels? short stories? poetry? [LOWERCASE]	___

Figure 1 - Sample Quick-Reference Chart Segment

The left-hand columns of the charts list style guidelines, organized alphabetically by categories, subcategories, and/or bold key words. Left-hand columns may also contain cautions, exceptions, and notes. In addition, they sometimes refer you to usage notes, which appear at the ends of chapters.

The columns to the right usually contain examples that illustrate each guideline. Sometimes these columns include bracketed text that clarifies information or identifies common standards.

Columns with a checkmark (✔) contain "write-on lines," on which you can record the options you prefer or rank your preferences by number. (Use *1* for your first preference, *2* for the next, and so on.)

Thin gray lines set off related information and multiple style options, such as "Up Style" versus "down style" capitalization. (Up Style favors capitalized words where down style favors lowercase.) Thick black lines set off individual guidelines.

Once you become familiar with the layout of these charts and determine which options you prefer, you will find them quite useful. If you prefer to edit on hard copy (paper), the appendix includes reproducible forms on which you can record additional guidelines. If you prefer to edit on a computer, this chapter explains how to create and maintain a simple electronic style guide.

Style Meister's Customizing Forms

In addition to the quick-reference charts, *Style Meister* provides a number of reproducible forms you can use to record and manage style decisions:

- Word List/Style Sheet

- Search-and-Replace Form

- Format Specifications Chart

This chapter introduces all three and discusses the Word List/ Style Sheet form in depth. Chapters 12 and 13 provide more information about the Format Specifications Chart. Chapter 14 explains the Search-and-Replace Form.

The Word List/Style Sheet. You can use one or more Word List/ Style Sheet forms to record preexisting conventions for a specific project or organization, as editors have done on similar forms for years. Or, you can use the forms as a framework to create a new style guide.

The two-page form includes six lettered boxes (A-B-C-D and so on) for recording specific words, including their capitalization, hyphenation, and spelling. For instance, in the I-J-K-L box of Figure 2, the term *Johari Window* is included both for the spelling of Johari and the capitalization of Window.

I-J-K-L	p.s.	pg.
Johari Window	*n*	*44*
Kanter, Rosabeth M.		*4*
Kübler-Ross, Elizabeth		*82*
Ladder of Inference	*n*	*44*
Linking Pin Model	*n*	*18*
linking pin [theory]	*m*	*18*
long term	*n*	
long-term	*m*	

Figure 2 - Sample Lettered Word List/Style Sheet Box

To the right of the lettered boxes are two columns. The first column (labeled p.s.) is for recording the part of speech when usage varies from one part of speech to another. For example, for this project—a nonfiction book entitled *Change at Work,* for which I provided editorial support—we hyphenated *long-term* when using it as a modifier (m) and set it as two words when using it as a noun (n). If you need clarification of grammar terms, Chapter 2 presents a refresher.

The second column to the right of the lettered boxes (labeled pg.) is for recording the first page (or, if you wish, all pages) on which a word appears. Page numbers come in handy if you change a decision and need to re-edit—particularly if you're working on hard copy rather than on a computer. If you're working on a computer, you might use this column to record the chapter number or file name instead of the page number. You can then rely on the computer's search-and-replace feature to locate words you need to change. Your word-processing software documentation should explain how to search and replace.

The Word List/Style Sheet also includes boxes for recording abbreviation, capitalization, footnote, number, punctuation, and reference styles. Chapters 4–11 address these topics in detail.

Because you can record a vast majority of style decisions on the Word List/Style Sheet, let's examine it a bit closer. Figure 3 (pages 6 and 7) shows how you might use the Word List/Style Sheet for a work of nonfiction. Figure 4 (pages 9 and 10) shows how you might use it for a work of fiction.

Nonfiction Applications. In works of nonfiction, Word List/Style Sheets come in handy for tracking details such as acronyms, people's names and job titles, product names and model numbers, references to other parts of the document, and so on.

In Figure 3, an *X* represents a variable letter or word, and a pound sign (#) represents a variable number. Thus, *Appendix X* on page 6 represents Appendixes A, B, C, and so on, with each appendix letter capitalized.

Likewise, *# percent* on page 7 means to use a numeral rather than a spelled-out number with the word percent.

Figure 3 shows a sample Word List/Style Sheet from the same book I used for Figure 2: *Change at Work*. This style sheet helped us remember the following details and more:

- Action Research Team is capitalized; action research is not.

- In American Television and Communication *and* is spelled out. Precision Grinding & Manufacturing uses an ampersand.

- CBAM stands for Concerns-Based Adoption Model (and Concerns-Based is hyphenated).

- Kanter's first name is Rosabeth, and Kübler-Ross's first name is Elizabeth.

- This book spells out most numbers below 100.

- This book uses "closed punctuation" (which uses more discretionary marks than "open punctuation") and "serial commas" (optional commas that precede a conjunction in a series). Chapter 4 and the glossary explain these terms in detail.

- Telecom, Australia appears under punctuation because this company name contains a comma; many other company-location combinations contain a hyphen.

Obviously, you need not record every single word that appears in a book. Simply use the form as a memory-jogger: Record only those decisions you (or others) might find difficult to remember or might otherwise treat a different way.

Word List/Style Sheet

Project: _Change at Work_   **Last Update:** _9/28/93_

A-B-C-D	*p.s.	pg.	**Abbreviations** **Acronyms & Initialisms**	*p.s.	pg.
A-1 Manufacturing		2			
action research	m, n	37	ART = Action Research Team		
Action Research Team		xiii	ARTs [plural]		xiii
American Television and Communication		2	CBAM = Concerns-Based Adoption Model		xiii
Appendix X		xiv			
concerns-based [game plans]	m	xii	LOU = Level of Use		183
cross-functional [groups]	m	37			
double-loop [learning]	m	208	PDCA = Plan-Do-Check-Act		227

E-F-G-H	*p.s.	pg.			
expectation-performance gap	n	3	TLT = Transformation Leadership Team		12
first-order [change]	m	54	TTMP = Total Transformation Management Process		xi
force-field [analysis]	m	xiii			

I-J-K-L	*p.s.	pg.
Johari Window	n	44
Kanter, Rosabeth M.		4
Kübler-Ross, Elizabeth		82
Ladder of Inference	n	44
Linking Pin Model	n	18
linking pin [theory]	m	18
long term	n	
long-term	m	

Capitalization Style

_X_ Up ___ Down

Contractions OK?

_X_ Yes ___ No

Footnote Scheme

not applicable

*p.s. = part of speech: m = modifier [adjective, adverb], n = noun, v = verb

Figure 3 - Sample Nonfiction Word List/Style Sheet

Word List/Style Sheet

Project: *Change at Work*   **Last Update:** *9/28/93*

M-N-O-P	**p.s.*	pg.	**Numbers**	**p.s.*	pg.
meta-learning	*n*		*Chapter One*		*xii*
Milestone chart		*100*	*Part One*		*xii*
Model I, II	*n*	*113*	*# percent*		*xi*
Open Organization Model	*n*	*16*			

Spell most numbers below ___ 10 ___ 20 _X_ 100

Q-R-S-T	**p.s.*	pg.	**Punctuation**
Precision Grinding & Manufacturing	*m*	*xiv*	*Telecom, Australia*
Royal Australian Air Force	*m*	*54*	
second-order [change]	*m*	*xiii*	
single-loop [learning]	*m*	*208*	
socioeconomic	*m*		

Basic scheme: _X_ Closed ___ Open
Serial commas? _X_ Yes ___ No
Space between initials? _X_ Yes ___ No

U-V-W-X-Y-Z	**p.s.*	pg.	**Reference Style**
world-class [products]	*m*	*4*	BOOKS: *Mink, O. G., Mink, B. P., and Owen, K. Q. Groups at Work. Englewood Cliffs, N.J.: Educational Technology Publications, 1987.*
Zeigarnik Effect	*n*	*162*	ARTICLES: *Sashkin, M. "True Vision in Leadership." Training and Development Journal, 1986, 40(5), 58–61.*

Alphabetize by: _X_ date ___ letter ___ word

*p.s. = part of speech: m = modifier [adjective, adverb], n = noun, v = verb

Figure 3 (continued) - Sample Nonfiction Word List/Style Sheet

Fiction Applications. In works of fiction, you can use Word List/ Style Sheets to track details such as character names, ages, and relationships; dialects and nonstandard English; important dates and locations; and any other information you might find helpful.

Figure 4 (on pages 9 and 10) provides a sample Word List/ Style Sheet for one of my favorite novels—*Pigs in Heaven* by Barbara Kingsolver. Because I work primarily with nonfiction, I'm using Kingsolver's book for a fiction illustration. Here are a few stylistic details from *Pigs in Heaven*:

- This sample contains information about several characters, including the main character, Taylor, and her six-year-old daughter, Turtle, and several minor characters.

- *Bengals* contains no apostrophe.

- In Bright Angel overlook, *Bright* and *Angel* are capitalized, but *overlook* is not.

- The *of* in Cornucopia Of Bowls is capitalized.

- The name of Harland's auto shop is El-Jay's Paint and Body.

- *Jimson weed* is set all lowercase.

- The abbreviation *I.D.* contains periods, but *TV* does not.

- The trademark *WD-40* is hyphenated rather than set solid (WD40).

- This book spells out times rather than setting them as numerals.

- Contractions are acceptable in this book.

- This book spells out most numbers below 100.

Word List/Style Sheet

Project: _Pigs in Heaven_   **Last Update:** _©1993_

A-B-C-D	*p.s.	pg.	**Abbreviations** **Acronyms & Initialisms**	*p.s.	pg.
Alice [age 61]		3	CNN [TV channel]	n	4
Angie Buster [Lucky's mom]		29			
Bengals [mug]	m, n	5			
Bright Angel overlook		11			
Cornucopia Of Bowls		6			
Creative Imaging	n	23			
Danny [Taylor's garbage man]		9			
Dodge Corona [Taylor's car]		14	I.D.	n	18

E-F-G-H	*p.s.	pg.			
El-Jay's Paint and Body [Harland's auto shop]		4	TV		4
Fay Richey [one of Alice's poker buddies]	m	6	WD-40	n	3
Formica [countertop]	m	4			
Harland [Alice's husband]		3			
Hester Biddle [Alice's neighbor]		5			
Home Shopping Channel		4			

I-J-K-L	*p.s.	pg.	**Capitalization Style**
Irascible Babies [Jax's band]		11	__ Up _X_ Down
Jax [Taylor's boyfriend]		11	
Jim Beam [liquor]	n	4	**Contractions OK?**
jimson weed		8	_X_ Yes __ No
Lou Ann [Taylor's friend]		14	
Lee Shanks [one of Alice's poker buddies]		6	**Footnote Scheme**
Lucky Buster [man with mental retardation]		13	not applicable

*p.s. = part of speech: m = modifier [adjective, adverb], n = noun, v = verb

Figure 4 - Sample Fiction Word List/Style Sheet

Word List/Style Sheet

Project: _Pigs in Heaven_   **Last Update:** _©1993_

M-N-O-P	*p.s.	pg.	Numbers	*p.s.	pg.
Mason jars	n	5	Arizona 93 [highway]		30
Minerva Stamper [Alice's mom]		5	four-fifteen [time]		4
Mutant Ninja Turtles		13	fifty cents		10
Naugahyde [recliner]	m	4	'59 Ford		20
Otis [Lucky's friend, Southern Pacific engineer]		13	sixty-one [age]		3
Old Miss slaughter pen		23	ten o'clock		20
			Spell most numbers below ___ 10 ___ 20 _X_ 100		

Q-R-S-T	*p.s.	pg.	Punctuation
Spelunking Club		20	
Sugar Marie Boss Hornbuckle [Alice's second cousin]		7	
Taylor Greer [Alice's daughter, lives in Tucson]		4	
time-zone [differences]	m	4	
time zone	n	22	Basic scheme: _X_ Closed ___ Open
Turtle [Taylor's 6-year-old]		9	Serial commas? _X_ Yes ___ No
			Space between initials? _X_ Yes ___ No

U-V-W-X-Y-Z	*p.s.	pg.	Reference Style
U-turns	v	15	not applicable
Vietnamese miniature pot-bellied pigs		5	
weak-kneed		16	
West Arizona	m	29	

*p.s. = part of speech: m = modifier [adjective, adverb], n = noun, v = verb

Figure 4 (continued) - Sample Fiction Word List/Style Sheet

The Search-and-Replace Form. Once you've made style decisions, you can track many of them with a Search-and-Replace Form. When styles change over the life of a project, I use such a form to make certain no old standards have accidentally survived.

Figure 5 shows a checklist that might be used to change uppercase to lowercase, British to U.S. spellings, hyphenated compounds to solid compounds, numerals to spelled-out numbers, and so on.

Search for	Replace with	✔
Psychology	psychology	—
behaviour	behavior	—
on-line	online	—
19	nineteen	—

Figure 5 - Sample Search-and-Replace Form

When making final changes, you can use such a list to search for problems, checking off each word as you go. Chapter 14 discusses considerations for performing a computerized search-and-replace (find-and-change) process. The appendix includes a reproducible version of the Search-and-Replace Form and other customizing forms.

The Format Specifications Chart. Another form, the Format Specifications Chart provides a place to record physical style decisions (page layout and type specifications). Chapters 12 and 13 cover these topics.

Reproducing the Forms

The Word List/Style Sheet, Format Specifications Chart, and several other forms in this book appear as reproducible forms in the appendix. While Castle Communications owns the copyright to these forms, you may make as many copies as you wish for your personal use. This does *not* include selling them to others, which is illegal.

If you do make copies, each reproduction must display this book's title. If you adapt the forms, please include this credit line: "Adapted from *Style Meister: The Quick-Reference Custom Style Guide*."

The Customizing Process

Now that you have a sense of the forms, let's examine a process for using them. The remainder of this chapter discusses the customization process and helps you create style guides tailored to your needs. If you have no particular need for customization, you may wish to skip ahead to Chapter 2 now and read about customization later. It is best, however, to read the narrative portion of each chapter before attempting to use its quick-reference charts.

Taking Some Preliminary Steps

Here's one approach to producing custom style guides:

First, determine who will use the guide and to what project or projects it will apply. This information will help put your task into perspective and guide your efforts.

Next, carefully analyze existing publications and correspondence. When possible, examine at least three samples of each type of communication to which the new standards will apply: three issues of a newsletter, three chapters of a book manuscript, three related brochures, and so on. You may be surprised how quickly potential problems will emerge.

Record your findings in a simple alphabetized list. Include the following:

- **Abbreviations.** Include their capitalization, their spacing, and their use or lack of periods (see Chapter 8).

- **Capitalization.** Note when words are capitalized versus lowercase and whether any words appear in all caps or small caps (see Chapter 7).

- **Hyphenation.** Record when compound words are hyphenated versus set as one word or as two words or more (see Chapter 6).

- **Numbers.** Note when numbers are spelled out versus set as numerals (see Chapter 9).

- **Spelling.** Include all variations used when more than one spelling is acceptable (see Chapter 5).

- **Word preferences.** Record words used for nonbiased language, plus any special terminology (see Chapters 10 and 11).

You will probably discover several variations for some words. Record each variation on your list. Also note the way the word is used (the part of speech), particularly for compounds, and where the word appears.

Compile the results of your initial examination in a two-column format. Your list can be as simple as the one in Figure 6, or it may consume several pages. In one column, record all the words that seem significant and all of their variations.

Words	Discussion
Manager manager	*Management capitalizes job titles.*
on line on-line online	*on-line preferred; easier to read*

Figure 6 - Sample Two-Column Alphabetized Word List

Next, share your findings with those who will use the new style guide. Look for patterns. Consider the implications of treating words one way versus another. If, for instance, you decide to hyphenate *work force* (or set it as one word), should you do the same for *work space*? Use the Discussion column to record people's opinions.

Choosing Between Conflicting Styles

Because people tend to hold on to their own opinions and preferences, reaching a consensus is perhaps the most difficult part of the endeavor. Everyone involved must realize that style tends to evolve over time. They must be prepared for the guide to be regularly revised and refined. This section gives some hints to help you choose between conflicting standards.

The Style Standards Continuum. The narrative in Chapters 2–11 will help you choose between specific style standards, but here's another thought to keep in mind: Style preferences tend to fall toward one end or another of a continuum, like that in Figure 7. (Don't worry if you're unfamiliar with the terms in this figure. I'll cover each of them in later chapters.)

A standard may fall anywhere on this continuum, but in general, those listed on the left end of the continuum tend to accompany each other. Those listed on the right end tend to go together as well. The continuum implies that large bureaucracies *generally* prefer more formal usage than small entrepreneurial concerns. Likewise, older audiences *tend* to prefer more formal usage than younger audiences, and so on.

"Formal" usage	"Informal" usage
Books, scholarly and professional journals, technical documents	Consumer magazines, newspapers, advertisements
Large organizations	Small organizations
Older audiences	Younger audiences
Traditionalists	Nontraditionalists
"Up Style" capitalization	"Down style" capitalization
"Closed" or "formal" punctuation	"Open" or "conversational" punctuation
Serial commas	No serial commas

Figure 7 - The Style Standards Continuum

Of course, exceptions do occur. For instance, I've noticed a growing trend over the past few years toward open punctuation and the omission of serial commas in trade fiction.

The Style Standards Continuum simply provides a place to start when you don't know which way to turn. If half of your data falls at one end of the continuum and the rest falls at the other end, go with a personal preference—your own or another person's.

Creating a Simple Style Guide

You can record much style information in a two-part form like the one shown in Figure 8. In the top part of the form, record information you can track easily with general guidelines, such as capitalization, contractions, numbers, and punctuation. In the bottom part, list words specific to your needs.

Number each page and set up an automatic revision date (an upper-right placement makes them easier to find). See your word-processing documentation to learn how to set up page numbers and dates. Now let's examine the bottom of the illustration.

I recommend a two-column format, with the words you prefer on the left and those you wish to avoid on the right. If you type your guide, you can either tab between the columns or type entries into the cells of a two-column table. An alphabetical list helps you locate specific words quickly, and recording alternatives makes it easier to search for problem words and replace them with words you prefer.

General Guidelines	Capitalization: X Up _ down	**Last Update: 1/10/98** **page 1**
	Contractions: X OK _ not OK	Punctuation: X closed _ open
	Numbers: _ 10 _ 20 X 100	Serial commas: X yes _ no
	USE	**NOT**
Word List	disc [CD]	disk, diskette
	disk [floppy disk, hard disk]	disc, diskette
	e-mail [1st: electronic mail (e-mail)]	email, Email, E-mail
	on-line [modifier], on line [noun]	online
	Pat Perez, Marketing Manager	Pat Perez, marketing manager
	sales rep, sales representative	salesman, saleswoman

Figure 8 - Simple Two-Part Style Guide

If your guide runs several pages, you might create a document with two sections, each with a different "header." (A *header* is a block of text that repeats at the tops of several pages.)

In the header of the first section, list your general guidelines and include the date and page number, as shown in Figure 8. In the header of the second section, list only the date and page number (and, if you wish, column heads for the word list), as shown in Figure 9.

Header for page 2–end		**Last Update: 1/10/98** **page 2**
	USE	**NOT**

Figure 9 - Sample Header for Page 2 and Beyond

This approach saves room and, when used on a computer, allows you to quickly highlight only the word list portion to alphabetize it automatically. Most word-processing manuals explain how to alphabetize lists automatically.

If you computerize your style guide, I strongly advise you to create a custom dictionary next. The spell-checking feature in most popular word-processing programs often allows one or more user-created dictionaries. The simplest way to create a custom dictionary is to *carefully* spell-check your refined word list, adding directly to the user dictionary any word the spell-checker doesn't recognize. Your word-processing documentation should explain this process in more detail.

To make it easier to locate answers quickly, put as much information as possible in graphic form. Choose and illustrate a basic punctuation scheme (see Chapter 4). Provide sample footnote schemes, reference citations, and the like (see Chapter 11). If your guide will cover physical formats, include samples for page layouts and type specifications (see Chapters 12 and 13).

Maintaining Your Style Guide

Finally, appoint a single "gatekeeper" to implement all changes. (This may very well be you!) Ensure that all changes and additions filter through this person. Date and distribute revised versions to all concerned parties, with the newest changes and additions highlighted each time.

Summary

This chapter has presented a basic approach for creating custom style guides and has explained several ways to use a Word List/ Style Sheet or a computerized list. The chapter has also introduced the Style Standards Continuum, which can help you choose between conflicting styles. The possibilities that these tools present will become clearer as we move along.

2

Grappling with Grammar

A Friendly Refresher

S tyle Meister is not a grammar book, nor am I a grammarian. Although people often confuse style and grammar, the two are not the same. Grammar addresses the underlying structure of language, while style addresses widely accepted, yet often conflicting, conventions.

Many people detest grammar and have difficulty relating to grammatical terms. That's perfectly all right; I'm not that fond of grammar terms myself. Provided we understand grammatical principles, most of us have little need to memorize grammar terms. Yet a rudimentary understanding of such terms is indispensable when navigating style guides and grammar books or compiling a customized guide. Many style guides index entries only by the part of speech, which makes using them a major headache if your knowledge of grammar is shaky.

This chapter is meant to help ease your way. It explains the eight parts of speech (along with some of their categories) and a bit about sentence structure. The chapter then discusses some common structural problems.

If your knowledge about the parts of speech and sentence structure is solid, you can skip this chapter. If you need a brief refresher, please read on.

The "Big Eight"—The Parts of Speech

The parts of speech are important building blocks of communication. These eight parts (in alphabetical order) include adjectives, adverbs, conjunctions, interjections, nouns, prepositions, pronouns, and verbs. Figure 10 briefly defines each term.

Adjectives	Compare, describe, emphasize, or limit nouns or pronouns.
Adverbs	Affirm, compare, describe, introduce, join, or negate verbs, adjectives, or other adverbs.
Conjunctions	Join words or groups of words and reveal their relationships.
Interjections	Exclaim or express emotion.
Nouns	Name or classify people, places, things, ideas, and qualities.
Prepositions	Position or show relationships between nouns and other words.
Pronouns	Substitute for names or classifications of nouns.
Verbs	Express an action or a state of being and often relate it to the past, present, or future.

Figure 10 - The Parts of Speech

The quick-reference charts in this chapter explain the parts of speech, break them down into categories, and provide examples of each part.

The Framework of Communication

The two most important building blocks of communication are the subject and the predicate. The *subject* is what the sentence is about. A subject consists of a noun, a noun phrase (a group of words acting as a noun), or a pronoun. The *predicate* is what we say about the subject. The predicate consists of a verb or verb phrase (a group of words acting as a verb). A predicate may also contain modifiers and/or the object that the subject acts upon.

To make use of all these building blocks, we need a framework in which to use them. Three types of frameworks are phrases, clauses, and sentences.

Phrases

A *phrase* is a group of words that lacks a related subject and predicate. Phrases come in several types:

- *Noun phrases* are groups of words that act like nouns (examples: the book-publishing business, my so-called agent, a well-known author).

- *Prepositional phrases* begin with prepositions (examples: at the next opportunity, in case of fire, over the transom).

- *Infinitive, participial*, and *verb phrases* use forms of verbs (examples: to publish widely, relieved of her duties, got rejected repeatedly).

- *Absolute phrases* modify the entire sentence (example: *Having completed his first novel,* Miguel felt a deep sense of satisfaction).

Phrases rarely make sense on their own. For instance, the prepositional phrase, "in case of fire," makes no sense on its own. It leaves us wondering what to do should a fire break out. That's a dangerous thought to leave unfinished!

Clauses

A clause contains both a subject and a predicate, and may or may not form a complete thought. "Celeste [subject] wants [predicate]" is an example of a clause that, in most cases, doesn't make sense on its own. We're left to wonder what, precisely, it is that Celeste wants. The clause "Celeste wants to be published," however, makes sense on its own and clarifies the situation.

A clause that makes sense on its own is called an *independent* (or main) *clause* when it appears with other elements, and a *simple sentence* when it appears alone. A clause that doesn't make sense on its own is called a *dependent* (or subordinate) *clause.*

A dependent clause requires an independent clause to complete its meaning. Examine the sentence, "If you study your markets well [dependent clause], you can sell most of your writing [independent clause]." The second clause, "you can sell most of your writing," completes the meaning of the first clause, "If you study your markets well." The dependent clause that follows rather than precedes an independent clause is no less dependent.

Sentences

In its simplest form, a complete sentence consists of a subject and a predicate. In the sentence, "Frances writes," *Frances* is the subject and *writes* is the predicate.

Some sentences have a subject, a predicate, and an object. The *object* completes the sense of the predicate—or tells us what the subject is acting upon. In the sentence, "Frances writes books," *books* is the object.

An object may be direct or indirect. A *direct object* answers the question, what. An *indirect object* answers the question, to whom or to what. In the sentence, "Dyanne submitted her manuscript to the publisher," *manuscript* is the direct object, and *publisher* is the indirect object.

The rest of the words in a sentence modify the subject, predicate, or object. *Modifiers* are adjectives or adverbs—or clauses or phrases that act like adjectives or adverbs.

In the sentence, "Jay submitted his nonfiction tale to the publisher," *nonfiction* modifies *tale*. In the sentence, "Jay submitted his nonfiction tale about his alien abduction to the publisher," *about his alien abduction* modifies *tale* as well.

Sentence Patterns. Most English sentences follow one of three patterns: 1) subject–predicate, 2) modifier–subject–predicate, or 3) predicate–subject. In the examples that follow, the subject is in bold type, the predicate is in italics, and the modifier is in roman (plain) type.

1. **Writers** *must learn to face rejection.*

2. Never one to toot her own horn, **Dottie** *failed to mention her Pulitzer nomination.*

3. *More unusual is* **having your first submission accepted**.

The first sentence illustrates the subject–predicate pattern. The second illustrates the modifier–subject–predicate pattern. The third illustrates the predicate–subject pattern.

Structural Problems

Now that we've refreshed our memories about phrases, clauses, and sentences, let's take a look at some structural problems. Two related problems that surface from time to time are run-on sentences and sentence fragments.

Run-on Sentences

When you join two independent clauses incorrectly, you produce a *run-on sentence*. To prevent this problem, you can either write two separate sentences, or you can join independent clauses in one of the ways shown in Figure 11.

Guideline	Example
Join two closely related independent clauses with a semicolon. (A comma alone produces an undesirable *comma splice*.)	I'm not in right now; leave a message after the tone.
Place a comma and a coordinate conjunction (*and, but, for, nor, or,* or *yet*) between two clauses.	I've completed the revisions, but I still need to proofread.
Place a conjunctive adverb (*also, however, anyhow, consequently,* etc.) between two clauses. NOTE: Use a semicolon before the conjunctive adverb and a comma after it.	I suppose editing can get tedious; however, I find it fascinating.

Figure 11 - Joining Independent Clauses

Never join two independent clauses without a coordinate conjunction, a conjunctive adverb, and/or the appropriate punctuation.

Sentence Fragments

When you use only a word or a phrase as a sentence, you produce a *sentence fragment*. There's nothing intrinsically wrong with sentence fragments, provided you use them intentionally and in an appropriate context. You can, for instance, freely use sentence fragments in advertisements, dialogue and quotes, and question-and-answer formats. In the following examples, the sentence fragments are italicized:

Advertisements
Flexible. Graphic presentation. Unique!

Dialogue & Quotes
"Oh, please." "You don't mean—" "Surely not!"

Question & Answer Formats
Do you write novels? *short stories? poetry?*

Q: What is the meaning of SASE?
A: *Self-addressed, stamped envelope.*

In all but the most formal writing, you can use sentence fragments for emphasis or effect. For example:

- Make no assumptions. *Really.*

- *Not for us.* Try another market.

Just make certain the context in which you place a sentence fragment makes its meaning clear.

How to Use Chapter 2's Quick-Reference Charts

The quick-reference charts for Chapter 2 outline and define the eight basic parts of speech and break them down by categories and subcategories.

The charts read essentially from left to right. Figure 12 shows a sample segment from a quick-reference chart.

PREPOSITIONS	*Position* or *show relationships* between people, places, things, ideas, qualities, and other words	
Simple	**Position**	**Examples**
• **Concede or exclude**	People, places, things, ideas, and qualities	but (except) except There's nobody here *but* us writers.
• Show **direction, place, or position**		above at behind in outside past toward Turn left *at* the corner, just *past* the gas station.

Figure 12 - Sample Quick-Reference Chart Segment

The left-hand column lists the parts of speech alphabetically, followed by categories and subcategories, then by bold key words. (In Figure 12, "Simple" is one category of prepositions, the other being "Compound or Phrasal.") This column sometimes contains cautions, exceptions, notes, and other information.

The center column describes the job or jobs each part of speech performs. The bold column heads in this column begin the statements that the words in each block of the column complete. In other words, read the center column of Figure 12 as

"Position people, places, things, ideas, and qualities." The right-hand column provides examples for each job.

Unlike most of *Style Meister*'s quick-reference charts, the charts in this chapter contain very few customizing features. These features are listed in the relative pronouns section. The columns with a checkmark (✔) contain "write-on lines," on which you can record the options you prefer or rank options when you find more than one acceptable.

The rest of the grammar charts are for reference—to jog your memory and illustrate grammar terms.

The charts provide a good foundation for addressing grammar questions, but as you use them, keep these points in mind:

1. Some words fit more than one category under the same part of speech,

2. Many words can be used as more than one part of speech, and

3. The charts provide examples, not complete listings of every possibility.

Usage notes appear at the end of the chapter, after the quick-reference charts. For further information, check the glossary or explore the sources in the annotated bibliography.

Summary

This chapter has reviewed some basic grammar terms and concepts to help you navigate more easily through any style guide. The chapter has defined the eight main parts of speech (adjectives, adverbs, conjunctions, interjections, nouns, prepositions, pronouns, and verbs). It has explained the differences between subjects, predicates, and objects and between phrases, clauses, and sentences. In addition, it has addressed two common structural problems: run-on sentences and sentence fragments.

The quick-reference charts that follow illustrate some of these grammar terms and concepts in more depth.

The Parts of Speech & Their Jobs

ADJECTIVES

Compare, describe, emphasize, or *limit* people, places, things, ideas, or qualities

Comparisons	Compare or Describe	Examples
• **Base or positive**	*One* person, place, thing, idea, or quality	good prolific sharp Elizabeth is a *prolific* poet.
• **Comparative**	*Two* people, places, things, ideas, or qualities	better more prolific sharper Elizabeth is a *more prolific* poet than Edgar is.
• **Superlative** (See *comparisons, p. 26.*) (See [1]*Usage Note, p. 38.*)	*More than two* people, places, things, ideas, or qualities	best most prolific sharpest Elizabeth is the *most prolific* poet I know.

Descriptive	Describe	Examples
• **Common** NOTE: *Do not capitalize* common adjectives. (See *proper, p. 31.*)	*Nonspecific* people, places, things, ideas, or qualities	amazing masterful talented *amazing* story *masterful* technique *talented* performer
• **Proper** NOTE: *Capitalize* proper adjectives. (See *common, p. 31.*)	*Specific* kinds of people, places, things, ideas, or qualities	African Christian Irish *African* folktale *Christian* magazine *Irish* poet

Limiting	Emphasize or Limit	Examples
• **Articles** NOTE: Some people classify articles as a separate part of speech.	*Individual* people, places, things, ideas, or qualities	a an [INDEFINITE] the [DEFINITE] Have you read *a* book on *the* English language? Wasn't that *an* interesting story?

Adjectives—Limiting	Emphasize or Limit	Examples
• **Demonstrative**	A *specific* person, place, thing, idea, or quality	that this [SINGULAR] *that* book *this* time
NOTE: Demonstrative adjectives require an object to complete their meaning. (See *demonstrative*, p. 33.)	*Specific* people, places, things, ideas, or qualities	these those [PLURAL] *these* songs *those* kids
• **Distributive** (See *indefinite/distributive*, p. 33.)	A *universal* person, place, thing, idea, or quality	each every [SINGULAR] *each* time *every* person
• **Indefinite** (See *indefinite*, p. 33.)	A *nonspecific* person, place, thing, idea, or quality	any either [SINGULAR] *any* day *either* one
	Nonspecific people, places, things, ideas, or qualities	some [PLURAL] *some* days
• **Numerical** – *Cardinal numbers* express amounts.	The *number* or *order* of people, places, things, ideas, or qualities	one two [CARDINAL] One lump or two?
– *Ordinal numbers* indicate order.		first second [ORDINAL] I get to go first!
• **Relative** NOTE: *Interrogative adjectives* are relative adjectives that introduce questions. (See *relative*, p. 35.)	*What* or *which* people, places, things, ideas, or qualities	what which Seja wondered *what* type of story would help her win the contest. *Which* entry won?

Predicate	Describe	Examples
NOTE: Predicate adjectives *describe* the *subject's condition* and complete the meaning of the predicate or linking verb that precedes them.	People, places, things, ideas, or qualities	accomplished sleepy unreasonable Jerome is so *accomplished*. You are getting *sleepy*. My boss is *unreasonable*.

ADVERBS

Affirm, negate, compare, describe, introduce, or *join* actions or states of being

Affirmative or Negative	Affirm or Negate	Examples
• **Affirmative**	Actions or states of being	yes *Yes*, I always spell-check!
• **Negative**		no not *No*, I'm *not* done yet.

Comparisons	Compare or Describe	Examples
• **Base or positive**	*One* action or state of being	smoothly quick well Ed's stories read *smoothly*.
• **Comparative**	*Two* actions or states of being	more smoothly quicker better Ed's stories read *more smoothly* than Lee's do.
• **Superlative** (See *comparisons, p. 24*.) (See [1]*Usage Note, p. 38*.)	*More than two* actions or states of being	most smoothly quickest best Ed's stories read the *most smoothly*.

Conjunctive or Linking	Join	Examples
• **Add, continue, or illustrate** (See *coordinate/simple, p. 28*.)	Independent clauses	also furthermore moreover namely I must edit this; *moreover*, I must proof it.
• **Compare or contrast** (See *subordinate/compare or contrast, p. 28*.)		conversely however still (but) I'm almost done editing; *however*, I need to proof.
• **Conclude or explain** (See *subordinate/conclude or explain, p. 28*.) (See [2]*Usage Note, p. 38*.)		anyhow consequently otherwise (or) therefore Shonda is terribly shy; *therefore*, she hates parties.

Adverbs—Expletive	Introduce	Examples
NOTE: Expletives fill a void but add no meaning. (See *expletives, p. 33.*)	Sentences	there *There* are over six billion people inhabiting this planet.

Simple	Describe	Examples
• **Flat** NOTES: – Flat adverbs lack an –*ly* ending.	Actions or states of being	fast hard too well Write *fast*. Work *hard*, but not *too hard*. Edit *well*.
– *Interrogative* adverbs are flat adverbs that introduce questions.		how what when where who why *Why* did you do that?
• Of **degree or size**	*How much* actions or states of being are performed	extensively less very Revise *extensively*.
• Of **direction, place, or position** (See *simple/direction, place, or position, p. 32.*) (See *subordinate/direction, place, or position, p. 29.*)	*Where* actions or states of being are performed	around here south through where work *around* sign *here* strike *through*
• Of **frequency or time** (See *simple/frequency or time, p. 32.*) (See *subordinate/frequency or time, p. 29.*)	*When* or *how often* actions or states of being are performed	eventually now rarely *eventually* publish *now* know *rarely* seen
• Of **manner** (See *subordinate/manner, p. 29.*)	*How* actions or states of being are performed	boldly feverishly wisely *boldly* go work *feverishly* *wisely* conclude
• Of **numerical order** (See *simple/number or order, p. 32.*)	*In what order* actions or states of being are performed	after first second last *After* completing your research, write *first*, edit *second*, and proofread *last*.

CONJUNCTIONS
Join words or groups of words and *reveal* their relationships

Coordinate	Join	Examples
• **Correlative**	*Equal* or *related pairs* or *series* of words or groups of words	both . . . and either . . . or if . . . then neither . . . nor not only . . . but also I like *both* writing *and* editing.
• **Simple** TIP: Think *and, or, nor, but, yet, for.* (See *conjunctive or linking,* p. 26.)	*Equal* or *related words* or *groups* of words	and but for nor or yet Mary never leaves home without her beeper, cell phone, *and* modem.
NOTE: *For* becomes a coordinate conjunction only when it connects independent clauses.		Cleo may not sell much work, *for* he's unwilling to promote it.

Subordinate	Join and Relate	Examples
• **Compare or contrast**	• *Unequal* clauses	than This is much harder *than* it looks.
• **Concede or exclude** (See *simple/concede or exclude,* p. 32.)	• *Unequal* clauses	although even if I'm dumping my agent, *even if* he begs me not to.
• **Conclude or explain** (See *conjunctive or linking/ conclude or explain,* p. 26.)	• *Why*	as because for since We're rejecting your work *because* it sucks.
• Show **condition** NOTE: Subordinate conjunctions join dependent clauses to independent clauses.	• *How*	if or provided unless You can sell most of your writing *if* you study the markets well.

Conjunctions—Subordinate	Reveal	Examples
• Of **direction, place, or position** (See *simple/direction, place, or position, p. 27*.) (See *simple/direction, place, or position, p. 32*.)	• *Where*	where whither Do not revise those segments *where* the editor has written "stet."
• Of **frequency or time** (See *simple/frequency or time, p. 27*.) (See *simple/frequency or time, p. 32*.)	• *When*	after as before since till until when while Don't edit your writing *until* you have completed the first draft.
• Of **manner** (See *simple/manner, p. 27*.)	• *How*	as as if Peter writes *as if* everyone understood astrophysics.
• Of **purpose** NOTE: Subordinate conjunctions join dependent clauses to independent clauses.	• *Why*	in order to so that that We left at seven *in order to* get there on time.

INTERJECTIONS   *Exclaim* or *express* emotion

Compound or Phrasal	As Phrases	Examples
• An interjection may be a compound word or phrase.		Goodness gracious Holy smoke Oh my Beepers and cell phones and modems, *oh my!*

Simple	As Single Words	Examples
• An interjection may be a single word.		alas eureka gee-whiz hey Lordy no oh well yee-haw yikes zounds HAMLET: "*Alas,* poor Yorick!" —Shakespeare

NOUNS

Name or *classify* people, places, things, ideas, and qualities

Collective	Name or Classify	Examples
NOTE: Collective nouns can be singular or plural, depending on one's intended meaning.	Groups of people, places, things, ideas, and qualities	audience committee couple faculty family minority number percent total variety
TIP: The word before a collective noun often tells us whether it's singular or plural. *The* signals singular; *a* signals plural.		*The* number of things I'd like to write increases every day. [SINGULAR] *A* number of revisions are required. [PLURAL]
CAUTION: Not all plural nouns are collective.		management [COLLECTIVE] Run that by management.
(See *plurals, p. 99.*)		managers [PLURAL] Some managers lack people skills.

Common	Name or Classify	Examples
• **Abstract** nouns	Ideas or qualities	creativity health quality tragedy
NOTE: Abstract nouns may be *capitalized* for emphasis.		Our organization has a great *Quality* program.
• **Concrete** nouns NOTE: *Do not capitalize* common nouns. (See *proper, p. 31.*)	*Nonspecific* people, places, and things	play playwright theater city music

Proper	Name or Classify	Examples
NOTE: *Capitalize* proper nouns. (See *common, p. 31.*) (See Chapter 7.)	*Specific* people, places, and things	Hamlet Shakespeare Globe Theatre London Pachelbel's Canon

PREPOSITIONS

Position or *show relationships* between people, places, things, ideas, and qualities, and other words

Compound or Phrasal	Show Relationships	Examples
NOTE: A preposition may be a compound word or phrase.	Of people, places, things, ideas, and qualities	aside from because of in case of together with *In case of fire,* break this glass to access fire hose.

Simple	Position	Examples
• **Concede or exclude** (See *subordinate/concede or exclude, p. 28.*)	People, places, things, ideas, and qualities	but (except) except There's nobody here *but* us writers.
• Show **direction, place, or position** (See *simple/direction, place, or position, p. 27.*) (See *subordinate/direction, place, or position, p. 29.*)		above at behind in outside past toward Turn left *at* the corner, just *past* the gas station.
• Of **frequency or time** (See *simple/frequency or time, p. 27.*) (See *subordinate/frequency or time, p. 29.*)		as (preceding a noun) at during past toward *After* Rebecca finishes proofing this book, she plans to chill out.
• Of **number or order** (See *simple/numerical order, p. 27.*)		below over under Carl's first advance was *over* fifty thousand dollars.
• Of **relationship** NOTES:		about among between concerning for of with
– Use *between* to refer to two people, places, things, ideas, or qualities.		Just *between* you and me, Gail's novels bore my socks off. [TWO]
– Use *among* to refer to more than two.		*Among* life's pleasures, good books rate near the top. [MORE THAN TWO]

PRONOUNS
Substitute for *names* or *classifications* of people, places, things, ideas, and qualities

Demonstrative	Name	Examples
(See *limiting/demonstrative,* p. 25.)	*Specific* people, places, things, ideas, and qualities	that this [SINGULAR] Please hold *this.*
		these those [PLURAL] Please hand me *those.*

Expletive	Introduce	Examples
NOTE: Expletives fill a void but add no meaning. (See *expletives, p.* 27.)	Sentences	it *It* is only a matter of time before I get a Pulitzer.

Indefinite	Imply	Examples
NOTES: • Such pronouns imply, but don't specify, the antecedent.	*Nonspecific* people, places, things, ideas, and qualities	another one [SINGULAR] If the first agent dislikes your work, try *another.*
• Indefinite pronouns often start with *any, every, no,* or *some.*		anybody everyone nothing [ALWAYS SINGULAR] *Everything* went smoothly.
• Distributive forms imply *individuals* or *pairs.*		each either neither [SINGULAR] Bruce doesn't like *either.*
• Some indefinite pronouns can be singular or plural.		all most none some [SINGULAR OR PLURAL]
TIP: Reserve *none* for plural and use *no one* or *not one* for singular.		Of the awards Jo received, she valued *none* more than her Violet Crown award.
(See *limiting/demonstrative & limiting/indefinite, p. 25.*) (See [3]*Usage Note, p.* 38.)		both few many several [ALWAYS PLURAL] Ted's biographies appeal to *many.*

Personal	Identify	Examples
• **Nominative or subjective case**	The subject	I you he/she/it [SINGULAR] *I* take writing seriously.
		we you they [PLURAL]
• **Objective case**	The object	me you him/her/it [SINGULAR] Could you fax *me* a copy?
		us you them [PLURAL]
• **Possessive case**	The possessor	my/mine your/yours her/hers his its [SINGULAR POSSESSIVE] That's *my* favorite book.
NOTE: Examples appear in first, second, then third person.		our/ours your/yours their/theirs [PLURAL POSSESSIVE] That's *their* problem.
(See *contractions vs. possessives, p. 110.*) (See *possessives, personal pronouns, p. 109.*)		whose [SINGULAR OR PLURAL POSSESSIVE] *Whose* manuscript is this?
Pronouns—Reciprocal	**Indicate Relationships**	**Examples**
NOTE: We form reciprocal pronouns by adding *other* or *another*.	Of people, places, things, ideas, and qualities	each other one another Be civil to *each other*.
Pronouns—Reflexive	**Reflect the Subject**	**Examples**
NOTES: • We form such pronouns with the suffix *–self* or *–selves*.	People, places, things, ideas, and qualities	myself yourself her/him/itself [SINGULAR] If you want it done right, you must do it *yourself*.
• Examples appear in first, second, then third person.		ourselves yourselves themselves [PLURAL] We'll publish this *ourselves*.

Pronouns—Reflexive	Reflect the Subject	Examples
• Reflexive pronouns that emphasize the subject are called *intensive pronouns*.		I *myself* laid out this book. Authors must promote their work *themselves*.

Relative	Link to Antecedent ✔	Examples ✔
• Use *that* or *which* for **animals and things**. (See [4]*Usage Note, p. 38.*)	Animals	Is that the dog *that* ___ bit you? Is that the dog *which* ___ bit you?
	Things	Is this article the one ___ *that* you wrote? Is this article the one ___ *which* you wrote?
• Use *that, who,* or *whom* **for people**.	Individual people	He is the agent *that* ___ I met. *or* He is the agent *who* ___ I met. [INFORMAL] He is the agent *whom* ___ I met. [FORMAL]
	People as a group	They are the team ___ *that* won today. *or* They are the team ___ *who* won today. [INFORMAL] They are the team for ___ *whom* I cheer. [FORMAL]
• Informal usage allows *who* unless it's the direct object of the clause it begins.		*Who* do you write ___ *for*? *but* *For whom* do you write? [INFORMAL]
• Formal usage requires *whom* for the object of a preposition. (See *who vs. whom, p. 62.*)		*Whom* do you write ___ *for*? *For whom* do you write? [FORMAL]

VERBS

Express an *action* or a *state of being* and often relate it to a *time*

Auxiliary or Linking	Help Complete	Examples
NOTE: Auxiliary or linking verbs (also called *helping verbs*) are words or phrases that complete other verbs and link the subject to its complement.	Actions or states of being	could be has had [PHRASES] We *could be* finished by tomorrow.
Auxiliary verbs include: – Forms of *be* [HELP FORM PASSIVE AND PROGRESSIVE CONSTRUCTIONS] TIP: Think *is, are, was, were, be, am, been, being.*		am are be been being is was were [FORMS OF *BE*] I *am going* to scream.
– Forms of *do*		did do does [FORMS OF *DO*] We *did* not *receive* your manuscript yet.
– Forms that express *mood*		can could may might should would [EXPRESS *MOOD*] I *could edit* that for you if you get it to me by Friday.
– Forms that express *sensing*		appear feel look seem smell sound taste [EXPRESS *SENSING*] You *look* tired.
– Forms that express *tense* CAUTION: Sometimes other words come between the verb and its helper. (See *tense, p. 55.*)		had has have shall will [EXPRESS *TENSE*] *Have* you ever even *dreamed* of such a helpful style book?

Verbs—Intransitive	Stand Alone	Examples
NOTE: Intransitive verbs do not require a direct object. (See *transitive, p. 37.*)	Actions or states of being	dance fire sigh muddles sells tried wiggled Judy's work really *sells*.

Transitive	Require Direct Object	Examples
NOTE: Transitive verbs require a direct object to complete the action. (See *intransitive, p. 37.*)	Actions or states of being	accomplish cite delete further (advance) verify The editor *deleted* half of Roger's column.

VERBALS	Used As	Examples
• **Gerunds** NOTE: Gerunds are verb-like forms that end in *–ing*. (See *participles, p. 37.*) (See [5, 6]*Usage Note, p. 38.*)	Nouns	*Writing* provides a great emotional release.
• **Infinitives** NOTE: Infinitives are verb-like forms preceded by the word *to*, which may appear either expressly or by implication.	Adjectives, adverbs, or nouns	This is the way *to write*. [AS AN ADJECTIVE, MODIFYING *WAY*] The book is going *to print*. [AS AN ADVERB] *To write* a best-seller is many a writer's dream. [AS A NOUN]
• **Participles** NOTES: • Participles take on characteristics of both verbs and adjectives. • Present participles end in *–ing*. • Past participles end in *–d, –ed, –en, –n,* or *–t*. (See *gerunds, p. 37.*)	Adjectives	*Holding* her breath, Alice ripped opened the publisher's reply. Please state your objections in *written* form.

USAGE NOTES

1 Adjectives and adverbs may appear in positive, comparative, and superlative forms. The *positive* (base) form describes one person, place, thing, idea, or quality. The *comparative* form describes two people, places, things, ideas, or qualities. The *superlative* form describes more than two people, places, things, ideas, or qualities.

2 *Conjunctive adverbs* are not true conjunctions; however, they may act like subordinate conjunctions.

3 *Antecedents* are the words that relative pronouns refer to. In the sentence, "I am the author who wrote this book," *I* is the antecedent of *who*.

4 Although many writers reserve *which* for nonrestrictive use, some writers use *which* restrictively.

5 *Verbals* are not true verbs, but they are formed from verbs.

6 Foreign audiences often find gerunds confusing.

3

But I Thought . . . ?

Common Problems & Outdated Rules

$\mathcal{E}$ very style guide should address recurrent grammatical problems. This chapter discusses some of the most common and most challenging. I've organized these as problems of clarity, consistency, conciseness, and precision. This chapter briefly discusses each of these categories and illustrates many of them further in the quick-reference charts.

Then, because old rules die hard, even when ill-conceived, the last set of charts illustrate some common misconceptions and outdated rules.

Problems with Clarity

Some common problems with clarity include dangling, misplaced, and squinting modifiers; missing prepositions; and unclear antecedents. The following sections explain these terms.

Dangling Modifiers

As mentioned in Chapter 2, *modifiers* affirm, compare, describe, emphasize, introduce, join, limit, or negate other words. Thus, they modify them. A modifier dangles when it appears to modify the wrong word or words. Dangling modifiers often occur when the subject precedes the predicate. Such modifiers may seem logical at first, but when examined closely lack accuracy or logic.

Example: "Having printed a fresh draft and attached an SASE, Virginia's manuscript was ready to submit." The phrase "Having printed a fresh draft and attached an SASE," dangles because a manuscript can't perform such work.

Alternative: "Having printed a fresh draft and attached an SASE, Virginia was ready to submit her manuscript." This phrase does not dangle because Virginia performed the work. (By the way, SASE stands for self-addressed stamped envelope.)

Misplaced & Squinting Modifiers

Misplaced and *squinting modifiers* pose similar problems. When a modifier could appear in more than one position and the sentence would still make sense, it's possible that modifier might be misplaced. Figure 13 illustrates this problem.

Variation	Meaning
Only I have eyes for you.	No one else can stand the sight of you.
I have *only* eyes for you.	I'll look at you, but I won't touch you.
I have eyes for *only* you.	You're the only one I want to see.

Figure 13 - Misplaced Modifiers

Similarly, if a modifier could modify either the word that precedes it or the one that follows, that modifier might be squinting. In the sentence, "Publishing regularly takes lots of work," *regularly* is a squinting modifier. We don't know whether the writer is referring to publishing on a regular basis or publishing in general. To prevent such problems, place modifiers closer to the words they modify or recast the sentence.

Missing Prepositions

English pairs certain prepositions with certain words, and dictionaries list these combinations (need *for*, interest *in*, and so on). Easy enough, right? However, compound subjects sometimes present a problem. To save space, we may try to get by with only one preposition where two or more are required. The sentence, "Professor Garza has a need and interest in publishing" doesn't quite make sense because *need* calls for a different preposition than *interest*. "Professor Garza has a *need for* and *interest in* publishing" does.

Unclear Antecedents

An *antecedent* is a noun that a pronoun refers to. Each pronoun must have a specific antecedent. Take the sentence, "Javier once aspired to become a famous poet, but he doesn't care much about it anymore." This sentence is unclear because we don't know whether *it* refers to fame or poetry. An alternative might read "Javier once aspired to become a famous poet, but he doesn't care much about fame [or poetry] anymore.

Watch out for unclear antecedents in sentences containing *he, she, it, one, that, these, they, this, those,* or *which.* Make certain they relate to the correct noun.

Problems with Consistency

Most problems with consistency boil down to disagreement. *Agreement* involves matching the case, gender, number, person, and tense of subjects and verbs or pronouns and antecedents. The following sections discuss these terms in more detail.

Subjective, Objective & Possessive Case

The *case* of a pronoun identifies it as the subject, the object, or the possessor. Figure 14 illustrates case, person, and number.

Case	Person	Singular	Plural
Subjective	First	I	we
	Second	you	you
	Third	he/she/it/ who/whoever	they
Objective	First	me	us
	Second	you	you
	Third	him/her/it/ whom/whomever	them
Possessive	First	my/mine	our/ours
	Second	your/yours	your/yours
	Third	his/her/hers/its/whose	their/theirs

Figure 14 - Case, Person & Number

In the *subjective* (or nominative) case, the pronoun is the subject. For example, *I* am the one who wrote this book. (Here, *I* is the subject.)

In the *objective* case, the pronoun is the object. For example, I wrote this book for *you*. (Here, *you* is the direct object.)

The *possessive* case describes ownership or possession. For example, If you don't appreciate it, that's *your* problem. (Here, you are the one who owns the problem.)

The pervasive error of confusing *I* with *me* occurs when people use the subjective case (I) in place of the objective case (me). It should be *Just between you and **me***, not *Just between you and **I*** because *you* and *me* are objects of the preposition *between*. To many of us, the subjective case sounds better—so much so that many grammarians call this error an overcorrection. But that doesn't mean the subjective case is correct in this example.

Note: The form of some possessive pronouns varies, based on whether they fall before or after the object (that's *her* manuscript; that manuscript is *her*s). The form for *his* and *its*, however, remains the same (that's *his* manuscript; that manuscript is *his*).

First, Second & Third Person

A story written from the *first person* point of view is written through the eyes of an individual, usually. Some authors use multiple narrators, who alternate from one segment to another but tell the story through their individual eyes. A piece written in the *second person* speaks directly to the audience (you!). Documents written in *third person* tend to be passive and less direct.

The first, second, and third person may be either singular or plural and may be subjective, objective, or possessive.

Singular & Plural Number

A *singular* subject relates to one person, place, thing, idea or quality; a *plural* subject relates to more than one. Singular subjects take singular verbs (he *writes*). Plural subjects take plural verbs (they *write*).

Sometimes, singular and plural verbs are the same; other times they vary. The form of the verb often varies with its tense—past, present, future, and so on (He *wrote*. He *writes*. He *will write*.) Figure 15 illustrates the singular and plural forms of the verb *write* in the simple past, present, and future tenses. Tenses are discussed in more detail in the next section.

Simple Tense	Singular	Plural
• Past	I wrote	We wrote
	You wrote	You wrote
	He/she/it wrote	They wrote
• Present	I write	We write
	You write	You write
	He/she/it writes	They write
• Future	I will write	We will write
	You will write	You will write
	He/she/it will write	They will write

Figure 15 - Simple Tense & Number

Tense

A verb's tense relates it to a time: past, present, or future, or a variation thereof. The tense may be simple, perfect, progressive, or perfect progressive.

Simple Tense. The *simple tense* of a verb is the "unembellished" form that relates the verb to the past, present, or future, as illustrated in Figure 15 and in the quick-reference charts.

Perfect Tense. The *perfect tense* conveys that actions were, are, or will be completed (or perfected). The perfect tense combines a linking verb with a past participle form of a verb. The past perfect tense uses *had*. The present perfect tense uses *has* or *have*. The future perfect tense uses *shall have* or *will have*.

Progressive Tense. The *progressive tense* represents action in progress. This tense combines a form of the linking verb *be* with an *–ing* form of the main verb. Remember, forms of *be* include *is, are, was, were, be, am, been,* and *being*.

Perfect Progressive. Sometimes, we combine the perfect and progressive tenses to form the perfect progressive tense. The past perfect progressive form combines *had been* with an *–ing* form. The present perfect progressive form combines *has been* or *have been* with an *–ing* form. The future perfect progressive form combines *will have been* with an *–ing* form.

Figure 16 illustrates the first person singular and plural forms of the verb *write* in the past, present, and future simple, perfect, progressive, and perfect progressive tenses. The quick-reference charts illustrate all three persons. (See *tense, p. 55.*)

Past Tense	Singular	Plural
• Simple	I wrote	We wrote
• Perfect *had*	I had written	We had written
• Progressive *was + –ing, were + –ing*	I was writing	We were writing
• Perfect Progressive *had been+ –ing*	I had been writing	We had been writing

Present Tense	Singular	Plural
• Simple	I write	We write
• Perfect *has, have*	I have written	We have written
• Progressive *am + –ing, are + –ing,* *is + –ing*	I am writing	We are writing
• Perfect Progressive *has been + –ing,* *have been + –ing*	I have been writing	We have been writing

Future Tense	Singular	Plural
• Simple *will*	I will write	We will write
• Perfect *shall have, will have*	I will have written	We will have written
• Progressive *will be + –ing*	I will be writing	We will be writing
• Perfect Progressive *will have been + –ing*	I will have been writing	We will have been writing

Figure 16 - Tense & Number

While you need not always use the same tense throughout a sentence, any shifts you make should be logical.

Pronoun–Antecedent Agreement

A pronoun's case, gender, number, and person should agree with that of its antecedent. In the statement, "Jill edited her work so tightly that she could justify every character," both the pronoun *she* and the possessive pronoun *her* clearly refer to the antecedent *Jill*.

Subject–Verb Agreement

A subject and verb must also agree in number and tense. In the majority of cases, you can ensure subject-verb agreement by mentally erasing all the words that fall between. For instance, examine the statement, "Rain, as well as hail, *is/are* expected here this evening." The phrase, *as well as hail,* is parenthetical. You can therefore mentally erase the words that fall between the subject (rain) and the verb (is/are) to decide between a singular or plural verb. This leaves you with "Rain *is* expected here this evening." You therefore need *is* rather than *are* in the original sentence.

Irregular Plurals. Although number and tense are the primary elements of subject–verb agreement, you should also be aware of irregular plurals. Greek and Latin derivations, in particular, make it challenging to maintain agreement. Because we spell the singular and plural forms of such derivations differently, they appear in Chapter 5.

Parallelism

A further consistency problem is the lack of parallelism. *Parallel* elements appear in similar form. Although many kinds of elements should be parallel, the concept is easiest to grasp by examining series or listed items. Figure 17 contrasts the nonparallel and parallel versions of a series.

Nonparallel	Parallel
Gina Maria plans to get published, to sell lots of articles, and she hopes for a Pulitzer prize.	Gina Maria plans *to get* published, *to sell* lots of articles, and *to win* a Pulitzer prize.

Figure 17 - Nonparallel & Parallel Lists

In the first example, the verb phrases *to get published* and *to sell lots of articles* are parallel, but the clause *she hopes for a Pulitzer prize* is not parallel with the phrases. Even if the clause were to read *she hopes to win a Pulitzer prize*, the words *she hopes* would make it non-parallel. To produce a parallel construction, each word, phrase, and/or clause should be used as the same part of speech.

Problems with Conciseness

Negative constructions and unnecessary doubling of prepositions are two factors that impair conciseness. The following sections discuss these problems.

Negative Constructions

Just as a frown requires more muscles, a negative construction requires more words. Note how I've rephrased the negative statement in Figure 18 to a positive statement. This not only yields a savings of seven words, but it's much less self-defensive.

Negative	Positive
The problem does not come from incompetence; it comes from not having enough people to do the job.	The problem comes from lacking enough people to do the job.

Figure 18 - Negative vs. Positive Construction

Unnecessary Prepositions

Some writers feel an inexplicable need to use two prepositions where one will suffice. In the statement, Jason picked the book *off of* the floor, for instance, there's no need for both *off* and *of*. It could and should read, Jason picked the book *off* the floor.

Three other enemies of conciseness deserve a bit more attention: extraneous words, wordy phrases, and the passive voice.

Extraneous Words

It's a rare writer who doesn't use more words than needed, at least occasionally. These extra words are frequently modifiers, paired with weak verbs, that attempt to perform the work of stronger verbs. Other times, writers pad their sentences with *expletives*. Although an expletive may be a swear word, it may also be a word like *it* or *there*. Expletives add no meaning to the sentences in which they appear.

Wordy Phrases

The trend in today's writing is away from wordiness toward conciseness. To that end, the quick-reference charts illustrate several words and phrases that lead to passiveness and wordiness: *it is, there are, that,* and *very*, plus numerous wordy phrases. For instance, you can almost always replace the phrase, *at the present time* with *now,* and *if this should prove to be the case* with *if*.

The quick-reference charts list other wordy phrases and suggest alternatives.

Active vs. Passive Voice

The *active voice* reveals who or what performs an action; the *passive voice* may or may not. For example, "Long inserts should be written on separate pages and be labeled on the manuscript" does not reveal who is performing the action.

You can rewrite this statement to reveal or imply who is performing the action: "*Authors* [or *You*] should write long inserts on separate pages and label them on the manuscript," or simply, "Write long inserts on separate pages and label them on the manuscript." In the second revision, the subject (you) is implied.

Figure 19 contrasts the active and passive voice in simple past, present, and future tenses.

Tense	Passive Voice	Active Voice
• Past	This book was written for you.	I wrote this book for you.
• Present	This book is dedicated to you.	I dedicate this book to you.
• Future	You will be shown how to create a custom style guide.	I will show you how to create a custom style guide.

Figure 19 - Active & Passive Voice

Although the passive voice tends to weaken writing, and for the most part you should avoid it, it is occasionally warranted. For instance, you might use the passive voice when you have reason not to name the performer of an action. "All employees and their spouses or partners are invited to the company picnic" doesn't say who is doing the inviting, nor does it need to.

Writing in the third person tends to lead to passive constructions. So does the use of the following:

- *am, are, be, been, being, is, was,* and *were*

- *give, have, hold, make, take,* and *or*

- words ending in *–ment* or *–tion*

If you're writing with a computer, note that grammar-checking software can often identify passive constructions and provide opportunities for you to correct them.

Problems with Precision

Problems with precision include mistaken meanings and mistaken usage. Nearly every style book addresses several words whose meanings people regularly confuse (affect/effect, lay/lie, precede/proceed, and so on). In addition, style books often point out words people sometimes use as the wrong part of speech. The quick-reference charts address some of these commonly confused words.

That vs. *Which*

One distinction of precision deserves a special mention—*that* versus *which* when used in a clause. Nearly every style guide agrees that restrictive clauses should begin with *that*. A *restrictive clause* is one that defines or restricts the word that precedes it. In the sentence, "We'll first stock the book that appeals to cake lovers" the clause, "that appeals to cake lovers" is necessary to complete our meaning. A *nonrestrictive clause* simply adds some "frosting." For example, "This book, *which contains one thousand cake recipes,* will appeal to cake lovers." We treat nonrestrictive clauses parenthetically and set them off with commas or equivalent marks.

Which can be used in both restrictive and nonrestrictive clauses. However, the number of folks who reserve *which* for nonrestrictive use has risen significantly over recent years. You might therefore follow suit to keep from getting caught up in "which hunts."

How to Use Chapter 3's Quick-Reference Charts

The quick-reference charts for Chapter 3 consist of four sections: 1) Conciseness, 2) Consistency, 3) Precision, and 4) Outdated Rules.

The left-hand columns of all these charts list style guidelines, organized alphabetically by categories, subcategories, and/or bold key words. These columns may also contain notes, exceptions, and cautions.

The center column of the Conciseness and Consistency charts lists typical problems. Similarly, outdated guidelines appear in the center column of the Outdated Rules charts. The right-hand columns suggest alternatives. Figure 20 shows a sample segment of a partial entry in the Conciseness chart.

Extraneous Words

it, there	**Extraneous**	**Alternative**
Limit *it is/isn't* and *there are/aren't* constructions.	*It isn't* easy to make a living as a writer.	Making a living as a writer isn't easy.
	There are too many writers who want to be published much more than they want to write.	Too many writers want to be published much more than they want to write.

Figure 20 - Sample Quick-Reference Chart Segment

The left-hand columns of the Precision charts contain sets of frequently confused words. The center columns illustrate the first word. The right-hand columns illustrate the second.

The charts in this chapter are almost exclusively for reference. The few customizable options include a "write-on" line. Use these lines to record your preferences. Figure 21 shows a sample segment from a Precision chart.

as, like	**As** ✔	**Like** ✔
• Informal usage accepts *like* as a conjunction when a comparison follows.	Nora's essays are ___ irreverent, *as* Dave Barry's work is. [FORMAL–COMPARISON]	Nora's essays are ___ irreverent, *like* Dave Barry's work is. [INFORMAL–COMPARISON]
• Formal usage does not.		

Figure 21 - Sample Quick-Reference Chart Segment

The charts provide a good foundation for addressing grammar questions, but as you use them, keep these points in mind:

1. Some words fit more than one category under the same part of speech,

2. Many words can be used as more than one part of speech, and

3. The charts provide examples, not complete listings of every possibility.

Usage notes appear at the end of the chapter, after the quick-reference charts. For further information, check the glossary or explore the sources in the annotated bibliography.

Summary

This chapter has addressed common grammatical problems related to clarity, conciseness, consistency, and precision.

- *Problems with clarity* include dangling, misplaced, and squinting modifiers; missing prepositions; and unclear antecedents.

- *Problems with consistency* include disagreement; inconsistent case, person, number, or tense; and nonparallel constructions.

- *Problems with conciseness* include negative constructions, unnecessary prepositions, extraneous words, wordy phrases, and passive constructions.

- *Problems with precision* relate primarily to confusing one word with another.

The quick-reference charts that follow illustrate some of these concepts in more depth, and in addition, address outdated rules.

Conciseness

EXTRANEOUS WORDS

it, there	Extraneous	Alternative
Limit *it is/isn't* and *there are/aren't* constructions. (See *expletives, p. 27.*) (See *expletives, p. 33.*)	*It* isn't easy to make a living as a writer. *There are* too many writers who want to be published much more than they want to write.	Making a living as a writer isn't easy. Too many writers want to be published much more than they want to write.

that	Extraneous	Alternative
Avoid extraneous *thats*	Angela thinks *that* there's no better calling than being a writer.	Angela thinks there's no better calling than being a writer.
CAUTION: Use *that* to clarify the relationship between verbs and times.		The boss reported Tuesday *that* sales fluttered a little.

very	Extraneous	Alternative
Avoid *very* with absolute terms such as *complete, final,* and *unique.*	I think you'll find I have a *very* unique imagination.	I think you'll find I have a unique imagination.
TIP: Use strong verbs in place of modifiers.	The editor was *very* mad when she saw the proofs.	The editor fumed when she saw the proofs.

Wordy Phrases	Wordy	More Concise
Substitute single words or shorter forms for wordy phrases.	• at the present time • at your earliest convenience • due to the fact that • in the majority of cases • if this should prove to be the case • it is probable that	• now • soon • because • usually • if • probably

Consistency

AGREEMENT

Pronoun–Antecedent	Vague	Specific
Each pronoun (noun substitute) should refer to a specific antecedent (original noun).	Jim told Matt *his* article was accepted. [WHOSE ARTICLE?]	Jim said, "Matt, *my* [or *your*] article was accepted."
TIP: Watch for nonspecific references when using *he, it, one, she, that, these, they, this, those,* and *which.*	Effective editors are objective, organized, and attentive to details. *This* ensures their success. [THIS WHAT?]	Effective editors are objective, organized, and attentive to details. *These skills* ensure their success.

Singular Subject–Verb	Inconsistent	Consistent
Company names, even those including several surnames	Holt, Rinehart, and Winston *are* a major textbook publisher.	Holt, Rinehart, and Winston *is* a major textbook publisher.
Compound subjects joined with *and,* when used as one unit	Peanut butter and jelly *are* Ralph's favorite sandwich combination.	Peanut butter and jelly *is* Ralph's favorite sandwich combination.
Singular subjects "supplemented" by *along with, and not, as well as, including, in addition to,* or *with*	Rain, as well as hail, *are* expected here tonight.	Rain, as well as hail, *is* expected here tonight.

Plural Subject–Verb	Inconsistent	Consistent
Compound subjects joined with *and,* when both parts are plural	All of Ken's manuscripts and query letters *has* returned unopened.	All of Ken's manuscripts and query letters *have* returned unopened.
Plural subjects "supplemented" by *along with, and not, as well as, including, in addition to,* or *with*	Short stories, and not her novel, *is* keeping Sally busy at nights.	Short stories, and not her novel, *are* keeping Sally busy at nights.

Singular/Plural Subject–Verb	Singular ✔	Plural ✔
Collective nouns, such as *audience, committee, couple, faculty, family, minority, percent,* and *variety,* can be singular or plural, depending on the author's intentions.	The *audience is* listening.	The *audience are* managers, supervisors, and work group leaders.
	A *variety* of foods *is* important for good health.	A *variety* of entries *are* expected.
The number of takes a singular verb, and *a **number of*** takes a plural.	*The* number of revisions that book has gone through *is* remarkable.	A number of additional revisions *are* needed before the book is done.
NOTE: British writers are less likely to accept plural collective forms.	The *faculty is* demanding an increase.	The *faculty are* demanding an increase.
Paired words: • Pair the verb with the nearest subject in ***either/or*** and ***neither/nor*** constructions.	*Either* three sample chapters *or* a proposal *is* due by Friday.	*Either* a proposal *or* three sample chapters *are* due by Friday.
Single words: • *Any* can be singular or plural, depending on the meaning.	*Is* there *any* other person who writes as well?	*Are* there *any* typos?
• Some writers use ***none*** as singular or plural.	*None* of you knows ___ what I've sacrificed.	*None* are happier ___ to be published than poets.
• Others reserve ***none*** for plurals and use ***not one*** for singulars.	*Not one* of Max's ___ stories *is* going to be published.	Max says *none* but ___ the best of his stories *were* submitted.
TIP: Match the verb to the true subject, not the expletive (*it is, there is, there are*). (See *expletives, p. 27.*) (See *expletives, p. 33.*)	The weather forecaster said *there is a few* storms in the area.	The weather forecaster said *there are a few* storms in the area.

PARALLELISM	Nonparallel	Parallel
A *parallel construction* uses the same part of speech or type of construction for related words, phrases, or clauses.	Gina Maria plans to get published, sell lots of articles, and she hopes to win a Pulitzer prize.	Gina Maria plans to get published, to sell lots of articles, and to win a Pulitzer prize.
TIPS: • You can often rewrite nonparallel statements in a variety of ways.	We will study writing, editing, and how to proofread.	We will study writing, editing, and proofreading.
• In addition to body text, check headings, subheadings, and tables of contents for parallel construction.		

TENSE	Singular	Plural
• **Simple Past** *(See British Usage, p. 62.)*	I wrote You wrote He/she/it wrote	We wrote You wrote They wrote
• **Simple Present**	I write You write He/she/it writes	We write You write They write
• **Simple Future**	I will write You will write He/she/it will write	We will write You will write They will write
• **Past Perfect** *had*	I had written You had written He/she/it had written	We had written You had written They had written
• **Present Perfect** *has/have*	I have written You have written He/she/it has written	We have written You have written They have written
• **Future Perfect** *shall have, will have*	I will have written You will have written He/she/it will have written	We will have written You will have written They will have written
• **Past Progressive** *was/were + –ing*	I was writing You were writing He/she/it was writing	We were writing You were writing They were writing
• **Present Progressive** *am/are/is + –ing*	I am writing You are writing He/she/it is writing	We are writing You are writing They are writing
• **Future Progressive** *will be + –ing*	I will be writing You will be writing He/she/it will be writing	We will be writing You will be writing They will be writing
• **Past Perfect Progressive** *had been + –ing*	I had been writing You had been writing He/she/it had been writing	We had been writing You had been writing They had been writing
• **Present Perfect Progressive** *have been + –ing* *has been + –ing*	I have been writing You have been writing He/she/it has been writing	We have been writing You have been writing They have been writing
Future Perfect Progressive *will have been + –ing*	I will have been writing You will have been writing He/she/it will have been writing	We will have been writing You will have been writing They will have been writing

Precision

MISTAKEN MEANING	Keep an eye open for similar words with different meanings and word choices that vary with usage.	
ability, capacity	**Ability**	**Capacity**
• *Ability* relates to the power to accomplish something. • *Capacity* relates to the power to contain or receive something.	Does this writer have the ability to complete the assignment? [POWER TO ACCOMPLISH]	Does this hard drive have enough capacity to meet our needs? [POWER TO CONTAIN/RECEIVE]
affect, effect	**Affect**	**Effect**
• *Affect* is almost always a verb. • *Effect* is a noun.	How do others' critiques affect your writing? [INFLUENCE]	What effect do others' critiques have on your writing? [RESULT]
CAUTION: In education and psychology, *affect* may be used as a noun to describe feelings/moods.	Her affect was depressed for several months. [FEELING/MOOD]	
allude, elude	**Allude**	**Elude**
• *Allude* refers to making an indirect reference. • *Elude* refers to escaping.	That's not what I mean to allude to. [INDIRECT REFERENCE]	Greg managed to elude a tax audit this year. [ESCAPE]
alternate, alternative	**Alternate**	**Alternative**
• *Alternate* refers to changing back and forth or taking turns. • *Alternative* refers to making a choice or being outside the norm. EXCEPTION: As adverbs, *alternate* and *alternative* are interchangeable.	I alternate between freewriting and editing my work carefully. [CHANGING BACK & FORTH] Jack and Jill will answer the grammar hotline on alternate days. [TAKING TURNS]	Your story was so implausible, we had no alternative but to reject it. [CHOICE] Mike writes for alternative papers. [OUTSIDE THE NORM]

Mistaken Meaning *(continued)*

assure, ensure, insure	Assure ✔	Ensure/Insure ✔
• *Assure* means convince. • *Ensure* means make certain.	I assure you that this book will sell. ___ [CONVINCE/U.S.]	Could you ensure that this book sells? [MAKE CERTAIN]
EXCEPTION: In British usage, *assure* means protect against loss.	Please assure this package when it ships. ___ [PROTECT/BRITISH]	
• *Insure* means protect against loss. (See *ensure, insure, p. 111.*)		Please insure this package when it ships. ___ [PROTECT/U.S.]

bimonthly, semimonthly	Bimonthly	Semimonthly
• *Bimonthly* means every other month. • *Semimonthly* means twice a month. NOTE: The same applies for *annually* and *weekly*.	We print this journal bimonthly, producing issues six times a year. [EVERY OTHER]	We print this newsletter semimonthly, producing two issues a month. [TWICE]

can, may	Can	May
• *Can* refers to ability. • *May* refers to permission or possibility.	I can write circles around you, Bub. [ABILITY]	We may run your article next week, if there's room. [PERMISSION OR POSSIBILITY]

complement, compliment	Complement	Compliment
• *Complement* means accompany or complete. • *Compliment* means praise.	Those colors complement each other nicely. [ACCOMPANY/COMPLETE]	Dayna received the nicest compliment about her column yesterday. [PRAISE]

continual, continuous	Continual	Continuous
• *Continual* means recurrent. • *Continuous* means uninterrupted.	That writer has continual difficulties writing a good lead. [RECURRENT]	To form a circle, you draw a continuous line. [UNINTERRUPTED]

Mistaken Meaning *(continued)*

device, devise	**Device**	**Devise**
• *Device* is a noun. • *Devise* is usually a verb.	How do you work this device? [NOUN]	Could you devise a better plan? [VERB]
NOTE: *Devise* also is a legal term related to the disposition of property.	You bequeath cars and jewelry in a will, but you devise real estate. [LEGAL]	

farther, further	**Farther**	**Further**
• *Farther* relates to distance • *Further* as an adjective relates to addition and as a verb relates to advancement.	I have come much farther than you. [DISTANCE]	I'll require nothing further. [ADDITION] A regular column would further your career. [ADVANCEMENT]

imply, infer	**Imply**	**Infer**
• *Imply* means suggest. • *Infer* means conclude.	Whatever are you implying? [SUGGESTION]	From the publisher's comments, I'd infer a strong interest. [CONCLUDE]

lay, lie	**Lay**	**Lie**
• *Lay* means place or put and needs a direct object. • *Lie* means recline or rest and needs no direct object.	Lay your work aside, and take a break. [PLACE/PUT] Do your hens lay good eggs? [DEPOSIT EGGS]	Could I lie down for a moment? [RECLINE/REST]
CAUTION: The past tense of *lie* is *lay*, while the past tense of *lay* is *laid*.	Ben laid the manuscript on the table. [PAST TENSE OF *LAY*]	Ben lay down and fell asleep after lunch. [PAST TENSE OF *LIE*]

people, persons	**People**	**Persons**
• Use *people* to emphasize a group. • Use *persons* to emphasize individuals.	". . . a government of the people, by the people, and for the people." [GROUP] —Abraham Lincoln	Use the phrase "persons with mental illness" in place of "the mentally ill." [INDIVIDUALS]

Mistaken Meaning *(continued)*

precede, proceed	**Precede**	**Proceed**
• Something that *precedes* something else comes before it. • *Proceed* implies advancement or going on.	Centuries labeled BC precede those labeled AD. [BEFORE]	Let's proceed with the questions. [GO ON]
shall, will	**Shall**	**Will**
• *Shall* refers to determination. • *Will* refers to inclination. NOTE: This distinction is rapidly disappearing. *Shall* is now rarely used.	I shall never submit another manuscript without an SASE. [DETERMINATION]	I will call you if any questions arise. [INCLINATION]
than, then	**Than**	**Then**
• *Than* is used for comparison. • *Then* relates to sequence or time.	We're all older than we used to be. [COMPARISON]	Brush your teeth, then floss them afterwards. [SEQUENCE]

MISTAKEN USAGE

Opinions are mixed about these points of usage. Indicate your preferences on the write-on lines.

as, like	**As** ✔	**Like** ✔
• Use *as*, *as if*, or *as though* with clauses. TIP: A clause has both a subject and a predicate (verb).	Do *as* I say, not *as* I do. [SUBJECT: *I*, PREDICATE: *SAY*.]	
• Use *like* when a noun or pronoun completes the object and no verb follows.		I 'd like to write *like* Barbara Kingsolver. [NO VERB AFTER *LIKE*]
• Informal usage accepts *like* as a conjunction when a comparison follows. • Formal usage does not.	Nora's essays are ___ irreverent, *as* Dave Barry's work is. [FORMAL–COMPARISON]	Nora's essays are ___ irreverent, *like* Dave Barry's work is. [INFORMAL–COMPARISON]
• Informal usage accepts *like* as a conjunction when an illustration follows. • Formal usage does not.	Rick writes works ___ of fiction, *such as* science fiction/fantasy. [FORMAL–ILLUSTRATION]	Rick writes works ___ of fiction, *like* science fiction/fantasy. [INFORMAL–ILLUSTRATION]

that, which	**That**	**Which**
• *That* helps identify the subject. • *Which* adds extraneous information. When used nonrestrictively, it is parenthetical and is punctuated accordingly.	Kim's favorite story that she wrote last year has not yet sold. [RESTRICTIVE—FAVORITE STORY WRITTEN LAST YEAR]	Kim's favorite story, which she wrote last year, has not yet sold. [NONRESTRICTIVE—FAVORITE OF ALL STORIES WRITTEN]
• Some people accept the restrictive use of *which*; others find it ambiguous. (See *descriptive or parenthetical information, p. 72*.)	Darrell liked the ___ book which is set in 1909. [RESTRICTIVE]	Darrell liked that ___ book, which is set in 1909. [NONRESTRICTIVE]

Outdated Rules

A vs. AN	THE OLD RULE: Use *an* before *historic*.	

Guidelines	Old Rule Example ✔	Alternative ✔
Using *an* before *historic* ties to a British tendency to drop the initial *h*. Instead—	This is *an* historic moment. ___	This is *a* historic moment. ___
• Use *a* when words begin with a consonant, a sounded *h* or an *o* with a *w* sound.		*a* hero [SOUNDED *H*] *a* one [O WITH A *W* SOUND]
• Use *a* when words begin with a long *u*.		*a* unique [LONG *u*]
• Use *an* when words begin with a silent *h* or a vowel sound (except a long *u*).		*an* honor [SILENT *H*]

BEGINNING A SENTENCE WITH A CONJUNCTION	THE OLD RULE: Never start a sentence with a conjunction.	

Guidelines	Old Rule Example ✔	Alternative ✔
In all but the most formal writing, you can start a sentence with a conjunction. (See *Usage Note, p. 62*.)	That would be all I have to say. ___	*And* that's that! ___
	The dish ran away with the spoon. ___	*And* the dish ran away with the spoon. ___

ENDING A SENTENCE WITH A PREPOSITION	THE OLD RULE: Never end a sentence with a preposition.	

Guidelines	Old Rule Example ✔	Alternative ✔
In all but the most formal writing, you can end a sentence with a preposition.	*To* what are you referring? ___	What are you referring *to*? ___
NOTE: You can follow the old rule or not, or simply write around the problem. (See *Usage Note, p. 62*.)	This is the best reference *of* which I am aware. ___	This is the best reference I know *of*. ___

SPLIT INFINITIVES	THE OLD RULE: Never split an infinitive. (Don't separate *to* and the main verb.)			
Guidelines	**Old Rule Example**	✔	**Alternative**	✔
This rule wrongly assumes you can't split infinitives in English since you can't do so in Latin. (See *Usage Note, p. 62*.)	We plan *to approve* the budget tentatively.	___	We plan *to* tentatively *approve* the budget.	___
NOTE: You can follow the old rule or not, or simply write around the problem.			We plan *to approve* a tentative budget.	___

WHO* vs. *WHOM	THE OLD RULE: Use *whom* as the object of a preposition, *regardless of its position*.			
Guidelines	**Old Rule Example**	✔	**Alternative**	✔
• In formal usage, *who* is always the subject. (*Who*, the "doer," equals *he, she,* or *they*.)	*Who* will publish your work? [SUBJECTIVE]			
• In formal usage, *whom* is the object. (*Whom*, the receiver, equals *her, him,* or *them*.)	*Whom* should I submit this *to*? [OBJECTIVE—FORMAL]	___	*Who* should I submit this *to*? [OBJECTIVE—INFORMAL]	___
• In informal usage, you can use *who* unless it's the direct object of the clause it begins.	*To whom* should I submit this ? [OBJECTIVE—FORMAL]	___	*To whom* should I submit this ? [OBJECTIVE—INFORMAL]	___
NOTE: In many cases, you can write around *who* and *whom*.	She is the agent *whom* I prefer.	___	She is the agent I prefer.	___

BRITISH USAGE

British usage sometimes calls for a past participle where U.S. usage calls for simple past. (Example: British usage may call for *got* where U.S. usage calls for *gotten*.)

USAGE NOTE

Don't follow an outdated rule when doing so will result in an awkward or stilted construction.

4

Does This Require a Comma?

Punctuation

*P*unctuation exists to clarify meaning, provide rhythm, and convey emotion. We haven't always had punctuation: As I understand it, Early Latin was written in all caps, with no spaces between words. If we still followed those standards, we'd conceivably be reading sentences like this:

IMAGINEHAVINGNOPUNCTUATIONOR
CAPITALIZATIONORSPACINGTODISTIN
GUISHONESENTENCEFROMANOTHER

Now, aren't you glad we have punctuation?

This chapter deals with sixteen types of punctuation marks: apostrophes, brackets, colons, commas, double quotation marks, single quotation marks, ellipses, em dashes, en dashes, exclamation points, hyphens, parentheses, periods, question marks, semicolons, and slashes. Figure 22, which appears on page 64, illustrates each of these marks. And the quick-reference charts that begin on page 71 provide numerous guidelines and examples for each mark.

Don't worry if you find some of these marks unfamiliar. When you've finished this chapter, you'll understand each one.

,	comma	**'**	apostrophe
;	semicolon	**( )**	parentheses
:	colon	**[ ]**	brackets
-	hyphen	**/**	slash
—	em dash	**. . .**	ellipsis
–	en dash	**.**	period
" "	double quotation marks	**?**	question mark
' '	single quotation marks	**!**	exclamation point

Figure 22 - Sixteen Types of Punctuation Marks

Common Punctuation Standards

Punctuation may be the most variable aspect of publication style. With few exceptions, publishers favor one of two basic styles:

- *Closed punctuation* (also called heavy, formal, or traditional)

- *Open punctuation* (also called light, informal, or conversational)

While the motto of closed punctuators might be "Punctuate where'er you hesitate," the motto of open punctuators might be "When in doubt, leave it out."

Writers who use the closed approach tend to use more discretionary marks, particularly optional commas. For example, they insert more commas after introductory words or phrases, before summations, or around interruptions.

Writers who use the open approach tend to limit discretionary marks. For example, they omit commas after introductory elements, before summations, and surrounding interruptions.

Yet, both types of punctuators insert commas for clarity and emphasis. For example, they both use commas when words, phrases, or clauses are "out of position" (A forty-year veteran of newscasting, Larry finally retired). The quick-reference charts on pages 71–96 illustrate both closed and open punctuation.

Identifying Closed vs. Open Punctuation

One of the most reliable ways to distinguish between closed and open punctuation is to examine whether *serial commas* are used. (Think of *serial* as meaning a series of three or more items.) Closed punctuators use serial commas: They insert a comma before the conjunction that precedes the last item in a series (beepers, cell phones, and modems).

> **Refresher:** A *conjunction* connects two or more words, phrases, clauses, or sentences. Conjunctions commonly used in series include *and, nor,* and *or.*

Although closed punctuators use serial commas most of the time, they do make exceptions, as detailed in the quick-reference charts. Open punctuators omit serial commas whenever the meaning is clear without them (beepers, cell phones and modems).

Choosing the Best Approach

Which school of thought is "best"? It depends. The style you choose should fit the situation. When used unconsciously, any style can cause problems. For instance, whether you use serial commas or not, you should treat items that constitute one unit differently than items that stand alone.

To illustrate, let's say you're writing about three types of sandwiches: 1) grilled cheese, 2) turkey, and 3) peanut butter and jelly. If you're an open punctuator, you might omit the comma after *turkey* automatically. Your readers might then conceivably believe that you were describing only two types of sandwiches: 1) grilled cheese, 2) turkey and peanut butter and jelly. (Bleah!) No matter what style you normally follow, you'd need the serial comma after turkey to convey your intended meaning.

But you're not off the hook if you're a closed punctuator either. If you're in the habit of inserting a comma in front of every conjunction, you just might place a comma after *peanut butter* simply because the conjunction *and* follows. Then you'd appear to be writing about four types of sandwiches: 1) grilled cheese, 2) turkey, 3) peanut butter, and 4) jelly. You can't punctuate effectively on automatic pilot.

Basic Considerations

When determining punctuation standards, consider the following factors:

- What the audience or market is used to

- The norm for the medium, organization, product, or publication

- The purpose of the communication

The most effective style retains the consistency of the whole as much as possible while communicating the writer's intention.

Closed Punctuation. Closed punctuation permeates most of the book publishing industry and is the approach recommended in *The Chicago Manual of Style* (Chicago)—the book publisher's "bible." Several other well-known authorities endorse closed punctuation:

- *Words Into Type* (WIT)—another book publishing manual

- The U.S. Government Printing Office's *A Manual of Style* (GPO)

- *The MLA Style Manual* (MLA) and the *Publication Manual of the American Psychological Association* (APA)—two guides used widely in academia and for scholarly journals

Open Punctuation. Most newspapers, magazines, and advertisements use open punctuation, with occasional exceptions. For instance, the Associated Press (AP) and United Press International (UPI) both insert a serial comma in series of longer phrases, even though they endorse open punctuation otherwise. Here's an example of this type:

> Writers who wish to be published must study the markets thoroughly, prepare their manuscripts carefully, and submit their work repeatedly.

As with any style, what's most appropriate depends upon the situation.

Geographic Considerations

A final factor to consider when deciding between closed and open punctuation is geography. U.S. and British usage approach punctuation differently. For instance, where U.S. writers use double quotation marks, British writers generally use single quotation marks, and vice versa. (Hey, I never claimed punctuation standards were simple!) The quick-reference charts in this book note other differences between U.S. and British usage. For further information about British usage, check the sources in the annotated bibliography.

Another geographic consideration is meeting the needs of audiences whose first language is not English. For such readers, it's often best to overpunctuate (use closed punctuation). In *Internationally Yours,* Mary A. De Vries says punctuation is "like a roadmap to foreign readers." She suggests you avoid ellipses, exclamation points, and slashes in two-word combinations (he/she, writer/editor, and so on) in works for foreign audiences.

General Considerations

As with any style decision, punctuation standards should be set with the audience, medium, and message in mind. Beyond those factors, what counts most is consistency.

The quick-reference charts in this chapter provide general punctuation guidelines, focusing primarily on closed versus open punctuation. You need not adhere exclusively to one approach or the other. However, it's helpful to choose one basic approach and make exceptions only when necessary to clarify meaning. Before exploring these charts, let's examine one further consideration—the jobs that punctuation marks perform.

The Jobs of Punctuation

People experiencing punctuation dilemmas often seek absolute rules about the placement of marks—context aside—instead of considering their purpose. I'm often asked questions such as "Does a compound sentence require a comma?" Without some sense of context and the circumstances involved, the only honest answer is, It depends.

Punctuation marks become much more meaningful when you consider the jobs they perform. Punctuation marks can 1) enclose, 2) end, 3) introduce, 4) join, 5) replace, or 6) separate letters, words, clauses, or phrases; they can also 7) indicate emotion or special usage.

Figure 23 associates the sixteen punctuation marks introduced earlier in this chapter with the jobs they perform. These jobs appear in the left-hand vertical column. The associated punctuation marks appear to the right of each job.

JOB	MARK					
Enclose	[ ] *brackets* [1]	, *comma*	— *em dash*	- *en dash* [2]	( ) *parentheses* [1]	" " ' ' *quotation marks* [3]
End	: *colon*	, *comma*	— *em dash*	- *en dash* [2]	! *exclamation point* [4]	. ? *period* *question mark*
Indicate	, *apostrophe*	. . . *ellipsis* [4]	— *em dash* [5]			
Introduce	: *colon*	, *comma*	— *em dash*	- *en dash*		
Join	, *comma*	— *em dash*	- *en dash*	- *hyphen*	; *semicolon*	/ *slash*
Replace	, *apostrophe*	: *colon*	, *comma*	— *em dash*	- *en dash*	- *hyphen* / *slash*
Separate	: *colon*	, *comma*	. . . *ellipsis* [4]	— *em dash*	- *en dash*	- ; / *hyphen* *semicolon* *slash* [4]

[1] British usage generally calls for parentheses within brackets rather than brackets within parentheses.

[2] British usage generally prefers en dashes in place of em dashes.

[3] British usage for both double and single quotation marks generally counters U.S. usage.

[4] Avoid ellipses, exclamation points, and slashes used with combinations such as writer/editor when communicating with audiences whose first language is not English.

[5] To avoid repetition, publishers sometimes use 2- and 3-em dashes to indicate missing letters and words, particularly in reference lists. For example:

Venolia, Jan. *Rewrite Right!* Berkeley: Ten Speed Press, 1987.
——. *Write Right!* (rev. ed.). Berkeley: Ten Speed Press, 1988.

Figure 23 - The Jobs of Punctuation

The "Feel" of Punctuation

As Figure 23 illustrates, sometimes more than one type of punctuation mark can perform the same job, and you must choose between them. For instance, you might enclose parenthetical information inside a pair of commas, parentheses, or em dashes.

But be careful: Just because two different punctuation marks can sometimes perform the same job does not mean you can always interchange them.

To choose between such alternatives, you need to consider each mark's "feel." Some marks blend quietly into the background; others make a loud outcry. Unless overused, commas and periods act like wallflowers, while ellipses and exclamation points leap into the limelight. Parentheses downplay their contents, while em dashes exclaim, "Hey, look at this!"

How to Use Chapter 4's Quick-Reference Charts

The quick-reference charts for Chapter 4 are organized by the jobs each punctuation mark performs (enclose, end, indicate, introduce, join, replace, separate). If you know what job a punctuation mark must perform but not which mark to use, scan the charts by job name. Figure 24 shows a sample segment from a quick-reference chart.

SEPARATE	Mark	Example	✔
Subtitles • Some writers use a colon.	‖ *colon*	*Style Meister: The Quick-Reference Custom Style Guide*	—
• Others use an em dash.	— *em dash (double dash)*	*Style Meister—The Quick-Reference Custom Style Guide*	—

Figure 24 - Sample Quick-Reference Chart Segment

The jobs appear alphabetically in large bold letters in the left-hand column. Text preceded by a round bullet (•) applies to the example with which it aligns horizontally. Flush-left text and notes preceded by dashes apply to the entire block of text that appears between one solid horizontal line and the next.

Often, two or more punctuation marks can perform the same job. For instance, you can separate a book subtitle from a main title with a colon or with an em dash. Thin gray lines set off interchangeable marks and common—but conflicting—style standards (closed versus open punctuation, and so on).

The second column displays oversized punctuation marks for easy reference. To answer questions about specific punctuationmarks,youcanquicklyscanthiscolumn.

The third column displays examples that illustrate the guidelines. Additional information occasionally appears in brackets.

The far-right column—the one containing a checkmark (✔)—displays "write-on lines," on which you can record the options you prefer or rank your preferences by number. (Use *1* for your first preference, *2* for the next, and so on.).

Unless you're marking up or producing final camera-ready copy, you need only skim the guidelines for em dashes and en dashes. If you're preparing a manuscript that someone else will produce, indicate em dashes by typing double hyphens; you probably won't need to deal with en dashes at all.

Once you become familiar with the layout of these charts and determine which options you prefer, you will find them quite useful. The appendix includes reproducible punctuation forms on which you can record additional guidelines.

Usage notes appear at the end of the chapter, after the quick-reference charts. For further information, check the glossary or explore the sources in the annotated bibliography.

The following abbreviation appears in this chapter's quick-reference charts.

A	answer (in Q&A format)
Q	question (in Q&A format)
Q&A	question-and-answer

Figure 25 - Abbreviation Key

Summary

This chapter has explained sixteen types of punctuation marks in terms of the jobs they perform and the "feel" of each mark. In addition, the chapter has suggested ways to choose between two common standards: closed and open punctuation.

The quick-reference charts that follow provide guidelines and examples for each of the sixteen marks.

Punctuation Guidelines

ENCLOSE	Mark	Example	✔
An alteration or elaboration within a quote • Some writers use brackets.	**[ ]** *brackets*	"Reading maketh a full man [or woman]; . . . writing an exact man [or woman]." <div align="right">—Francis Bacon</div>	—
• Others use parentheses. NOTES: • Brackets more clearly define additions to a quote. • Punctuate both ends. (See *brackets, p. 95.*)	**( )** *parentheses*	"Reading maketh a full man (or woman); . . . writing an exact man (or woman)."	—
A cross-reference to a chapter or section, page, piece of art, reference, or other element • Some writers use brackets.	**[ ]** *brackets*	[see Chapter 4] [continued on page 8] [Smith & Jones, 1992]	— — —
• Others use parentheses. NOTE: Punctuate both ends. (See *brackets, p. 95.*)	**( )** *parentheses*	(see Chapter 4) (continued on page 8) (Smith & Jones, 1992)	— — —
A definition or translation • Some writers use double quotation marks.	**" "** *double quotation marks*	Editors place the Latin term *stet,* "let it stand," next to reversed editorial decisions.	—
• Others use single.	**' '** *single quotation marks*	Editors place the Latin term *stet,* 'let it stand,' next to reversed editorial decisions.	—
• Still others use parentheses. NOTE: Punctuate both ends. (See *new term, word, or phrase, p. 74.*) (See [3]*British Usage, p. 96.*)	**( )** *parentheses*	Editors place the Latin term *stet* (let it stand) next to reversed editorial decisions.	—

Enclose *(continued)*

	Mark	Example	✔
Descriptive or parenthetical information • Some writers use commas.	**,** *comma*	She began writing**,** which was her passion**,** at the tender age of six.	——
• Others use em dashes. (See *brackets, p. 95*.) (See [1]*British Usage, p. 96*.)	**—** *em dashes* *(double dashes)*	She began writing**—**which was her passion**—**at the tender age of six.	——
• Still others use parentheses. (See [3]*British Usage, p. 96*.) NOTES:	**( )** *parentheses*	She began writing **(**which was her passion**)** at the tender age of six.	——
• Punctuate both ends. • Use em dashes or parentheses when the enclosed text contains commas.		A *serial comma* precedes the conjunction before the last item in a series **(**beepers, cell phones, and modems**)**.	
Dialogue, exact quotes, or implied speech (but not indented excerpts, internal monologue, or Q&A formats) (See *single-word summation, p. 75*.)	**" "** *double quotation marks*	**"**In matters of style, swim with the current; in matters of principle, stand like a rock.**"** —Thomas Jefferson	
The **dialogue or speech of one person**, when it spans two or more paragraphs NOTE: Use opening quotation marks before each paragraph but closing only after the last.	**" "** *double quotation marks*	**"**My signature isn't worth very much right now. **"**But some day—maybe—it will increase in value!**"** —Tennessee Williams	
An **editorial aside or comment** • Editors' comments usually appear in brackets.	**[ ]** *brackets*	Wise writers study their markets **[**if they want their work published**]**.	——
• Authors' comments usually appear in parentheses. (See *alteration or elaboration, p. 71*.)	**( )** *parentheses*	Good writing takes practice, patience, and perseverance **(**really!**)**.	——

Enclose *(continued)*

	Mark	Example	✔
An interjection or interruption • Some writers use commas.	**,** *comma*	Why, of course, I spell-checked! [CLOSED]	___
• Others omit the commas.		Why of course I spell-checked! [OPEN]	___
• Some writers use em dashes.	▬ *em dashes* *(double dashes)*	Please try to remember—if only for accuracy—to spell my byline right this time.	___
• Others use parentheses. NOTE: Punctuate both ends.	**( )** *parentheses*	Please try to remember (if only for accuracy) to spell my byline right this time.	___
• Some writers enclose transitional words such as *moreover, nevertheless, unfortunately,* and so on.		I'm certain, nonetheless, that my book will sell. [CLOSED]	___
• Others use no parenthetical punctuation.		I'm certain nonetheless that my book will sell. [OPEN]	___
A letter or number preceding a listed item • Some writers use parentheses.	**( )** *parentheses*	Three character formats often used for emphasis are **(a)** bold, **(b)** italics, and **(c)** underlines.	___
• Some writers omit opening parentheses and set only closing parentheses after letters.	**)** *single* *parenthesis*	Three character formats often used for emphasis are a**)** bold, b**)** italics, and c**)** underlines.	___
• Some writers set vertical lists with letters followed by periods and reserve parentheses for lists run in with text. (See *item numbers, p. 191.*)	**•** *period*	Three character formats often used for emphasis are a. bold, b. italics, and c. underlines.	___

Enclose *(continued)*

	Mark	Example	✔
A **location** inserted within a proper name	**( )** *parentheses*	The following article first appeared in *The Wichita* **(**Kansas**)** *Eagle*.	——
A **new term, word, or phrase** on first use • Some writers use double quotation marks.	**" "** *double quotation marks*	A **"**byline**"** is an author credit line above or below a title.	——
• Others use single. (See [2]*British Usage, p. 96.*) (See *quotation marks, p. 95.*)	**' '** *single quotation marks*	A '**byline**' is an author credit line above or below a title.	——
• Still others use special formatting, such as bold, italics, or small caps. NOTE: Terms following *called, so called, known as,* and so on need no special treatment. (See *conveying meaning & creating emphasis, p. 237.*)		A **byline** is an author credit line. [BOLD] A *byline* is an author credit line. [ITALICS] A BYLINE is an author credit line. [SMALL CAPS]	—— —— ——
A **nickname** (except when it substitutes for a real name) • Some writers use double quotation marks. (See [2]*British Usage, p. 96.*)	**" "** *double quotation marks*	This here is Bradley "Bubba" Brown. Bubba knows all about style.	——
• Others use parentheses. (See [3]*British Usage, p. 96.*) (See *quotation marks, p. 95.*)	**( )** *parentheses*	This here is Bradley **(**Bubba**)** Brown. Bubba knows all about style.	——
Parenthetical information that already appears **within parentheses** (See *brackets, p. 95.*) (See [3]*British Usage, p. 96.*)	**[ ]** *brackets*	Status verbs (*is, are, was, were, be, am, been,* and *being* **[**all forms of *to be***]**) often lead to passive writing.	——

Enclose *(continued)*	**Mark**	**Example**	✔
A **quote within a quote** (See [2]*British Usage, p. 96.*) (See *definition or translation, p. 71.*) (See *quotation marks, p. 95.*)	❛ ❜ *single quotation marks*	"Don't utilize 'utilize'; use 'use'!" —ANONYMOUS	—
A **single-word summation** (*yes, no, maybe, never*) only when it is a direct quote (See [2]*British Usage, p. 96.*)	❝ ❞ *double quotation marks*	Have I always loved to write? In a word, "Yes!"	—
A **subjective or unconventional word or phrase** CAUTION: When overused, this style looks sophomoric. (See [2]*British Usage, p. 96.*) (See *quotation marks, p. 95.*)	❝ ❞ *double quotation marks*	No style standard is ever set "for good."	—
A **title** of an article or essay; a lecture, painting, short story, short poem, song, speech, or book chapter or section (See *Figure 49, p. 235.*)	❝ ❞ *double quotation marks*	Jay's story, "My Alien Abduction," appeared in Saturday's paper.	—

END	Mark	Example	✔
A **complete sentence or thought**, or an **indirect question or request**	• *period*	Make no assumptions. Really. Would you please fax your changes by Friday.	
• You can omit the period from a complete sentence enclosed within a sentence.		Some writers (I'm sure *you'd* never do this) submit their manuscripts with no SASE.	—
A **complete sentence that introduces a list** (See *list, p. 79.*) (See *list, p. 80.*)	• *period*	You can do a great deal to become a successful writer. 1. Study your markets thoroughly, 2. Prepare your manuscripts carefully, and 3. Keep submitting work.	—
A **complimentary close** in a letter	, *comma*	Sincerely yours, All my love,	—
• Some writers omit the complimentary close and precede the signature with an em dash alone. (See *greeting, business, p. 77.*) (See *greeting, personal, p. 77.*)	— *em dash (double dash)*	Richard, Let's do lunch. —Helen	—
A **direct question** or an **interrogative clause or statement**	? *question mark*	Have you obtained permission to print this quote?	
• Use a question mark even after incomplete questions.		Will I ever find a publisher? is what most every writer wonders.	
• Use a period after a paraphrased question. (See *indirect question or request, p. 76.*)		The editor asked if I could fax my column by Friday.	

End *(continued)*	Mark	Example	✔
An **expression of strong emotion or surprise**, or an **imperative statement** (See *quotation marks, p. 95.*) (See *exclamation point, p. 95.*)	**!** *exclamation point*	The publishing industry will rave about my book**!** You're kidding**!!** Yee-haw**!!!**	—— —— ——
The **greeting in a formal business letter** (See *complimentary close, p. 76.*) (See *greeting, personal, p. 77.*)	**:** *colon*	Dear Mr. Doe**:**	——
A **greeting in a personal letter** • Some writers use a comma.	**,** *comma*	Dear John**,**	——

• Others use an em dash. (See *complimentary close, p. 76.*) (See *greeting, business, p. 77.*)	**——** *em dash (double dash)*	Richard**—**
		    Let's do lunch.
		         Love, Helen
			——

An **interrupted or incomplete sentence** (See *hesitation, p. 78.*)	**——** *em dash (double dash)*	You don't mean**—**	——

Lettered **items or numbers in an outline** (except when enclosed in parentheses)	**.** *period*	I. Style and Grammar
		    A. A Friendly Refresher
		         not
		 I) Style and Grammar
		    A) A Friendly Refresher
			——

Items in a series, when each requires special **emphasis** • Some writers capitalize the words right after each question mark.	**?** *question mark*	Do you write novels**?** Short stories**?** Poetry**?** [INITIAL CAPS]	——
• Others leave them lowercase.		Do you write novels**?** short stories**?** poetry**?** [LOWERCASE]	——

INDICATE	Mark	Example	✔
Hesitation (See *interrupted or incomplete sentence, p. 77.*) (See *omission from a quote, p 78.*) (See *quotation marks, p. 95.*)	▬▬ *em dash (double dash)*	What a—unique idea.	___
An **omission from a quote** • Some writers space ellipses.	• • • *ellipsis*	"Of every four words. . .,I strike out three." —Nicolas Boileau [SPACED]	___
• Others set ellipses with no space. (See *hesitation, p. 78.*) (See *shift in thought/passage of time, p. 78.*)	••• **ellipsis**	"Of every four words...,I strike out three." [UNSPACED]	___
A possessive (See *common nouns, p. 108.*) (See *personal pronouns, p. 109.*)	**'** *apostrophe*	writer's work [ONE WRITER] writers' work [TWO OR MORE]	
A shift in thought or the **passage of time** • Some writers add a period when an ellipsis ends a sentence.	• • • *ellipsis*	Not for us. . . . Try another market. [PERIOD PLUS ELLIPSIS]	___
• Others use an ellipsis alone.		Not for us. . . Try another market. [ELLIPSIS ALONE]	___
• Still others use em dashes. • Some capitalize the word after the em dash.	▬▬ *em dash (double dash)*	Not for us—Try another market. [CAPITALIZED]	___
• Others set it in lowercase. CAUTION: Some publishers object to these forms. (See *omission from a quote, p 78.*) (See *ellipsis/em dash, p. 95.*)		Not for us—try another market. [LOWERCASE]	___

INTRODUCE	Mark	Example	✔
Dialogue in plays, scripts, and transcripts • Some writers use a colon.	**:** *colon*	HAMLET**:** To be, or not to be: that is the question. 　　　　　—William Shakespeare	___
• Others use an em dash.	**——** *em dash (double dash)*	HAMLET**—**To be, or not to be: that is the question.	___
• Still others use a period.	**.** *period*	HAMLET**.** To be, or not to be: that is the question.	___
An **elaboration, quotation, restatement, or summary** • Some writers use a colon.	**:** *colon*	Here's how to get your work to sell**:** Show, don't tell.	___
• Others use an em dash.	**——** *em dash (double dash)*	Here's how to get your work to sell**—**Show, don't tell.	___
An **example or illustration** • Some writers use a colon.	**:** *colon*	Two marks cause the majority of punctuation problems**:** commas and hyphens.	___
• Others use a comma. 　CAUTION: In some contexts, people may interpret such a comma as part of a series.	**,** *comma*	Two marks cause the majority of punctuation problems**,** commas and hyphens.	___
• Still others use an em dash.	**——** *em dash (double dash)*	Two marks cause the majority of punctuation problems**—**commas and hyphens.	___
A **list**, especially when any of the listed items could complete the sentence (See *complete sentence that introduces a list, p. 76.*) (See *list, p. 80.*)	**——** *em dash (double dash)*	To be a successful writer**—** 1. Study your markets thoroughly, 2. Prepare your manuscripts carefully, and 3. Keep submitting work.	___

Introduce *(continued)*	Mark	Example	✔
A **list**, especially one **preceded by words such as** *as follows, follow, the following*, and so on	• • *colon*	Three common character formats used for emphasis follow: 1) bold, 2) italics, and 3) underlines.	
• When any of the listed items could complete the sentence, many writers omit the colon.		Three common character formats used for emphasis are 1) bold, 2) italics, and 3) underlines. [NO COLON]	___
• Some writers retain the colon even when the text that follows completes the sentence. (See *complete sentence that introduces a list, p. 76.*) (See *list, p. 79.*)		Three common character formats used for emphasis are: 1) bold, 2) italics, and 3) underlines. [WITH COLON]	___
Information in **question-and-answer** format	• • *colon*	Q: What is the meaning of SASE? A: Self-addressed, stamped envelope.	___
A **quote** (See *quote, p. 90.*)	, *comma*	As E.M. Forster said, "I never understand anything until I have written about it."	___
A **summary**	━━ *em dash* *(double dash)*	Beeper, cell phone, and modem—Mary considers each a necessity.	___

JOIN	Mark	Example	✔
Many **compound fractions and numbers**	━ *hyphen*	two-thirds eighty-nine forty-five hundred	
Most **compound modifiers** EXCEPTIONS:	━ *hyphen*	black-and-white photo first-rate editor thought-provoking essay	— — —
• When the compound itself is modified, do not hyphenate between its parts.		Maria is a *very well known* novelist.	
• When the first part of a modifier ends in *–ly* and the second in a participle or an adjective, set the compound as two separate words. (See Chapter 6 for other compounding guidelines.)		That is a *fully indexed* volume. Jim consistently produces *widely read* works.	
Special **compound modifiers**	━ *en dash* (*¹⁄₂ em dash*)	ex–student publication editor [FORMER EDITOR OF STUDENT PUBLICATION]	—
(See ¹*British Usage, p. 96.*)		ex-student publication editor [EDITOR OF ALUMNI PUBLICATION]	—
(See *em dash/en dash, p. 95.*)		post–World War II novel	—
Most **compound nouns**	━ *hyphen*	best-seller self-expression writer-illustrator	— — —
Many **compound verbs**	━ *hyphen*	self-publish spell-check	— —
Otherwise **confusing combinations**	━ *hyphen*	costly-looking glass vs. costly looking-glass short-story editor vs. short story-editor	

Join (*continued*)	**Mark**	**Example**	✔
Closely related **independent clauses joined with a conjunctive adverb or an adverbial phrase** • Some writers use a semicolon.	**;** *semicolon*	I suppose editing can get tedious; however, I find it fascinating.	—
• Others use an em dash.	**▬** *em dash* *(double dash)*	I suppose editing can get tedious—however, I find it fascinating.	—
Independent clauses joined with a coordinate conjunction (*and, or, nor, but, yet, or for*)	**,** *comma*	I've completed the revisions, but I still need to proofread. [CLOSED]	—
• When two short, closely related, noncontradictory clauses share a subject, you can omit the comma as long as the meaning is clear.		I've completed the revisions but I still need to proofread. [OPEN]	—
CAUTIONS: • Do not use a comma *after* a coordinate conjunction.		I've completed the revisions, but I still need to proofread. [NO COMMA AFTER *BUT*]	
• Do not insert a comma between the parts of a compound predicate unless it's needed to clarify the meaning.		I'll revise this now and proofread later on. [NO COMMA AFTER *NOW*]	
• Use a semicolon to join long independent clauses or clauses that already contain commas.	**;** *semicolon*	Some writers write with computers, word processors, and typewriters; others use pencils, pens, and markers.	

Join (*continued*)	**Mark**	**Example**	✔
Closely related **independent clauses** *not* **joined by a conjunction** • Some writers use a semicolon.	**;** *semicolon*	We're not in right now; please leave a message after the tone.	___
• Others use an em dash.	▬▬ *em dash* *(double dash)*	We're not in right now— please leave a message after the tone.	___
Compound **occupational titles** • Some writers use an en dash.	▬ *en dash* (*¹/₂ em dash*)	poet–novelist secretary–treasurer writer–illustrator	___
• Others use a hyphen.	▬ *hyphen*	poet-novelist secretary-treasurer writer-illustrator	___
• Still others use a slash. CAUTION: Some publishers object to this use of a slash. (See [1]*British Usage, p. 96.*) (See *slash, p. 95.*)	**/** *slash*	poet/novelist secretary/treasurer writer/illustrator	___
• An unabsorbed or easily misunderstood **prefix and its root** (See Chapter 6 for other compounding guidelines.)	▬ *hyphen*	co-op cross-reference pre-publication re-form	___ ___ ___ ___

REPLACE	Mark	Example	✔
Letters missing from a contraction or dialect (See *contractions, p. 98.*)	**'** *apostrophe*	Aren't you writin' today?	
Letters missing from an expletive • Some writers use hyphens.	**-** *hyphen*	Well, sh--!	——
• Others use an em dash (only when replacing two or more missing letters). (See *em dash/en dash, p. 95.*)	**▬** *em dash (double dash)*	Well, sh—!	——
The word ***namely*** before a list or an example • Some writers use a colon.	**:** *colon*	Beth's editor requested some revisions: massive changes in Chapters 2 and 3.	——
• Others use a comma.	**,** *comma*	Beth's editor requested some revisions, massive changes in Chapters 2 and 3.	——
• Still others use an em dash.	**▬** *em dash (double dash)*	Beth's editor requested some revisions—massive changes in Chapters 2 and 3.	——
The word ***of*** between a person's name and place of residence	**,** *comma*	James Michener, Austin, Texas, was one of the state's most prolific writers.	
The word ***or*** or ***per*** in certain combinations CAUTION: Some publishers object to these forms.	**/** *slash*	he/she Sir/Madam $50/hr	—— —— ——
The word ***that***, only when it precedes a direct quote • Some writers use a comma.	**,** *comma*	Kay's editor proclaimed, "This book is destined to be a best-seller."	——
• Others use an em dash.	**▬** *em dash (double dash)*	Kay's editor proclaimed— "This book is destined to be a best-seller."	——

Replace *(continued)*	**Mark**	**Example**	✔
The word *to* or *through* in ranges • Some writers use a hyphen. (See *ranges, p. 197.*)	**-** *hyphen*	A-Z 9-5 ages 5-8 Emily Dickinson (1830-1886) Chapters 1-5 pages 3-9	—— —— —— —— —— ——
• Others use an en dash. NOTES: – Most publishers set ranges with no space before or after the en dash.	**—** *en dash* *(¹/₂ em dash)*	A–Z 9–5 ages 5–8 Emily Dickinson (1830–1886) Chapters 1–5 pages 3–9	—— —— —— —— —— ——
– Spell out *to* or *through* if the word *from* precedes the range.		I aim for six productive hours of writing every day, sometime from 9 A.M. to 11 P.M.	——
– When a sentence ends with an abbreviation that ends with a period, do not add another period after the abbreviated form. (See *em dash/en dash, p. 95.*) (See *times of day, p. 167.*)		I aim for six productive hours of writing every day, sometime from 9 A.M. to 11 P.M. *not* I aim for six productive hours of writing every day, sometime from 9 A.M. to 11 P.M..	——
A **word that appeared earlier** in the sentence and can be implied rather than repeated NOTE: The comma in this example substitutes for the word *prefer.*	**,** *comma*	Some publishers prefer closed punctuation; others, open. [CLOSED]	——
• Some writers may omit such a comma when the sentence is clear without it.		Some publishers prefer closed punctuation; others open. [OPEN]	——

SEPARATE	Mark	Example	✔
Latin **abbreviations** NOTES: • If no other mark precedes the abbreviation, place a comma before it.	**,** *comma*	I have one dream in life, i.e., to write great books. [CLOSED]	___
• The comma after the abbreviation is optional.		I have one dream in life, i.e. to write great books. [OPEN]	___
The elements of **addresses** (except between states and ZIP codes or at the ends of stacked lines)	**,** *comma*	1501 W. 5th, # E-2 Austin, TX 78703 U.S.A. [STACKED]	___
(See *house & street numbers, p. 195.*)		1501 W. 5th, # E-2, Austin, TX 78703, U.S.A. [RUN-IN]	___
A nonessential **adjectival clause or phrase** that immediately follows the noun it modifies	**,** *comma*	The editor's assistant, sitting behind a three-foot stack of manuscripts, sorted through the slush pile.	___
Consecutive **adjectives** that modify the same noun	**,** *comma*	The report consisted of one long, boring, tedious passage after another.	___
EXCEPTION: Omit the comma when the first adjective modifies both the second adjective and the noun.		We found a dusty old manuscript in the attic. [*DUSTY* MODIFIES *OLD MANUSCRIPT.*]	
An **affirmative or negative**	**,** *comma*	Yes, I always spell-check! No, I'm not done yet.	___
An **alternative combination** CAUTION: Some publishers object to these forms. (See *slash, p. 95.*)	**/** *slash*	and/or audio/visual true/false	___ ___ ___

Separate *(continued)*	Mark	Example	✔
An **author's first and last name** in a bibliography or reference list entry	**,** *comma*	Judd, Karen. *Copyediting: A Practical Guide.* Menlo Park, CA: Crisp Publications, 1990.	
Brief entries in a news flash column • Some writers space ellipses.	**• • •** *ellipsis*	Joe Smith's new book will be out in May. . . Anna Sanchez signed a contract for three new novels. . . [SPACED]	___
• Others set ellipses with no space. (See *ellipsis, p. 95.*)	**•••** *ellipsis*	Joe Smith's new book will be out in May... Anna Sanchez signed a contract for three new novels... [UNSPACED]	___
A **combination of words** that could otherwise confuse or obscure meaning	**,** *comma*	Thoughts of fame terrify him so, he won't submit a thing. *vs.* Thoughts of fame terrify him, so he won't submit a thing.	
The parts of a **compound declarative sentence**	**,** *comma*	Style involves continuous improvement, and standards evolve over time.	
EXCEPTION: You can omit the comma when both parts are short clauses.		Shirley edited and Tom proofread.	
A **"conditional" clause or phrase** (one starting with a word such as *after, because, before, if, since, unless, when, while,* and so on), followed by an independent clause	**,** *comma*	If I were you, I'd keep my day job. [CLOSED] If I were you I'd keep my day job. [OPEN]	___ ___
• Some writers omit such commas or use them only after a set number of words (e.g., five or more). Record such limits on the ✔ line.		When space is a problem, avoid all caps. [CLOSED] When space is a problem avoid all caps. [OPEN]	___ ___

Separate *(continued)*	Mark	Example	✔
A **conjunctive adverb or adverbial phrase**	**,** *comma*	I suppose editing can get tedious; however, I find it fascinating. [CLOSED]	___
NOTE: Even open punctuators may insert such a comma for emphasis or clarification.		I suppose editing can get tedious; however I find it fascinating. [OPEN]	___
A **courtesy title**	**,** *comma*	Hope you like my book, sir.	
A bit of **dialogue** from its tag line	**,** *comma*	"I'd have been here sooner," Jay said, "but I got abducted by some aliens."	
A **direct address**	**,** *comma*	Look, Mom! I got another six-figure contract!	___
A light **exclamation**	**,** *comma*	Why, your byline is enormous!	___
A run-in **head** • Some writers end a run-in head with a colon.	**:** *colon*	**Run-in:** The preceding bold letters form a run-in head.	___
• Others use an em dash.	**——** *em dash (double dash)*	**Run-in—**The preceding bold letters form a run-in head.	___
• Still others use a period.	**.** *period*	**Run-in.** The preceding bold letters form a run-in head.	___
The elements of a **home page address**	**/** *slash*	http://www.apple.com	

Separate *(continued)*	Mark	Example	✔
A **house number** from a street address	**—** *en dash* *(¹/₂ em dash)*	801–34th Street	
Identical or similar consecutive words, to clarify meaning	**,** *comma*	If you want to write, write.	
An inverted **index entry**	**,** *comma*	printers, laser . . . . p. 9	
An **infinitive phrase** used independently	**,** *comma*	Few people can expect to make a living as a novelist, to tell you the truth.	
Interpolations and summations	**,** *comma*	Proofread carefully, too. [CLOSED]	___
• Some writers omit this comma, provided the meaning is still clear. (See *single-word summation*, *p. 75*.)		Proofread carefully too. [OPEN]	___
An **introductory word, clause, or phrase** that precedes the main clause	**,** *comma*	First, write a quick draft. [CLOSED]	___
• Some writers omit such commas.		First write a quick draft. [OPEN]	___
• Some writers use a comma only after a set number of words (e.g., five or more). Record such limits on the ✔ line.		From a publisher's point of view, art includes everything that will print on the final page. [AFTER A SET WORD COUNT]	___
The **letters of a spelled-out word**	**-** *hyphen*	M-i-s-s-i-s-s-i-p-p-i	

Separate *(continued)*	**Mark**	**Example**	✔
Pairs of words in a series of three or more	**,** *comma*	Your audience might be adults or children, teachers or students, technical experts or novices.	
Lines of **poetry** within blocks of prose • In this usage, set a space on both sides of the slash.	**/** *slash*	Roses are red. / Violets are blue. / I'm not a poet. / How about you?	___
• Two or more lines of poetry are often indented farther from the margins than the other text.		I wrote this poem myself: Roses are red. Violets are blue. I'm not a poet. How about you?	___
A name and a **professional title**	**,** *comma*	Pam Hong, submissions editor, urged me to submit more work.	
EXCEPTION: Omit the commas when a title precedes a name.		Submissions Editor Pam Hong urged me to submit more work.	
A **quote** from its tagline . . .	**,** *comma*	"Our city is growing by leaps and bounds," the mayor said in last night's speech.	
. . . but *not* a partial quotation		The mayor said this area was "growing by leaps and bounds."	
CAUTION: Do not allow a comma to separate a verb from its object. (See *dialogue, p. 88.*) (See *dialogue, exact quotes, or implied speech, p. 72.*) (See *quote, p. 80.*)		The editor declared my poem "the best poem of the year." [NO COMMA AFTER DECLARED]	
A mild **reversal or summary**	**,** *comma*	Don't worry, be happy. In conclusion, the end is near.	

Separate *(continued)*	Mark	Example	✔
Words, phrases, or clauses in a **series** of three or more • Some writers use a comma before the conjunction.	**,** *comma*	Mary never leaves home without her beeper, cell phone, and modem. [CLOSED, WITH SERIAL COMMA]	___
• Others omit the comma (*except* when its absence obscures meaning).		Mary never leaves home without her beeper, cell phone and modem. [OPEN/BRITISH, NO SERIAL COMMA]	___
• You can omit the serial comma when items are joined by conjunctions, and the series is simple and lacks internal punctuation.		Fred is a writer and an editor and a desktop publisher. [CLOSED OR OPEN]	___
CAUTIONS: • Do not create false series by using commas where dashes are needed.		While between assignments, some freelancers perform other work—editing and proofreading.	
• Do not use a comma *after* the final item.		Mary always carries her beeper, cell phone, and modem when she leaves the house. [NO COMMA AFTER *MODEM*]	
Sets of items in a series when commas already appear in one or more sets	**;** *semicolon*	Writers can write with computers, word processors, and typewriters; or pencils, pens, and markers.	
Subtitles • Some writers use a colon.	**:** *colon*	*Style Meister: The Quick-Reference Custom Style Guide*	___
• Others use an em dash.	**—** *em dash* *(double dash)*	*Style Meister—The Quick-Reference Custom Style Guide*	___
Supplementary title information	**–** *en dash* *(1/2 em dash)*	*House Style Guide–Revised*	

Combined Punctuation

With Brackets/ Parentheses	**Mark**	**Example**	✔
In general, omit punctuation marks that fall just **before opening parentheses**.	*all punctuation marks*	Punctuation isn't at all important **(**unless you want others to get your point**)**. [NO PUNCTUATION AFTER *IMPORTANT*]	
When the enclosed text ends the surrounding sentence, the **full stop** goes *outside*.*	**.** *period*	Punctuation isn't at all important **(**unless you want others to get your point**).**	___
• Some writers include the full stop when the enclosed text is a complete thought.	**!** *exclamation point*	Good writing takes practice, patience, and perseverance **(**really**!).**	___
• Others omit the full stop.		Good writing takes practice, patience, and perseverance **(**really**).**	___
	? *question mark*	Don't you think **(**really**?)** that this book could win a Pulitzer prize?	___
In U.S. usage, the **full stop** goes *inside* only when it ends the enclosed text.*	*all full stops*	**(**A *run-in head* is also called a *side head***.)** [U.S.]	___
• In British usage, the full stop goes *outside* unless it is part of a direct quotation.		**(**A *run-in head* is also called a *side head***)**. [BRITISH]	___
• All other punctuation marks go outside parentheses or brackets.		The words of T.S. Eliot **(**"This is the way the world ends, not with a bang but a whimper**.")** foretell a defeated ending.	___

*A *full stop* is an exclamation point, a period, or a question mark.

Style Meister: The Quick-Reference Custom Style Guide

With Quotation Marks	Mark	Example	✔
Colons generally go *outside*.*	**:** *colon*	Scott's agent expects him to "really produce": to write one best-seller after another.	___
In U.S. usage, **commas** generally go *inside*.	**,** *comma*	"You're nuts," Nicki said. [U.S.]	___
• In British usage, commas generally go *outside*.* (See *periods/special terms, p. 93.*)		"You're mad", Nichole said. [BRITISH]	___
Em dashes generally go *outside*.*	**—** *em dash (double dash)*	"Not for us"—the editor wrote. "Try another market."	___
En dashes generally go *outside*.*	**–** *en dash (½ em dash)*	"Not for us"–the editor wrote. "Try another market."	___
Exclamation points generally go *outside*.*	**!** *exclamation point*	I can't believe they called my work "astounding"!	___
In U.S. usage, **periods** generally go *inside*.	**.** *period*	"In matters of style, swim with the current; in matters of principle, stand like a rock." —Thomas Jefferson [U.S.]	___
• In British usage, periods generally go *outside*.*		"To be, or not to be: that is the question". —William Shakespeare [BRITISH]	___
• In U.S. usage with **special terms**, commas and periods may go inside or outside.		The Latin term for 'let it stand' is 'stet.' [U.S. INSIDE]	___
• In British usage, commas and periods go outside.		The Latin term for 'let it stand' is 'stet'. [U.S. OUTSIDE, BRITISH]	___

With Quotation Marks *(cont)*	Mark	Example	✔
Question marks generally go *outside.**	**?** *question mark*	Will your article include a "sidebar"**?**	——
Semicolons generally go *outside.**	**;** *semicolon*	Don't utilize 'utilize'; use 'use.' —ANONYMOUS	——

*When part of a direct quotation, any punctuation mark goes inside.

USAGE NOTES

[ ] *brackets*	Brackets will not transmit over news wires. If writing for the media, use parentheses or revise.
, *comma*	Serial commas often appear in books, journals, and formal documents. Magazines, newspapers, and advertisements often omit them.
: *colon*	Use a colon after an introductory statement containing the words *as follows, follow,* or *the following.* (Mary always carries the following: beeper, cell phone, and modem.)
. . . *ellipsis*	The overuse of ellipses irritates many editors. Audiences whose first language is not English may be less accustomed to ellipses. Unspaced ellipses are common in British and Continental usage.
—— *em dash* *(double dash)*	The overuse of em dashes irritates many editors. To avoid repetition, publishers often use 2- and 3-em dashes to indicate missing letters and words, particularly in reference lists. Example: Venolia, Jan. *Rewrite Right!* Berkeley: Ten Speed Press, 1987. ———. *Write Right!* (rev. ed.). Berkeley: Ten Speed Press, 1988.
— *en dash* *(1/2 em dash)*	When submitting manuscripts to publishers, do not mark or set en dashes unless requested to do so. Use hyphens instead.
! *exclamation point*	Audiences whose first language is not English may be less accustomed to exclamation points. Using too many exclamation points dilutes their impact!!!
" " *double quotation marks*	Avoid using quotation marks for emphasis. Use bold or italics instead.
/ *slash*	Audiences whose first language is not English may be less accustomed to slashes used with combinations (such as writer/editor).

BRITISH USAGE

[1] British usage often prefers en dashes in place of em dashes and often sets dashes open (with one space on each side). In the U.S., spacing varies, although many publishers set em and en dashes closed.

[2] British usage for both double and single quotation marks generally counters U.S. usage.

[3] British usage often calls for parentheses within brackets rather than brackets within parentheses.

5

I Before E Except After C?

Spelling

It's not so much the rules of spelling that cause trouble; it's the exceptions. Most people educated in the U.S. can readily quote the old jingle, "*I* before *e* except after *c*," but few of them can go beyond. Sheryl Lindsell, author of *Proofreading and Editing for Word Processors*, presents the rhyme like this:

> Put *i* before *e* except after *c*,
>
> Or when sounding like *a* as in *neighbor* and *weigh*,
>
> And except *seize* and *seizure*, and also *leisure*,
>
> *Weird, height*, and *either, forfeit* and *neither*.

And we might as well add *ancient, caffeine, foreign, protein, sheik*, and *their*. And, by all means, let's not overlook *meister*! This should aptly demonstrate why there aren't many spelling guidelines in this chapter. If you have the slightest doubt about a spelling, check a dictionary.

This chapter will increase your awareness about common spelling problems—particularly those a spell-checker may not catch. The chapter also addresses contractions, possessives, and plurals; words with alternative spellings; Greek and Latin derivations; and words with diacritical marks.

Guidelines for hyphenation and capitalization, two issues many people relate to spelling, appear in Chapters 6 and 7, respectively.

Common Spelling Problems

A great number of spelling errors can be attributed to the widespread confusion (or unconsciousness) about contractions and possessives. Possessives and plurals are often confused as well. Even if you aren't confusing possessives and plurals, you may wonder how to form a plural from time to time. The following sections clarify the differences.

Contractions

A contraction is simply a "scrunched up" or *contracted* word in which an apostrophe represents a missing character or characters. Contractions include such words as *he'd* (he had, he would), *I'm* (I am), *it's* (it is, it has), *she's* (she is), *we're* (we are), and *you'll* (you will).

We form contractions from a verb alone or from a pronoun plus a verb. Those formed from verbs (aren't, can't, didn't, haven't, wouldn't, and so on) rarely cause problems. Those formed from a pronoun-verb combination are another matter. Check out the quick-reference charts at the end of this chapter, and y'all'll see what I mean. (By the way, *y'all'll* is the Texas contraction for *you all will*.)

While we're talking about contractions, I'd like to mention a couple of things. First, many people disapprove of contractions in formal writing. What constitutes "formal" however is a matter of opinion. My interpretation of formal writing includes most legal, scholarly, scientific, and technical documents.

Second, contractions are not appropriate for international audiences. English is confusing enough without them, so always spell out contractions in international communications.

Possessives

Because contractions are frequently confused with possessives, this seems a good time to point out the differences. While the apostrophes in contracted words represent missing characters, the apostrophes in *possessives* represent ownership (possession). We form most possessives by adding an apostrophe and an *s* or an apostrophe alone. This does not hold true for possessive *personal pronouns* (her/hers, his, its, my/mine, our/ours, their/theirs, whose, your/yours). Many people mistakenly add apostrophes to pronouns out of the belief that all possessives require apostrophes. Others add apostrophes simply out of carelessness. Even when we know better, we may go a bit unconscious at times.

The quick-reference charts list guidelines for forming possessives of both singular and plural forms.

Plurals

For most native English speakers, plurals come fairly naturally. (*Plurals*, as opposed to *singulars*, are words that indicate more than one.) We form most plurals by adding an *s* (indent/indents) or *es* (boss/bosses) or by changing *y* to *ies* (copy/copies). Other plurals take irregular forms (child/children).

In English, we spell some words the same in both singular and plural form (Chinese, corps, deer, salmon, wheat). Some words always appear in singular form (mathematics, music, news, statistics). Some always appear in plural form (pants, proceeds, remains, scissors, thanks).

It's no wonder we have so much trouble with spelling! Fortunately, most of us adjust to these differences fairly easily, but it's more of a challenge when words have variable spellings.

Variable Spellings

Most words in English that have variable spellings fall into one of four categories:

- Irregular noun and verb forms (foot/feet, write/wrote/written),

- British versus U.S. spellings (centre/center, labour/labor, programme/program),

- Greek and Latin derivatives (analysis/analyses, criterion/criteria, medium/media), and

- Words with diacritical marks (El Niño, l'Hôtel Française, qué, schönen).

For native English speakers, irregular nouns and verbs rarely cause a problem. Non-native speakers, however, often experience more difficulty. I urge you to consult a dictionary whenever you have the slightest doubt about a word's spelling. The quick-reference charts address both British versus U.S. usage and Greek and Latin derivatives.

Because not all writers need diacritical marks, I will mention them only briefly. *Diacritical marks* (é, ç, ô, è, ü, ñ, and so on) are accent marks or characters that denote phonetic distinctions. They appear in many foreign languages.

Basic Considerations

For the most part, words are either spelled correctly or they're not, which certainly simplifies life. Sometimes, however, more than one spelling is equally accepted or relatively minor variations represent specialized meanings. For instance, some people in high tech distinguish between *disc, disk,* and *diskette* (though the latter term is losing favor). *The Microsoft Manual of Style for Technical Publications* and *Wired Style* use *disk* to describe hard disk drives and floppies (or diskettes) and *disc* to describe compact discs (CD-ROMs).

Other examples of word preference are intentionally misspelled words. For instance, some people misspell words or use outdated spellings on purpose to make their companies or products stand out. Some examples include *Kountry Kitchen* and *Ye Olde Soda Shoppe.*

Custom style guides should therefore include word-preference information for their particular audience, market, medium, organization, product, or publication. One simple way to record such information is in a two-column format like that shown in Figure 26.

Words	Definition
disk	*hard disk drive*
disc	*compact disc*
diskette	*floppy disk*

Figure 26 - Sample Word Preferences

When working with computerized documents, you can verify that such preferences have been followed by searching for alternatives and replacing them with preferred words. Chapters 1, 10, and 14 contain further information about word preferences and automation.

Beyond word preferences, spelling standards tend to vary most with geography.

Geographic Considerations

By now you probably already know that, in British usage, some words are spelled differently. (In some cases, the words are altogether different, like *lift* instead of *elevator*.) To learn more, check the sources in the annotated bibliography.

If you're using foreign words, or even some English words of foreign derivation, you may need to use diacritical marks. The English words that contain diacritical marks come primarily from French. Some of the most common include *café, entrée,* and *résumé.*

As we've absorbed words into English, we've dropped the marks from most other words. However, some writers retain the marks when two words that are otherwise spelled the same have different meanings. *Résumé* (vita) versus *resume* (continue) is one example. If you're working with international communications or documents that include foreign words, familiarize yourself with diacritical marks and use them carefully.

These days, a chapter on spelling isn't complete unless it mentions spell-checking. I'll mention it here, but because it relates to computer automation, I'll cover it in Chapter 14.

While use of a computer spell-checker usually reduces the number of errors that slip through, a spell-checker alone cannot catch everything. Careful proofreading is a necessity. I can't stress this enough. See Chapter 14 for more information.

How to Use Chapter 5's Quick-Reference Charts

The quick-reference charts for Chapter 5 contain four sections: 1) Plurals, 2) Possessives, 3) Frequently Confused Words, and 4) British vs. U.S. Spellings. Figure 27 shows a segment from the Plurals chart.

COMPOUNDS	Singular	Plural
NOTES:		
• Add an *s* to the most important part.	attorney general mother-in-law	attorneys general mothers-in-law
• Use singular forms for **measurements**.	six-month contract	six-month contract [NOT SIX-MONTHS CONTRACT]

Figure 27 - Sample Plurals Chart

Style guidelines, organized alphabetically by categories, subcategories, and/or bold key words appear in the left-hand column. This column sometimes also contains notes, exceptions, and cautions. The center and right-hand columns illustrate contrasting forms. The Possessives charts are organized similarly.

The left-hand column of the Frequently Confused Words charts lists words organized alphabetically in bold type. (See Figure 28.) The center column provides examples using the first words. The right-hand column provides examples using the second.

Category	First Word	Second Word
aid, aide		
• *Aid* relates to assistance.	The emergency crew provided first *aid*.	Our *aide* will get back to you soon.
• *Aide* names the assistant.	[ASSISTANCE]	[ASSISTANT]

Figure 28 - Sample Frequently Confused Words Chart

The British vs. U.S. Spellings charts are organized similarly.

Some of the quick-reference charts in this chapter contain customizing features; others are strictly for reference. The customizable charts contain a column with a checkmark (✔) and "write-on lines," on which you can record the options you prefer.

Usage notes appear at the end of the chapter, after the quick-reference charts. For further information, check the glossary or explore the sources in the annotated bibliography.

Summary

This chapter has introduced three areas where spelling problems often occur: contractions versus possessives, possessives versus plurals, and words with variable spellings. The quick-reference charts that follow list guidelines and further illustrate these areas. While grammar and style books offer many spelling rules, the number of exceptions is so high that it's hardly worthwhile to memorize them. The best defense against spelling errors is to consult a dictionary regularly and be aware of common problem words.

Plurals

ABBREVIATIONS	Singular	✔	Plural	✔
Some writers add an **s** alone.	CPA MFA	___	CPAs MFAs [ADD AN *S* ALONE]	___
	C.P.A. M.F.A.	___	C.P.A.s M.F.A.s [ADD AN *S* ALONE]	___
• Some use **'s** for multiple-letter abbreviations with periods.	C.P.A. M.F.A.	___	C.P.A.'s M.F.A.'s [MULTIPLE LETTERS WITH PERIODS]	___
• Others use **'s** every time.	CPA MFA	___	CPA's MFA's [ADD AN *'S* EVERY TIME]	___
CAUTION: If you also need possessives, form plurals without apostrophes.	C.P.A. M.F.A.	___	C.P.A.'s M.F.A.'s [ADD AN *'S* EVERY TIME]	___

COMMON NOUNS	Singular		Plural	✔
• Add *es* if the word ends in *s, x, z, ch,* or *sh*.	class box buzz inch wish		classes boxes buzzes inches wishes	
• For some words that end in *o,* add an *s*. For others, add *es*.	folio piano ratio hero tomato		folios pianos ratios heroes tomatoes	
NOTE: Some words take either ending.	motto zero		mottos zeros mottoes zeroes	___ ___
• For some words that end in *f* add an *s*. For others, change the *f* to *ves*.	belief chief gulf elf leaf shelf		beliefs chiefs gulfs elves leaves shelves	
• For some words that end in *y* add an *s*. For others, change the *y* to *ies*.	attorney day galley ability company industry royalty		attorneys days galleys abilities companies industries royalties	
• For other words, add an *s*. (See *irregular plurals,* *p. 104.*)	manuscript publisher year		manuscripts publishers years	

Common Nouns *(cont.)*	**Singular**	**Plural**
EXCEPTIONS: **Irregular plurals** and plurals that match singular forms.	child foot man mouse tooth woman Chinese corps deer salmon wheat	children feet men mice teeth women Chinese corps deer salmon wheat

COMPOUNDS	**Singular**	**Plural**
NOTES: • Add an *s* to the most important part. • Use singular forms for **measurements**.	attorney general mother-in-law six-month contract	attorneys general mothers-in-law six-month contract [NOT SIX-MONTHS CONTRACT]

FRACTIONS	**Singular**	**Plural**
• Use singular forms for fractions of one.	$^3/_8$	$^3/_8$ *not* $^3/_8$s, $^3/_8$'s, or $^3/_8$ths

GREEK & LATIN DERIVATIVES	**Singular**	✔	**Plural**	✔
analysis, analyses	analysis		analyses	
appendix, appendices	appendix		appendices	—
appendix, appendixes			appendixes	—
NOTE: Some writers reserve *appendices* for math and *appendixes* for books.			appendices [MATH] appendixes [BOOKS]	— —
cactus, cacti	cactus		cacti	—
cactus, cactuses (See *Usage Note*, p. 115.)			cactuses	—
crisis, crises	crisis		crises	
criterion, criteria	criterion		criteria	

Greek & Latin *(cont.)*	Singular	✔	Plural	✔
curriculum, curricula	curriculum		curricula	——
curriculum, curriculums			curriculums	——
data, data NOTE: Many people accept *data* as singular or plural.	*This* data *reveals.*		*These* data *reveal.*	——
datum, data NOTE: This option is the more traditional choice.	*This* datum *reveals.*		*These* data *reveal.*	——
datum, datums NOTE: *Datums* offers another alternative.	*This* datum *reveals.*		*These* datums *reveal.*	——
formula, formulae	formula		formulae	——
formula, formulas (See *Usage Note, p. 115.*)			formulas	——
index, indexes	index		indexes	——
index, indices			indices	——
NOTE: Some writers use *indexes* for publications and reserve *indices* for math.			indexes [PUBLICATIONS] indices [MATH]	—— ——
medium, media	medium		media	——
medium, mediums (See *Usage Note, p. 115.*)			mediums	——
memorandum, memoranda	memorandum		memoranda	——
memorandum, memorandums (See *Usage Note, p. 115.*)			memorandums	——

Greek & Latin *(cont.)*	Singular	✔	Plural	✔
nucleus, nuclei	nucleus		nuclei	
parenthesis, parentheses	parenthesis		parentheses	
phenomenon, phenomena	phenomenon		phenomena	—
phenomenon, phenomenons (See *Usage Note, p. 115.*)			phenomenons	—
referendum, referenda	referendum		referenda	—
referendum, referendums (See *Usage Note, p. 115.*)			referendums	—
synopsis, synopses	synopsis		synopses	
thesis, theses	thesis		theses	

LETTERS	Singular		Plural	✔
Some writers form **multiple-letter plurals** with *'s*.	*ABC*		*ABC***'s** [ADD *'s* EVERY TIME.]	—
• Others use an *s* alone. NOTES: – When single letters appear in italics, the *s* that follows does not.			*ABC*s [ADD *s* ALONE.]	—
– We form plurals of some abbreviations by doubling a letter.	*l.* (line) *ms.* (manuscript) *p.* (page)		*ll.* (lines) *mss.* (manuscripts) *pp.* (pages)	
Some writers form all **single-letter plurals** with *'s*.	I made an *A* in English.		I made *A*'s in English.	
EXCEPTION: Use *'s* when needed for clarity.			*p*'s [FOR CLARITY]	

NUMBERS	**Singular**	**Plural**	✔
• Some writers add only an *s*, provided their meaning will be clear.		8s 100s 1960s	___
• Some writers always add *'s*.		8's 100's 1960's	___

PROPER NAMES	**Singular**	**Plural**	✔
NOTE: For most names— • Some writers add an *s*.	Austen Browning Frost Orwell	the Austens the Brownings the Frosts the Orwells	___ ___ ___ ___
• Some writers add *es* if the name ends in *s, x, z, ch, or sh*, unless it's likely to result in a mispronunciation.	Jones Cox Perez Church Bush	the Joneses the Coxes the Perezes the Churches the Bushes	___ ___ ___ ___ ___
• Other writers add an apostrophe alone when a name ends in *s, x, or z*. EXCEPTION: Avoid this choice if you'll also need the possessive form.	Jones Cox Hernandez	the Jones' the Cox' the Hernandez'	___ ___ ___
CAUTION: Do not change a name that ends in *y* to *ies*. (See *common nouns, p. 108.*)	Kennedy	the Kennedys [NOT KENNEDIES]	

Possessives

ABBREVIATIONS	Singular/Plural	✔	Possessive	✔
• To form a **singular possessive**, add 's.	CPA MFA	—	CPA's MFA's Drop these records by my CPA's office.	—
	C.P.A. M.F.A.	—	C.P.A.'s M.F.A.'s Drop these records by my C.P.A.'s office.	—
• To form a **plural possessive**, add ' alone.	IOUs IRAs	—	IOUs' IRAs' These IRAs' terms aren't clear.	—
	I.O.U.s I.R.A.s	—	I.O.U.s' I.R.A.s' These I.R.A.s' terms aren't clear.	—
TIP: Changing plurals to singulars may prevent awkward wording.			These IRA terms aren't clear.	
(See *acronyms & initialisms, p. 165.*)			These I.R.A. terms aren't clear.	

COMMON NOUNS	Singular/Plural	Possessive Case	✔
• When common nouns don't end in *s*, add 's.	person/people woman/women	person's/people's woman's/women's	
• When common nouns end in *s*, some writers add 's to singulars and ' **alone** to plurals.	boss/bosses class/classes witness/witnesses	boss's/bosses' class's/classes' witness's/witnesses'	—
• Others add ' **alone** to both forms. (See *proper names, p. 107.*)		boss'/bosses' class'/classes' witness'/witnesses'	—

HYPHENATED COMPOUNDS	Singular/Plural	Possessive Case
• Add 's.	mother-in-law mothers-in-law	mother-in-law's mothers-in-law's

OPEN COMPOUNDS	Individual Ownership	Joint Ownership
• Add 's after each noun to show individual ownership and after only the last noun to show joint ownership.	Siskel's and Ebert's opinions [INDIVIDUAL]	Siskel and Ebert's movie review [JOINT]

ORGANIZATIONS	Examples	Exceptions
NOTE: Many such names contain no apostrophe.	Editorial Freelancers Association National Writers Union	American Medical Writers' Association Austin Writers' League

PERSONAL PRONOUNS	Singular Possessive	Plural Possessive
NOTE: Personal pronouns show possession without an apostrophe.	her his its my our their your whose	hers his its mine ours theirs yours whose

SURNAMES	Singular	✔	Possessive Case	✔
When names end in *s, x, z,* or in an *s* or *z* **sound**— • Some writers add *'s* for one-syllable names and **' alone** for two syllables or more.	Burns Yeats [ONE SYLLABLE] Dickens Williams [TWO OR MORE]	——	Burns's Yeats's [ONE SYLLABLE] Dickens' Williams' [TWO OR MORE]	——
• Other writers use **' alone** for any number of syllables.	Burns Yeats Dickens Williams	——	Burns' Yeats' Dickens' Williams' [ANY SURNAME]	——
• When names do not end in *s, x, z,* or in an *s* or *z* **sound**, add *'s*.	Carroll Huxley Whitman		Carroll's Huxley's Whitman's	

Frequently Confused Words

CONTRACTIONS VS. POSSESSIVES	Contraction	Possessive
it's **vs.** *its*	*It's* only a matter of time before I get a Pulitzer prize. [IT IS]	This book lost *its* cover. [BOOK'S COVER]
they're, their, there NOTE: People often confuse *there* with *their* or *they're*.	*They're* shipping the galleys (typeset copy) on Friday. [THEY ARE]	Authors often review *their* galleys before *their* work goes to print. [AUTHORS' GALLEYS, WORK]
who's **vs.** *whose*	We haven't decided *who's* designing the cover. [WHO IS]	We haven't decided *whose* cover design we'll use. [ARTIST'S DESIGN]
you're **vs.** *your*	*You're* the artist whose work I most admire. [YOU ARE]	Could I get *your* autograph? [PERSON'S SIGNATURE]

HOMONYMS	First Word	Second Word
accept, except • *Accept* has several meanings, none of which relates to exclusion. • *Except*, on the other hand, does relate to exclusion.	Don't blindly *accept* all suggested revisions. [APPROVE] They couldn't *accept* that he was abducted. [BELIEVE] I'm thrilled to *accept* this award. [RECEIVE]	Writing is great, *except* for the paperwork! [EXCLUSION]
aid, aide • *Aid* relates to assistance. • *Aide* names the assistant.	The emergency crew provided first *aid*. [ASSISTANCE]	Our *aide* will get back to you soon. [ASSISTANT]
all ready, already • *All ready* relates to completeness. • *Already* means before.	Is the job *all ready* to go? [COMPLETENESS]	We *already* ran this piece. [BEFORE]

Homonyms *(continued)*	First Word	Second Word
capital, capitol • *Capital* has several meanings, none of which relates to a building. • *Capitol* refers only to a building.	Words with "initial caps" begin with *capital* letters. [LETTER CASE] Businesses get *capital* from stockholders. [MONEY] He committed a *capital* crime. [PUNISHMENT]	The Texas *capitol* is taller than our nation's *capitol* in Washington, D.C. [BUILDING]
complement, compliment • *Complement* means completion or enhancement. • *Compliment* relates to admiration or praise.	A good sidebar would *complement* your article nicely. [COMPLETION] That color *complements* your eyes. [ENHANCEMENT]	Dayna just got the nicest *compliment* on her column! [ADMIRATION] Some people can't take *compliments*. [PRAISE]
conscience, conscious • *Conscience* relates to morality. • *Conscious* relates to awareness.	Doesn't all your lying wear on your *conscience*? [MORALITY]	Some writers can write for hours without being *conscious* of a thing around them. [AWARENESS]
council, counsel • A *council* is a governing body. • *Counsel* refers to advice.	The city *council* passed an ordinance against smoking in restaurants. [GOVERNING BODY]	The writer sought the editor's *counsel*. [ADVICE] Could you *counsel* a novice writer? [ADVISE]
ensure, insure • Some writers use *ensure* to mean make certain. • Others use *insure*.	✔ Please *ensure* that this report gets out. — [MAKE CERTAIN/U.S.]	✔ Please *insure* that this report gets out. — [MAKE CERTAIN/U.S.]
• U.S. writers use *insure* to mean protect against loss, even if they also use it to mean make certain.		If you buy a home, you need to *insure* it — for its value. [PROTECT/U.S.]
• British writers use *assure*. (See *assure, ensure, insure,* p. 57.)		If you buy a home, you need to *assure* it — for its value. [PROTECT/BRITISH]

Homonyms *(continued)*	**First Word**	**Second Word**
foreword, forward • *Foreword* relates to a section of a book. • *Forward* relates to movement or progress. (See *–ward*, p. 115.)	The *foreword* serves as a book's endorsement or introduction. [BOOK]	Are we going *forward* with this project or not? [MOVEMENT OR PROGRESS]
precedence, precedents • *Precedence* means preference or priority. • *Precedents* are customs or examples.	Changes to content take *precedence* over changes to format. [PRIORITY OR PREFERENCE]	We hate to set *precedents* for meeting such impossible deadlines. [CUSTOMS OR EXAMPLES]
principal, principle • *Principal* means primary or chief. • *Principle* means rule or belief.	The *principal* reason we rejected your story is, it sucks. [PRIMARY] The school hired a new principal. [CHIEF]	You'll never go wrong if you follow this *principle*. [RULE] Our Constitution is based on the *principle* of freedom. [BELIEF]
reign, rein • *Reign* means govern or rule. • *Rein* means control or restrain.	King Louis XVI's *reign* over France ended when he was beheaded. [GOVERN OR RULE]	Could you please *rein* in your little hoodlums? [CONTROL OR RESTRAIN]
stationary, stationery • *Stationary* means immobile or unchanging. • *Stationery* refers to writing materials.	Mother exercises on a *stationary* bicycle. [IMMOBILE OR UNCHANGING]	I've nearly run out of business *stationery*. [WRITING MATERIALS]
to, too, two NOTE: People sometimes confuse *two* (the number) with *to* or *too*.	I've always loved *to* write. [PREPOSITION]	Many people believe writing is *too* hard. [ALSO]

British vs. U.S. Spellings

To "Britainize" a Word—	British	✔	U.S.	✔
Use *ae* in place of *e*.	encyclopaedia	—	encyclopedia	—
	haemoglobin	—	hemoglobin	—
	leukaemia	—	leukemia	—
Use *ce* in place of *se*.	defence	—	defense	—
	pretence	—	pretense	—
NOTE: • In British usage, these endings often vary, depending on the part of speech. • Some U.S. dictionaries accept either form.	licence [NOUN]	—	license [NOUN]	—
	license [VERB]	—	license [VERB]	—
• Use *dge* in place of *dg*.	acknowledgement	—	acknowledgment	—
	judgement		judgment	—
• Use *ea* in place of *a*.	sizeable	—	sizable	—
• Use *ise* in place of *ize*.	authorise	—	authorize	—
	legalise	—	legalize	—
	maximise	—	maximize	—
	organise	—	organize	—
	standardise	—	standardize	—
	visualise	—	visualize	—
CAUTIONS: Many U.S. words use *ise* rather than *ize*. When in doubt, consult a dictionary.	advertise		advertise	
	compromise		compromise	
	despise		despise	
	exercise		exercise	
	revise		revise	
	supervise		supervise	
	surprise		surprise	

To "Britainize" a Word—	British	✔	U.S.	✔
• Use *ll* in place of *l*.	cancelled	___	canceled	___
	jewellry	___	jewelry	___
	labelled	___	labeled	___
	marvellous	___	marvelous	___
	travelled	___	traveled	___
• Use *mme* in place of *m*.	programme	___	program	___
• Use *ogue* in place of *og*.	catalogue	___	catalog	___
	dialogue	___	dialog	___
NOTE: Many U.S. writers prefer the British form.			catalogue	___
			dialogue	___
• Use *ou* in place of *o*.	behaviour	___	behavior	___
	colour	___	color	___
	favour	___	favor	___
	honour	___	honor	___
	labour	___	labor	___
	mould	___	mold	___
	neighbourhood	___	neighborhood	___
• Use *pp* in place of *p*.	worshipped	___	worshiped	___
• Use *que* in place of *ck*.	cheque	___	check	___
• Use *re* in place of *er*.	calibre	___	caliber	___
	centre	___	center	___
	fibre	___	fiber	___
	goitre	___	goiter	___
	litre	___	liter	___
	lustre	___	luster	___
	manoeuvre	___	maneuver	___
	metre	___	meter	___
	spectre	___	specter	___
	theatre	___	theater	___

To "Britainize" a Word—	British	✔	U.S.	✔
• Add an *s* to compounds ending in the suffix *–ward*.	afterwards	___	afterward	___
	backwards	___	backward	___
	forwards	___	forward	___
	towards	___	toward	___
• Use *sation* in place of *zation*.	organisation	___	organization	___
• Use *se* in place of *ce*.	practise [VERB]	___	practice [VERB]	___
	practice [NOUN]	___	practice [NOUN]	___
• Use *se* in place of *ze*.	analyse	___	analyze	___
	or			
	analyze	___		
	paralyse	___	paralyze	___
• Use *ss* in place of *s*.	biassed	___	biased	___
	focussed	___	focused	___
• Use *t* in place of *ed*.	learnt	___	learned	___
	spelt	___	spelled	___
• Use *tt* in place of *t*.	benefitted	___	benefited	___

USAGE NOTE

In the listings for Greek and Latin derivatives, unless otherwise stated, the first of two options represents the more traditional.

6

Should I Hyphenate Anal Retentive?

Compound Words & Word Division

A huge proportion of style problems can be attributed to "Hyphenation Hell," but judicious use of a word list/style sheet can certainly ease the pain. If you record each hyphenation decision carefully, you'll rarely be left puzzling over whether to hyphenate *copyedit* or to set it as one word or two.

This chapter explains the factors that make compound words so confounded confusing and presents some basic compounding guidelines. By *compound word*, I mean combinations of two or more words that express a single idea: download, proofreader, telecommuting; cross-reference, full-time, hands-on; artificial intelligence, desktop publishing, word processor. This chapter also includes words formed with prefixes (non-native, overtime, reboot), even though such words are not true compounds.

In addition, this chapter addresses word division. By *word division*, I mean hyphenation used to indicate that a word continues from one line to another when the entire word won't fit on one line. Although this topic is most relevant for those who produce final pages, an understanding of word division can help all writers prepare their work in a way that prevents production problems down the line.

Compound Words

Of all the points of style, hyphenation tends to cause the most frustration. There are essentially three types of compound words: 1) hyphenated, 2) solid (often called closed), and 3) split (often called open). Although many style guides refer to compounds as "closed" and "open," I've chosen to refer to them as "solid" and "split," in order to contrast them with the punctuation conventions used in Chapter 4. Closed and open punctuation have nothing to do with closed (solid) and open (split) hyphenation.

Three factors intensify hyphenation problems: 1) the evolutionary process that compounds tend to go through, 2) the variations in hyphenation with different parts of speech, and 3) the differences between British and U.S. usage.

The Evolution of Compounds

Compound words tend to evolve from unassociated words to hyphenated compounds to solid compounds. Occasionally, they then evolve into split compounds—but only when their parts have become so closely associated that there's no risk of ambiguity. Figure 29 illustrates this progression.

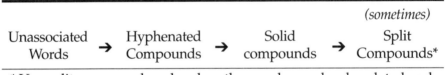

(sometimes)

| Unassociated Words | → | Hyphenated Compounds | → | Solid compounds | → | Split Compounds* |

* Use split compounds only when the words are closely related and unambiguous.

Figure 29 - The Evolution of Compounds

For many words, this progression takes place so gradually that most people don't notice it's happening. This fact solidified for me when I read Willa Cather's *Death Comes for the Archbishop*, which was published in 1927. Cather hyphenated the words to-day, to-morrow, and to-night—forms I saw frequently in childhood but see only in British works these days. She also hyphenated other compounds that most of us now write in solid form: candle-light, court-yard, door-sill, hand-made, mountain-side, pillow-case, sky-line, and table-cloths, among others.

The extent to which we use a compound influences the rate at which it evolves. The information age has escalated the rate of evolution for many words. Some words evolve so rapidly, they skip the hyphenation stage altogether. A few compounds whose evolution I've observed in recent decades include database, laptop, microprocessor, wordwrap, and workspace. The Internet in particular has had a profound influence on the rate at which people accept solid compounds. Internet users tend to opt for quickness and convenience. Thus, they lean toward solid compounds and open punctuation.

The varying speeds at which compounds evolve make it difficult to say just where a word is in the process. You must be a keen observer and rely on the most current authorities to track the evolution of compound words.

Another factor that confuses hyphenation has to do with the part of speech a compound plays at any particular time.

Variations with Different Parts of Speech

We often treat the same compound differently when used as a different part of speech—or when it's positioned differently in the sentence. For example, a compound modifier that precedes a noun often contains a hyphen, particularly when it would be ambiguous otherwise. That same compound following the noun may be split or solid.

Here's an example of such a variation: In the sentence, "Glen is a well-known poet," the hyphen clarifies the fact that we're using *well-known* as an adjective to modify the noun *poet*. When we move the modifier after the noun, we can write either "Glen's poems are well known" (no hyphen required) or "Glen's poems are well-known."

There's one tricky aspect to hyphenating modifiers that precede nouns: Adverb–adjective compounds rarely need a hyphen because they fall in "normal" word order. The adverb modifies the adjective, which in turn modifies the noun. Some examples include compounds that contain the adverb *very* or compounds whose first portion ends in *ly*. The statements, "Maria writes highly acclaimed novels" and "Jim is very widely published" need no hyphens because they offer little risk for confusion.

Watch out, however, for words that fall in adverb–adjective–noun order but could still be misinterpreted. For instance, the message, "Please spell check" could be literally interpreted as a request to spell the word *check* (although it's pretty unlikely). Hyphenating the verb *spell-check* or setting it solid clarifies the meaning.

A third factor that confuses hyphenation (as well as other style issues) is the difference between U.S. and British usage.

U.S. vs. British Usage

U.S. writers usually accept compounds more readily than British writers do. When British writers use compounds, they tend to hyphenate or split those that many U.S. writers would set solid. The annotated bibliography cites several sources that address British usage.

Choosing a Basic Approach

Enough with the bad news; let's explore the good: Compounding guidelines aren't nearly as arbitrary as they appear. Don't compound your problems (as it were) by making such decisions in a void. Many dictionaries and style books list compound words. Check a recent reference whenever you have doubts. If a compound isn't listed, this general rule of thumb will usually suffice: Hyphenate modifiers (adjectives and adverbs) before a noun, but split them after a noun.

As you make hyphenation decisions, keep four things in mind: 1) the audience you're writing for, 2) the type of document you're producing, 3) the points you wish to emphasize, and 4) the current compounding trends.

Audience

Your audience's needs must take priority over esthetics. In general, the less familiar a compound might be for your audience, the better it is to hyphenate. On the other hand, when a hyphen falls at the end of a line, foreign readers may have trouble determining whether a hyphen indicates a compound or is simply there to continue the word. When writing for those whose first language is not English, pay special attention to the treatment of compounds.

Type of Document

If you're producing a technical document, you may wish to limit the number of hyphenated forms. If you don't, it may result in choppy-looking pages because technical terms lend themselves to many more optional hyphens. In nontechnical documents, you may wish to use more hyphens because they may be needed for clarity.

Points of Emphasis

The judicious placement of a hyphen can help emphasize or de-emphasize certain words in a sentence. Because the beginnings and endings of sentences are the parts that stand out most, using a hyphenated compound word in one of these locations can help emphasize your point. Note the difference in these statements:

- I write a monthly column that totals 750 words.

- Each month I write a 750-word column.

Say I'm pitching my credentials to a monthly publication and I want to emphasize that I'm experienced in meeting a monthly deadline. By using the compound *750-word,* I can place *Each month* at the beginning, where it will draw more attention.

Compounding Trends

Where guidelines are less defined, current trends favor solid compounds over hyphenated or split forms. I imagine we're in for more solid forms, especially because of their popularity on the Internet, but this trend could change at any time. Check the most current sources you can get your hands on when determining your hyphenation style.

Some writers confuse hyphenation with word division, which is what we'll look at next.

Word Division

Although it's best to avoid breaking a word (carrying it over from one line to another), sometimes that's the only way to make text fit. Dividing a word at the end of a line also helps smooth the edges of ragged-right copy and prevents unsightly spaces in justified text.

Although many word-division guidelines exist for esthetic reasons, a sensible approach can also enhance clarity. This holds true especially when a compound word falls at the end of a line.

Publishers commonly set a limit to the number of consecutive lines that end with a hyphen. Two- or three-line maximums are typical limits. Many publishers also avoid dividing first and last lines of paragraphs, headlines, titles, columns, and pages. Never break abbreviations or initials that fall at the end of a line. Instead, break the line before or after. The quick-reference charts address some word-division guidelines.

Most any dictionary can assist you with syllabication (dividing words based on their syllables). If you need to make frequent hyphenation decisions, you may wish to invest in a special word-division book, such as *Webster's New World Speller-Divider.*

Automatic Hyphenation Programs

If you use a computer, you probably already know that word-processing and page-layout programs can hyphenate automatically. This can be a great time-saver, but computers don't always break lines (insert hyphens) at the most appropriate points. The quick-reference charts therefore provide guidelines to help you decide where to break a word.

You can prevent hyphenation problems by not inserting hard hyphens. *Hard hyphens* are inserted with a hyphen key (-), generally located to the right of the zero on a standard keyboard. Since hard hyphens remain where you put them, they sometimes wind up in the middle of revised lines. Make it easier on production people (or yourself) by reserving hard hyphens for compound words.

Most word-processing programs have a special key or key combination (such as COMMAND + - or CONTROL + -) that allows you to insert "soft" or "discretionary" hyphens. These appear on your computer screen but print only when they're needed.

Breaking Up Need Not Be Hard To Do

If you're preparing a manuscript for publication, use hyphens at the ends of lines only for hyphenated compounds. Do not use them to indicate that a word continues on the next line. This applies to word-processed, typed, and handwritten work.

On a computer, turn off the automatic hyphenation. Use hyphens only when needed to form compound words. When you prepare a manuscript for publication, confirm that every hyphen in it connects a compound. Don't fret over a jagged margin; line endings usually change when the text is typeset anyway.

The Word-Division Guidelines in the quick-reference charts apply to work you are producing in final form yourself.

Variations Between U.S. & British Usage

U.S. writers divide words based on pronunciation; British writers, based on derivation. When in doubt, consult a dictionary.

How to Use Chapter 6's Quick-Reference Charts

The quick-reference charts for Chapter 6 contain two major sections: Compounding Guidelines and Word-Division Guidelines.

The columns with a checkmark (✔) contain "write-on lines," on which you can record the options you prefer or rank options when you find more than one acceptable.

The Word-Division Guidelines use a backslash symbol (\) to indicate the best place to break a word that won't fit on one line. The examples with multiple backslashes represent alternative points where you might break a line. Any hyphens in that section print regardless of their position on the line. Figure 30 illustrates a segment from the Word-Division Guidelines.

Word-Division Guidelines	Examples	✔
Break words between **adjacent vowels** that are pronounced separately.	co \ author re \ address	

Figure 30 - Sample Quick-Reference Chart Segment

For further information, check the glossary or explore the sources in the annotated bibliography.

Summary

This chapter has explained the three types of compounds: solid (closed), split (open), and hyphenated. It has also introduced some issues that make hyphenation challenging: the evolutionary process compounds go through, the variations in hyphenation with different parts of speech, and differences in U.S. versus British usage.

A few factors to consider when choosing a hyphenation approach include the audience, the type of document, the points you wish to emphasize, and general compounding trends.

The chapter has also covered principles of word division. The quick-reference charts provide further guidelines and examples.

Compounding Guidelines

Compounding Guidelines	Example	✔
Set compounds **beginning** *with any,* *every,* **or** *some* solid. EXCEPTION: Split such words when used in a narrower sense.	anyone everyplace somewhere any body [ANY ONE BODY] every time [EVERY SINGLE TIME] some thing [SOME SPECIFIC THING]	
Hyphenate compounds formed with two **colors or a color plus a noun.**	The clouds were yellow-gray. Sandi uses an emerald-green pen.	
EXCEPTION: Split such compounds when the first color ends with *ish.*	The clouds were yellowish gray.	
Hyphenate **comparative or superlative** modifiers. (See [1]*Usage Note, p. 38.*)	wider-read novel [COMPARATIVE] best-selling novel [SUPERLATIVE]	
U.S. writers generally set compound **compass directions** solid.	southeast northwest [U.S.]	——
• British writers generally hyphenate all compass directions.	south-east north-west [BRITISH]	——
NOTE: Hyphenate words combining three or more directions.	south-southeast [U.S./BRITISH]	
Hyphenate **compound numbers** unless one or both of the number's parts already contains a hyphen. (See *fractional modifiers, p. 125.*) (See *fractional nouns, p. 125.*)	eighty-three dollars three million dollars eighty-three million dollars [NO HYPHEN BEFORE MILLION]	
Hyphenate potentially **confusing combinations.**	ex-human-services chief thought-provoking theory	
U.S. writers set most compounds with **duplicate consonants** solid.	bookkeeping [U.S.]	——
• British writers hyphenate them. (See *triple consonants, p. 128.*)	book-keeping [BRITISH]	——

Compounding Guidelines *(continued)*	**Example**	✔
U.S. writers set most compounds with **duplicate vowels** solid.	preestablish reenter [U.S.]	—— ——
EXCEPTION: Hyphenate *awkward* duplicate-vowel compounds.	de-emphasize semi-independent	
• British writers hyphenate duplicate vowels.	pre-establish re-enter [BRITISH]	—— ——
Split most compound modifiers or nouns formed from widely known **foreign phrases**.	*bona fide* offer *nom de plume* *sine qua non*	
EXCEPTION: Some foreign phrases may contain hyphens. Consult a dictionary.	*fleur-de-lis* *laissez-faire*	
Hyphenate **fractional modifiers**, unless one or both parts of the fraction already contain a hyphen. (See *compound numbers, p. 124.*) (See *fractional nouns, p. 125.*) (See *mixed numbers, p. 126.*)	This project is nine-tenths completed.	
Split **fractional nouns**.	The ghostwritten portion of his book totaled two thirds. [U.S.]	——
CAUTION: British usage calls for hyphenating both fractional modifiers and fractional nouns, unless one part of the fraction is a compound number.	The ghostwritten portion of his book totaled two-thirds. [BRITISH]	——
EXCEPTION: Retain the hyphen if the compound follows a form of *be* (*is, are, was, were, be, am, been,* or *being*). (See *compound numbers, p. 124.*) (See *fractional nouns, p. 125.*) (See *mixed numbers, p. 126.*)	The ghostwritten portion of his book *was* two-thirds.	
Split modifiers when their second part consists of a **letter or numeral**.	grade B movie Level 2 head Type A personality	

Compounding Guidelines *(continued)*	**Example**	✔
Split **mixed numbers** consisting of whole numbers and fractions. In other words, do not use a hyphen before or after *and*.	eight and two-thirds [NUMBER PLUS FRACTION] eighty-nine and two-thirds [HYPHENATED NUMBER PLUS FRACTION]	
Hyphenate compound **modifiers preceding nouns**, but not necessarily following them.	That is a well-known poem. [PRECEDING NOUN]	
• Some writers hyphenate some modifiers that follow nouns.	That poem is well-known. [FOLLOWING NOUN, HYPHENATED]	——
• Others split some modifiers that follow nouns.	That poem is well known. [FOLLOWING NOUN, SPLIT]	——
NOTES: • Omit the hyphen when the first part of a compound is modified itself.	That poem is *very* well known. [MODIFIED, SPLIT]	
• Split compound adverbial modifiers when the first part ends in *ly* and second part has a participial ending.	That is a fully illustrated volume. That volume is fully illustrated.	
• An adjectival modifier may require a hyphen to prevent ambiguity.	That is a costly-looking glass.	
Hyphenate compound modifiers consisting of a **number** (whether a numeral or a word) **plus a measurement**.	5-year-old printer 24-hour time two-page spread	
EXCEPTION: Word and symbols relating to money, percentages, and so on, are not modifiers and need no hyphens.	Many writers dream of writing that million dollar best-seller.	
Split modifiers formed from a **number plus a possessive**.	two weeks' vacation	
Some writers hyphenate double **occupational titles**.	poet-novelist secretary-treasurer [HYPHEN]	——
• Others use en dashes or slashes. (See *occupational titles, p. 83.*)	poet–novelist [EN DASH] poet/novelist [SLASH]	—— ——

Compounding Guidelines *(continued)*	Example	✔
Hyphenate most compound modifiers with **participial endings** (*–ed, –en, –ing*).	middle-aged person	—
	write-protected disk	—
	ghost-written book	—
	God-given talent	—
	copy-editing skill	—
	proof-reading job	—
• Some writers set some such compounds solid.	ghostwritten book	—
	copyediting skill	—
	proofreading job	—
Set compound **personal pronouns** solid.	herself himself itself oneself themselves yourself	
Set most compounds formed with **prefixes** solid, unless the result will be ambiguous or awkward.	*anti*climactic *mini*mum *over*print *pseudo*nym *sub*head *tri*logy	
EXCEPTIONS:		
• Some compounds with prefixes can take hyphenated or solid forms.	bi-weekly semi-annual non-fiction pre-publication [BRITISH/U.S.]	— —
	biweekly semiannual nonfiction prepublication [U.S.]	— —
• Hyphenate most compounds formed with a prefix plus a proper noun. (See *hyphenated prefixes, p. 141*.)	anti-American neo-Darwinism	
• Hyphenate most compounds formed with *ex–, first–, half–, quasi–,* or *self–*.	ex-spouse first-rate half-tone quasi-official self-publish	
RECOMMENDATION: Look up any unclear compounds formed with a prefix. (See *duplicate consonants, p. 124*.) (See *duplicate vowels, p. 125*.) (See *repeated prefixes, p. 128*.) (See *triple consonants, p. 128*.)		

Compounding Guidelines *(continued)*	Example ✔
Hyphenate compounds formed with three or more words and containing **prepositions**, unless misreading is very unlikely.	brother-in-law up-to-the-minute *but* partners in crime point of view stream of consciousness
CAUTION: Do not hyphenate overly long compounds containing prepositions.	coming of age in New York City tale
Hyphenate compound modifiers formed from **proper names**.	Dallas-Fort Worth airport Twain-like humor
EXCEPTION: Split two-word proper names unless they are hyphenated in their original form.	New York publishing scene North American author
Hyphenate compounds with **repeated prefixes**.	re-revise sub-subplot
Set **scientific or technical modifiers** open or solid, unless one of their parts normally contains a hyphen.	barcode scanner deoxyribonucleic acid touchscreen display
Hyphenate compounds starting with a **single letter**, whether capitalized or not. (See *single letters, p. 150*.)	S-curve T-square U-turn X-height *or* x-height
Set most compounds containing **suffixes and suffix-like endings** solid.	break*age* vign*ette* book*ish* protago*nist* home*less* abridge*ment* censor*ship*
EXCEPTION: Hyphenate compounds ending in *odd*. RECOMMENDATION: Look up any unclear compounds formed with a suffix.	My publisher receives fifty-odd submissions a day (though all fifty may very well be odd).
Hyphenate compound words that would otherwise result in **triple consonants**. (See *duplicate consonants, p. 124*.) (See *duplicate vowels, p. 125*.)	cross-section full-length well-liked

Compounding Guidelines *(continued)*	Example	✔
Hyphenate compound modifiers formed from **two or more ideas describing the same noun**.	leftist-intellectual newspaper	
Hyphenate compound modifiers formed from **two or more numbers or words describing the same noun**.	first-place award part-time job 500-word article	
NOTE: When the noun follows only the last part of the modifier, suspend the hyphens after the preceding parts.	first- or second-place award full- or part-time job 500-, 750-, and 1,000-word articles	
Split compounds consisting of **two or more words commonly considered a single concept**.	book review literary agent news release social security trade book virtual reality	
NOTE: Split such compounds regardless of their part of speech or position in the sentence.	post office box [ADJECTIVE] post office [NOUN]	
Some writers hyphenate compound **verbs** when both parts would have a different meaning on their own.	double-space spell-check [HYPHENATE]	___ ___
• Others split such words.	double space spell check [SPLIT]	___ ___
• Still others set them solid.	doublespace spellcheck [SOLID]	___ ___
NOTES: • U.S. writers generally set compound modifiers and some compound nouns formed with a verb/adverb or verb/preposition combination solid.	backup layout makeup [NOUN] back up lay out make up [VERB] [U.S.]	___ ___
• British writers generally hyphenate compounds with verb/preposition combinations as nouns and verbs. (See *confusing combinations, p. 124.*)	back-up make-up [NOUN] *but* layout back-up make-up [VERB] [BRITISH]	___ ___

Word-Division Guidelines

Word-Division Guidelines	Examples	✔
Try not to divide **abbreviations**. (See *middle names or initials, p. 131*.)	M.B.A. Op-Ed [NO BREAK]	
Break words between **adjacent vowels** that are pronounced separately.	co \ author re \ address	
Break words in ways that **clarify their meaning, pronunciation, or part of speech**.	proj \ ect [NOUN] pro \ ject [TRANSITIVE VERB]	
For esthetic reasons, limit the number of **consecutive divided lines**. • Some publishers aim to divide no more than three consecutive lines.	Xxxxx xx xxx xxxxx xxxx xxxx xxxx-xxx. Xx xx xxxxxx xxx xxxx xxxxxx-xxx. Xxxxx xx xxx xxxxx xxxx xxxx-xxxx xxxxx. [3-LINE MAXIMUM]	——
• Others aim to divide no more than two consecutive lines.	Xxxxx xx xxx xxxxx xxxx xxxx xxxx-xxx. Xx xx xxxxxx xxx xxxx xxxxxx-xxx. Xxxxx xxx xxx xxxxx xxxx xxx. [2-LINE MAXIMUM]	——
Break words between **consonants** when possible.	anec \ dote paper \ work per \ mis \ sions	
NOTE: When words contain three or more consecutive consonants, keep one attached to the preceding vowel.	dis \ trib \ u \ tor	
CAUTION: Avoid breaks that might result in a misreading.	mul \ tiply *not* multi \ ply roy \ alties *not* royal \ ties	
Try not to divide **contractions**.	haven't I'd they're you'll [NO BREAK]	
Do not divide numbers containing **decimals**. (See *decimals, p. 190*.)	3.14159265 [NO BREAK]	

Word-Division Guidelines (*cont.*)	**Examples**
Break lines after **ellipses** rather than before them.	The end is near. . . . \ But that doesn't mean I'm pessimistic.
Break lines after an **em dash or en dash** rather than before it.	She began writing— \ which was her passion— \ at the age of nine.
Try not to divide words with **endings pronounced as single syllables**.	cre \ den \ tials *not* credenti \ als ju \ di \ cious *not* judici \ ous
Try not to divide **first and last names**.	Lewis Carroll *not* Lewis \ Carroll
EXCEPTIONS: When necessary, divide compound surnames after the hyphen or the first surname. (See *middle names or initials, p. 131.*) (See *surnames & abbreviations, degrees, or titles, p. 133.*)	Claire Kehrwald \ Cook *not* Claire \ Kehrwald Cook
Break **hyphenated compounds** after the hyphen. NOTE: In narrow columns, this may not be possible.	two- \ column *not* two-col \ umn best- \ seller *not* best-sell \ er poet- \ novelist *not* poet-novel \ ist
Try not to divide lines between **introductory letters or numbers** and their associated **listed items**.	Three common character formats used for emphasis are: 1) bold, 2) italics, and 3) underlines. *not* Three common character formats used for emphasis are: 1) bold, 2) italics, and 3) underlines.
Try not to divide **large numbers**	5,000,000 [UNDER ONE BILLION]
EXCEPTION: You can divide 1 billion and higher *after* the third comma.	5,000,000, \ 000 [AT/OVER ONE BILLION]
Break names after **middle names or initials** only when necessary. (See *first and last names, p. 131.*) (See *surnames & abbreviations, degrees, or titles, p. 133.*)	Karen Elizabeth \ Gordon *not* Karen \ Elizabeth Gordon E. B. \ White *not* E. \ B. White

Word-Division Guidelines *(cont.)*	Examples	✔
Do not divide between **months and days** or **months and years**.	December 31 December 1999 [NO BREAK]	
Do not divide between **numbers** and associated **abbreviations, symbols, or text**.	AD 1998 12:30 PM 32°F $30 15% Chapter 9 page iii 15 percent [NO BREAK]	
Break words after rather than before a **one-syllable vowel**, unless it will result in an inaccurate pronunciation.	idi \ om *not* id \ iom solilo \ quy *not* solil \ oquy	
CAUTION: Never break right after a single vowel that starts a word.	agent *not* a \ gent ital \ ics *not* i \ talics	
Break compounds with **prefixes** before their root or base.	anti \ climax *not* anticli \ max co \ author *not* coau \ thor	
EXCEPTIONS: In narrow columns, such a break may not be possible. (See *prevent confusion or unintentional humor, p. 132.*) (See *suffixes, p. 133.*)		
Break words in ways that **prevent confusion or unintentional humor**.	com \ edies *not* come \ dies roy \ alties *not* royal \ ties ste \ reotype *not* stereo \ type	
TIP: Check each portion of the divided word to see if it is pronounceable.	Editors like good bottom-line analy \ ses of competitive books. *not* Editors like good bottom-line anal \ yses of competitive books.	
Try not to divide most **short or one-syllable words** (five or fewer letters).	agent clips style [NO BREAK]	
CAUTION: Watch out for one-syllable words ending in *ed*.	closed shipped watched [NO BREAK]	

Word-Division Guidelines *(cont.)*	Examples	✔
Break words with **suffixes** before the suffix rather than within in. EXCEPTIONS:	censor \ ship *not* cen \ sorship protagon \ ist *not* protag \onist	
• Break words ending in *able* or *ible* in a way that preserves their original root.	publish \ able *not* pub \ lishable flex \ ible *not* flexi \ ible [*ABLE/IBLE*]	
• When words contain double consonants, break them between the duplicated letters.	novel \ la *not* no \ vella syl \ lable *not* syll \ able [DOUBLE CONSONANT]	
• In narrow columns, breaking within a root may be necessary. (See *prefixes, p. 132.*) (See *prevent confusion or unintentional humor, p. 132.*)		
Do not divide between **surnames and abbreviations, degrees, or titles**.	Martin Luther King, Jr. *not* Martin Luther King, \ Jr.	—
(See *first and last names, p. 131.*) (See *middle names or initials, p. 131.*)	Dr. Jane \ Doe *or* Jane Doe, M.D. *not* Dr. \ Jane Doe *or* Jane Doe, \ M.D.	—
Break words only between **syllables**.	ac \ knowl \ edg \ ment for \ mu \ la	

7

The Ups & Downs of It All

Capitalization

*C*apitalization is (thankfully!) one of the more straightforward areas of publication style. This chapter discusses common capitalization standards and a few exceptions and variations. It also explains the use of capitalization for emphasis and other special applications.

In this book, the term *capitalize* refers to the first letter of a word—the *initial cap*—unless specifically stated otherwise. Acronyms and initialisms, which generally appear in all caps or small caps, are an exception and are explained in Chapter 8.

As do most other chapters in this section, this chapter ends with customizable quick-reference charts.

Common Capitalization Standards

Similar to closed and open punctuation, there are two primary styles of capitalization: "Up Style" and "down style." In situations where either style is acceptable, *Up Style* leans toward capitalizing every important word, while *down style* leans toward lowercase.

Some words are capitalized or set in lowercase no matter which style you chose. For instance, the first letter of a sentence is almost invariably capitalized. Names of economic or social groups, such as *the middle class*, are almost always lowercase. Nouns that are capitalized when part of a proper name (the Colorado River, the Globe Theater) may be upper- or lowercase when used as plurals (the Colorado and Mississippi River [or rivers], the Globe and Paramount Theaters [or theaters]).

Another capitalization style is what newspaper columnist L.M. Boyd refers to as "nerd capitalization"—capitalizing a letter in the middle of a compound word or name. This development, which is especially prevalent in business, matches the manufacturer's capitalization (and spacing and hyphenation) for a trademark. *CorelDRAW!, PostScript, QuarkXPress,* and *X-Acto* are examples of "nerd capitalization."

Choosing the Best Approach

Which approach is "best"? It depends upon the situation. Sometimes, space is a significant consideration. Lowercase letters simply consume less space than capital letters. But, most of the time, it's wise to base a decision on more than space alone.

Basic Considerations

When determining capitalization standards, consider the following factors:

- What the audience or market is used to

- The purpose of the communication

- The norm for the medium, organization, product, or publication

The most effective style retains the consistency of the whole as much as possible while communicating the writer's intention.

Capitalization standards tend to vary more with the types of organizations that set them than with the medium in which they appear. Large organizations and academic and government bureaucracies often lean toward Up Style capitalization.

Many organizations determine a basic approach (Up Style or down style) and then make exceptions as individual needs arise. Personal preferences tend to influence capitalization standards more than they do other points of style.

British usage leans toward fewer caps than U.S. usage. The British capitalize names of organizations and institutions (European Commission, Labour Party, Parliament, World Bank) but rarely people's titles (chairman, defence secretary, president, prime minister). There are, of course, a number of exceptions.

When in doubt, check an authoritative guide. The annotated bibliography cites sources that address British usage.

Current Trends

The trend today leans toward down style, though many organizations still capitalize extensively. Those who use down style generally prefer it for two reasons: 1) It looks more casual and therefore comes off as more friendly, and 2) It helps readers focus on what's most important. When too many words are capitalized, they look equally important, and nothing stands out.

Emphasis & Special Applications

Some people use all caps for emphasis (LIKE THIS). On the whole, I'd discourage such use. All caps can be overbearing and are actually more difficult to read.

Small caps are somewhat more useful. For instance, many publishers use small caps for AD and BC with years and AM and PM with times. Signage frequently employs small caps. Some publishers use small caps for acronyms. Publishers of computer manuals sometimes use small caps for keyboard keys and command names. Chapter 12 discusses all caps and small caps in more detail.

A further consideration is the capitalization scheme for addressing envelopes. OCR (optical character recognition) scanners can read and sort mail more quickly when addresses appear in all caps, with no punctuation. Figure 31 illustrates a format recommended by the United States Post Office.

```
Your Name
Your Company
Your Street
Your City, State  ZIP


                          ADDRESSEE'S NAME
                          ADDRESSEE'S COMPANY
                          ADDRESSEE'S STREET
                          ADDRESSEE'S CITY  STATE  ZIP
```

Figure 31 - Preferred Addressing Format

How to Use Chapter 7's Quick-Reference Charts

The quick-reference charts for Chapter 7 contain two major sections. The General Guidelines section addresses capitalization conventions that relate more to form than to content. The Specific Guidelines section addresses capitalization conventions for specific categories or words. Celestial bodies, compass points, ethnic groups and nationalities, job titles, parts of publications, scientific names, and signage are just a few of the categories addressed.

The categories appear in the left-hand column, organized alphabetically by bold key words. The right-hand column provides examples that illustrate each guideline. Brackets contain clarifying information. Figure 32 shows a sample segment from a quick-reference chart.

Guidelines	Example	✔
Some writers capitalize **common adjectives** derived from proper names.	Italic type	——
	Manila folder	——
	Roman numeral [UP STYLE]	——
• Others set them in lowercase.	italic type	——
	manila folder	——
	roman numeral [DOWN STYLE]	——

Figure 32 - Sample Quick-Reference Chart Segment

Frequently, more than one capitalization scheme is acceptable. Dotted lines set off common, but conflicting, style standards (Up Style versus down style, and so on). The column with the checkmark (✔) contains "write-on lines," on which you can record the options you prefer or rank your preferences by number.

Once you become familiar with the layout of these charts and determine which options you prefer, you will find them quite useful. For short jobs, you may need only to record your capitalization preferences on a Word List/Style Sheet form or in a simple computerized style guide (see Chapter 1). For further information, check the glossary or explore the sources in the annotated bibliography near the end of the book.

The following abbreviations appear in this chapter's quick-reference charts:

caps	capital letters
GPO	U.S. Government Printing Office's *A Manual of Style*
w/	with

Figure 33 - Abbreviation Key

This chapter has introduced two primary approaches to capitalization: "Up Style" and "down style." It has also examined the current trend toward down style and has talked about the use of capitalization for emphasis and special applications.

The quick-reference charts that follow present capitalization guidelines and provide further examples.

GENERAL GUIDELINES	Example	✔
Capitalize **abbreviations** of capitalized words. NOTE: Abbreviations of lowercase words are sometimes capitalized.	Aug. (August) Mon. (Monday) St. (Street) Tex. (Texas)	
(See *abbreviation formats, p. 165.*) (See *capitalization of abbreviations, p. 168.*) (See *measurements, p. 142.*)	No. (number) P.S. (post script) SE (southeast) TV (television)	____ ____ ____ ____
Some writers set **acronyms** in all caps.	DOS (disk operating system) ZIP (Zone Improvement Program) [ALL CAPS]	____
• Others set them in small caps.	DOS (disk operating system) ZIP (Zone Improvement Program) [SMALL CAPS]	____
EXCEPTION: Set common nouns derived from acronyms in lowercase. (See *capitalization of abbreviations, p. 168.*) (See *capitalization schemes, p. 236.*) (See *measurements, p. 142.*)	modem pixel radar [DERIVATIONS]	
Some writers capitalize **common adjectives** derived from proper names.	Italic type Manila folder Roman numeral [UP STYLE]	____ ____ ____
• Others set them in lowercase. (See *proper adjectives, p. 142.*)	italic type manila folder roman numeral [DOWN STYLE]	____ ____ ____

General Guidelines *(continued)*	**Example**	✔
In general, capitalize the first word of **complete sentences**.	The check is in the mail. Is this story publishable?	
Capitalize the first word of *complete lines of* **dialogue**, but not interrupted dialogue. (See *direct quotes, p. 141.*)	"You're crazy," Linda said. Then Alex snarled, "You bet I am!" *but* "You're crazy," Linda said, "and I've had enough of you."	
In general, capitalize the first word of **direct quotes**, but not indirect quotes. NOTE: Capitalization of quoted material can be altered to fit new contexts. (See *dialogue, p. 141.*)	"Our city is growing by leaps and bounds," the mayor said in last night's speech. *but* In last night's speech the mayor said that our city is experiencing tremendous growth.	
Set **hyphenated prefixes** in lower-case, no matter what their root is.	anti-Communist non-Western pre-publication	
Some writers set **initialisms** in all caps.	CPU (central processing unit) FYI (for your information) [ALL CAPS]	——
• Others set them in small caps. (See *acronyms, p. 140.*)	CPU (central processing unit) FYI (for your information) [SMALL CAPS]	——
Some writers capitalize **listed items**—whether they form complete sentences or not.	1. Insert disk 2. Double click on file name 3. Edit file, saving often [UP STYLE]	——
• Others capitalize only those items that form complete sentences. NOTE: This guideline holds true whether the listed items begin with bullets, with letters, or with numbers.	1. insert disk 2. double click on file name *but* 1. Insert your disk. 2. Double click on the file name. [DOWN STYLE]	——

General Guidelines *(continued)*	**Example**	✔
Set **measurements** in lowercase.	dpi in. lb sq. ft wpm	
In general, capitalize individual lines of **poetry**—whether they form complete sentences or not.	Roses are red. Violets are blue. I'm not a poet. How about you?	—
EXCEPTION: Some poets use lowercase throughout a poem to create a distinctive style.	i shall imagine life is not worth dying, if (and when) roses complain their beauties are in vain <div align="right">—e.e. cummings</div>	—
Capitalize **proper adjectives**. (See *common adjectives, p. 140*.)	British usage Texas writer	
Some writers capitalize **sentence fragments** following a colon or a question mark. Some use lowercase when—	Are you most interested in writing novels? Short stories? Poetry? [UP STYLE]	—
• The parts before and after the mark are closely related, or	Are you most interested in writing novels? short stories? poetry? [DOWN STYLE]	—
• The part following the colon or question mark is less important than what precedes it.	Three styles often used for emphasis follow: bold, italics, underlines. [DOWN STYLE]	—
Some writers capitalize **sentences within sentences**, particularly direct thoughts or questions.	You may wonder, Which style guide is the most authoritative? [UP STYLE]	—
• Others use lowercase.	You may wonder, which style guide is the most authoritative? [DOWN STYLE]	—
• Some writers capitalize sentences within sentences when enclosed in brackets, dashes, or parentheses.	Editors place the Latin term *stet* (Let it stand) next to reversed editorial decisions. [UP STYLE]	—
• Others use lowercase.	Editors place the Latin term *stet* (let it stand) next to reversed editorial decisions. [DOWN STYLE]	—

Specific Capitalization Guidelines

SPECIFIC GUIDELINES	Example	✔
Capitalize *specific* **academic course titles** and set subjects in lowercase.	Creative Writing Psychology 101 *but* writing psychology	——
EXCEPTION: Always capitalize names of languages and language courses.	English French Spanish	
Capitalize *specific* **academic degrees** following proper names, whether the degrees are abbreviated or not.	Emily Chang, B.A., M.F.A., Ph.D. Emily Chang, Doctor of Philosophy	
• Set *general* terms in lowercase.	bachelor's degree doctorate master of fine arts	
Set **academic years** in lowercase.	freshman sophomore junior	
• Capitalize those used as proper adjectives.	Senior Prom	
Capitalize *specific* **astronomical terms**, particularly those containing proper names.	Big Dipper Hale-Bopp comet Milky Way galaxy	
• Set general terms in lowercase.	asteroid meteor solar system star	
Capitalize names of individual **buildings and bridges**.	Globe Theatre Library of Congress Golden Gate Bridge London Bridge	
• Some capitalize plural forms.	Golden Gate and London Bridges	——
• Others do not.	Golden Gate and London bridges	——
Capitalize all **celestial bodies**, including *Earth, Moon,* and *Sun*. . .	The Sun is about 389 times farther from Earth than the Moon. July 20, 1969, was the first Moon walk.	——
. . . but set *moon* and *sun* in lowercase when not referring to our own. (See *celestial bodies*, p. 144.)	Jupiter has several moons. [UP STYLE]	——

Specific Guidelines *(continued)*	**Example**	✔
Celestial bodies *(continued)*		
• Some writers capitalize *Earth* with other planets, but not *moon* or *sun*.	The moon orbits Earth, between Venus and Mars. [DOWN STYLE]	——
• Some writers set *earth* in lowercase when the word *on* precedes it.	This is the greatest show on earth! [DOWN STYLE—ON EARTH]	——
• Some writers set *earth* in lowercase when the word *the* precedes it.	The earth's inner core is solid iron. [DOWN STYLE—THE EARTH]	——
Some writers set **centuries** in lowercase, except in a title, before a proper name, or when starting a sentence.	twentieth century Twentieth Century Club	——
• Others capitalize them every time.	Twentieth Century	——
Capitalize names of **cities**. (See *states, p. 151.*)	Austin New York City	
Capitalize **compass points**, when used in reference to major regions or specific cultures.	the Deep South the East Coast the Midwest the Pacific Northwest	
• Set them in lowercase when they are used as directions.	Turn north at the second light.	
• Capitalize compass points used in proper names, but set them in lowercase if another word falls between them.	Eastern States *but* eastern seaboard states	
Capitalize names of **continents**.	Africa Antarctica Asia Australia Europe North America South America	
Capitalize names of **counties**.	Travis County Williamson County	
• Plural forms are often lowercase.	Travis and Williamson counties	
Capitalize names of **countries**.	Canada Mexico United States	
Capitalize **days** of the week, whether they are abbreviated or not.	Monday Thursday Saturday Mon. Thurs. Sat.	

Specific Guidelines *(continued)*	**Example**	✔
Capitalize names of **deities and revered persons**.	Buddha Christ God Jehovah Jesus Mohammed the Holy Spirit *but* the gods	
Set **disease names** that aren't proper names in lowercase EXCEPTIONS:	arthritis diabetes hypertension	
• Retain the capital for proper names used in disease names, but set the common part, including *disease, phenomenon, syndrome,* and similar words, in lowercase.	Alzheimer's disease Down syndrome [NOT DOWN'S] Raynaud's phenomenon	
• Set acronyms in all caps or small caps.	CP (cerebral palsy) [ALL CAPS] CP (cerebral palsy) [SMALL CAPS]	___ ___
Set **economic and social groups** in lowercase. (See *ethnic groups & nationalities,* p. 145.)	blue-collar workers the homeless middle class the urban poor	
Capitalize **epithets** used in place of personal names.	Language Maven	
NOTE: Enclose in quotation marks epithets that appear with full names.	William Safire, the "Language Maven"	
Capitalize most **ethnic groups and nationalities**.	African American Asian Hispanic Native American	
• Some writers also capitalize *black* and *white*.	Black White [UP STYLE]	___
• Others use lowercase.	black white [DOWN STYLE]	___
NOTE: In certain languages, some word ending vary based on sex. (In Spanish, *–a* indicates female, *–o*, male.) (See *economic & social groups, p. 145.*)	Chicana/Latina [FEMALE] Chicano/Latino [MALE]	

Specific Guidelines *(continued)*	Example	✔
Set **foreign particles** to match the individual's preference, or match the style most commonly seen. NOTE: The capitalization of particles and the spacing between them and last names are individual preferences.	da Vinci Du Maurier La Fayette de Maupassant De Vries	
Capitalize **geographic features** only when they are part of a proper name.	Chisos Mountains San Andreas Fault Yucatán Peninsula	
• Some writers capitalize plural geographic features.	Colorado and Mississippi Rivers North and South Poles	——
• Others set them in lowercase.	Colorado and Mississippi rivers North and South poles	——
NOTE: Avoid adding words that mean the same as foreign terms.	Rio Grande [OMIT *RIVER. RIO* MEANS *RIVER.*]	
Capitalize official names of **geological eras and historic events and periods**.	Mesozoic Era Jurassic Period Ice Age [PLEISTOCENE ONLY] Great Depression the Sixties	
NOTE: Set unofficial names in lowercase. (See *GPO*.)	ice age [OTHER THAN PLEISTOCENE]	
Capitalize the names of **governing bodies** (*city, federal, state*) when used as part of a proper name.	Austin City Council Federal Bureau of Investigation State Capitol Building	
• Some writers also capitalize names of governing bodies used as modifiers or as common nouns.	City services Federal income tax employees of the State	—— —— ——
• Others use lowercase. (See *political divisions, p. 149.*)	city services federal income tax employees of the state	—— —— ——

Specific Guidelines *(continued)*	**Example**	✔
Capitalize the official names of **historic doctrines, documents, and legislation**, but not unratified amendments and treaties.	Bill of Rights United States Constitution Copyright Revision Act of 1976	
• Set the names of unofficial descriptions of legislation in lowercase.	the treaty at Versailles *but* Versailles Treaty	
Capitalize names of **holidays**.	New Year's Day Fourth of July Halloween Thanksgiving Day	
Some writers capitalize both parts of **hyphenated compounds in titles**.	*Style Meister: The Quick-Reference Custom Style Guide* [UP STYLE]	—
• Some set the second part in lowercase. (See *Figure 49, p. 235.*)	*Style Meister: The Quick-reference Custom Style Guide* [DOWN STYLE]	—
Capitalize the pronoun *I*, except when making an exception for poetic license.	Why of course I spell-checked! i shall imagine life is not worth dying, if (and when) roses complain their beauties are in vain —e.e. cummings	— —
Capitalize **kinship names** followed by or used as proper names.	I love Grandma Castle's chocolate mayonnaise cake. Is Dad home yet?	
• When used as common nouns or as possessives, set kinship names in lowercase.	That man is my uncle. Our daughter's performance was outstanding.	
Capitalize major words in a **letter's salutation** and the first word in a **complimentary close**. (See *complimentary close, p. 76.*) (See *greeting, business, p. 77.*) (See *greeting, personal, p. 77.*)	Dear Ms. Doe: Sincerely yours,	

Specific Guidelines *(continued)*	**Example**	✔
Set most names of **medical operations and procedures** and the like in lowercase when they appear without a proper name.	appendectomy dialysis gastric lavage tracheotomy *but* Bosworth procedure Heimlich maneuver Kazanjian operation	
EXCEPTION: Set acronyms in all caps or small caps.	CT (computerized tomography) EKG (electrocardiogram) [ALL CAPS] CT (computerized tomography) EKG (electrocardiogram) [SMALL CAPS]	—— ——
Capitalize **military titles** that precede a name or are used in direct discourse.	Captain James Bowie General Ulysses S. Grant "Ready to set sail, Admiral."	
• Set general references to military rank and military titles that follow names in lowercase.	admiral captain colonel general Ulysses S. Grant, commanding general	
EXCEPTION: Some government and military titles are capitalized both before and after a name and when used without one. (See *occupational titles, p. 148.*) (See *titles of honor, p. 152.*) (See *GPO* or *Words into Type.*)	Commander in Chief General of the Army Supreme Allied Commander Chairman, Joint Chiefs of Staff Chief of Staff Admiral of the Navy, Fleet Admiral	
Capitalize **months**, whether they are abbreviated or not.	January April July October Jan. Apr. Jul. Oct.	
Most writers capitalize **occupational titles** that precede proper names, but not those that follow them.	Submissions Editor Pam Hong Pam Hong, submissions editor	——
• Some capitalize in both positions. (See *military titles, p. 148.*) (See *titles of honor, p. 152.*)	Submissions Editor Pam Hong Pam Hong, Submissions Editor	——

Specific Guidelines *(continued)*	Example	✔
Capitalize the official names of **organizations** (agencies, associations, clubs, companies, departments, divisions, and institutes).	The American Red Cross United Way Boy Scouts of America General Electric United States Navy Publications Division Smithsonian Institute	
• Set organization names used as adjectives and not preceded by proper names in lowercase.	army surplus naval base	
• Set abbreviated forms of organization names in lowercase.	scout camp scouts	
Some writers capitalize significant **parts of larger elements** when they precede a letter, number, or title.	Appendix A Chapter 3 Figure 8 Room 101 Volume II: N–Z	—— —— —— —— ——
• Others set them in lowercase.	appendix A chapter 3 figure 8 room 101 volume II: N–Z	—— —— —— —— ——
EXCEPTION: Set variables in lowercase.	trial *n* item *x*	
• Set smaller elements in lowercase, unless they're the first word of the sentence.	lines 80–86 page 300 paragraph 7.1.3	
Capitalize **political divisions** only when they are part of proper names.	Travis County 21st Congressional District	
• Some writers capitalize plural political divisions.	Travis and Williamson Counties [UP STYLE]	——
• Others set them in lowercase.	Travis and Williamson counties [DOWN STYLE]	——

Specific Guidelines *(continued)*	Example	✔
Capitalize **proper names and initials**.	John Fitzgerald Kennedy Martin Luther King, Jr. JFK MLK	
Capitalize the official names of **religions**.	Buddhism Christianity Confucianism Hinduism Judaism Shintoism Taoism	
Capitalize the first words of **rules and slogans**.	Castle's law: *Make no assumptions.* The primary rule of style is *It depends.*	
Some writers use all caps for the **salutation, *To Whom It May Concern***.	TO WHOM IT MAY CONCERN:	—
• Others use initial caps.	To Whom It May Concern:	—
Capitalize **scientific names** of *phyla, classes, orders, families*, and their related subcomponents.	Chordata [PHYLUM] Vertebrata [SUBPHYLUM] Mammalia [CLASS] Eutheria [SUBCLASS] Primate [ORDER] Anthropoidea [SUBORDER] Hominidae [FAMILY]	
• Capitalize and italicize *genera*.	*Homo* [GENUS]	
• Set *species* and *varieties* in italicized lowercase—even those derived from proper names.	*sapiens* [SPECIES] *Lupinus texensis* or *L. texensis* [GENUS/SPECIES FOR TEXAS BLUEBONNET]	
• Some writers capitalize names of *kingdoms*.	Animalia [KINGDOM—UP STYLE]	—
• Others set names of kingdoms in lowercase.	animalia [KINGDOM—DOWN STYLE]	—
In general, use small caps for **signage**.	BEWARE OF BOA CONSTRICTOR	—
In general, capitalize **single letters** that name things or indicate shapes. (See *single letter, p. 128*.)	A-frame T-square U-turn	—

Specific Guidelines *(continued)*	**Example**	✔
Capitalize **states**. (See *cities, p. 144*.)	New York Texas	
Capitalize individual **streets and highways**.	Pecan Street Sixth Street IH 35 U.S. 183	
Capitalize major words in **titles of artistic and literary works**. NOTES: • Some writers capitalize the *first* and *last words* and all *proper nouns*.	*Publishers Weekly* "The Tonight Show" *The Wizard of Oz* "Waiting for Godot" *Whistler's Mother*	—— —— —— —— ——
• Others capitalize only the *first word* and all *proper nouns*.	*The wizard of Oz* "Waiting for Godot" *Whistler's mother*	—— —— ——
• In general, set *articles, conjunctions,* and *short prepositions* in lowercase.	*The Elements of Style* *Of Mice and Men* [CAP FIRST WORD]	
• Some writers capitalize *conjunctions* and *prepositions with four or more letters*. Record such limits on the ✔ line.	"The Bridge *Over* the River Kwai" "Desire *Under* the Elms" *Enough About Grammar* *Writing With Precision* [CAP PREPOSITIONS W/ FOUR OR MORE LETTERS]	——
• Some writers always capitalize *as, if, once, than, that,* and *till*.	*Writing That Works*	——
• In general, set *to* in lowercase.	*A Writer's Guide to Research*	——
EXCEPTION: Some writers capitalize *to* when it's used as an infinitive.	*How To Get Control of Your Time and Your Life*	
• Some writers capitalize all major words in titles of references.	*The Careful Writer: A Modern Guide to English Usage*	——
• Others capitalize only proper nouns and the first words of titles and subtitles. (See *Figure 49, p. 235*.)	*The careful writer: A modern guide to English usage*	——

Specific Guidelines *(continued)*	Example	✔
Capitalize **titles of honor** that precede proper names. • When such titles follow the name, appear without a name, or appear outside of formal context, set them in lowercase.	Pope John Paul II Reverend Jesse Jackson Governor George W. Bush President Bill Clinton Representative Lloyd Doggett	
EXCEPTIONS: Do not capitalize a title when the word *former* precedes it. (See *occupational titles, p. 148.*) (See *military titles, p. 148.*)	former Texas governor Ann Richards former president George Bush	
Capitalize **trademarks**, but not the common nouns they identify. NOTES:	Rolodex rotary card file X-Acto knife	
• Some writers match the manufacturer's capitalization, hyphenation, and spacing *every time* they use a trademark.	CorelDRAW! Ko-Rec-Type UNIX WordPerfect [MATCH EVERY TIME]	——
• Others match the manufacturer the *first time, then* use *initial caps* and *match* the *spacing.*	CorelDRAW! *then* CorelDraw [MATCH ON FIRST USE, THEN USE INITIAL CAPS & MATCH SPACING]	——
• Some match the manufacturer the *first time, then* just use *initial caps.*	CorelDRAW! *then* Corel Draw [MATCH ON FIRST USE ONLY]	——
• Words that have lost official protection can be set in lowercase. (See Chapter 11 for more information about trademarks.)	aspirin escalator mimeograph zipper [UNPROTECTED TRADEMARKS]	
Capitalize the names of **vehicles:** *aircraft, automobiles, spacecraft, ships,* **and** *submarines.*	Boeing B-52 Concorde DC-10 Honda Accord Mercedes-Benz *Flyer Apollo 13 Sputnik II Calypso*	
• Many writers italicize names of vehicles, but not the abbreviations that precede them.	HMS *Pinafore* USS *Bowfin*	——

8

S.O.S.!

Abbreviations, Acronyms & Initialisms

*A*t first glance, you might think the only decision you need to make about abbreviations is whether to use them or not. This is certainly the most significant decision, but you must also consider how to capitalize, punctuate, and space the abbreviations you use. And, occasionally, you may need to form plural or possessive abbreviations. This chapter discusses these points in relation to three types of abbreviations: 1) basic abbreviations, which include clipped or truncated words, 2) acronyms, and 3) initialisms. The next few sections define these terms and explain them in more detail.

Types of Abbreviations

An *abbreviation* is a shortened form of a word or phrase used in place of its complete form. For the most part, this chapter uses the term in a generic sense to include all types of abbreviations.

Basic Abbreviations

To form some abbreviations, we clip or truncate the beginning or ending of a word. Some examples include bus (omnibus), Feb. (February), fig. (figure), logo (logotype), misc. (miscellaneous), and vol. (volume). We truncate some abbreviations at both ends fridge (refrigerator).

We form other basic abbreviations by contracting words, or by using hybridizations or phonetic forms. Some examples include bldg. (building), fax (facsimile transmission), hi (high), infomercial (information commercial), and pixel (picture element). Note that, unlike contractions (can't, it's, we're, and so on), abbreviations rarely contain apostrophes to show where something's missing.

Acronyms and initialisms are two other types of abbreviations.

Acronyms

An *acronym* consists of the first letter or letters of the main parts of a compound word. Articles and prepositions are usually excluded. We pronounce acronyms as words in their own right: ASCII ("ask-ee": American Standard Code for Information Interchange), NAFTA ("naf-ta": North American Free Trade Agreement), WYSIWYG ("whizzy wig": what you see is what you get), laser ("la-zer": light amplification by stimulated emission of radiation), and sonar ("so-nar": sound navigation ranging) are examples of acronyms. The origins of most of these examples are self-apparent. Sonar is an exception, for it incorporates the first two letters of the first two words (*so*und *na*vigation *r*anging).

Initialisms

An *initialism* is constructed like an acronym but is pronounced as individual letters. Some initialisms include ABA (American Booksellers Association), ISBN (International Standard Book Number), PC (personal computer, politically correct, *or* postal code), and e.t.a. (estimated time of arrival).

And we mustn't leave out the computer-inspired PCMCIA, which, according to journalist Michelle Quinn, means "People Can't Memorize Computer Industry Acronyms." Although quite a few folks would agree, PCMCIA actually stands for "Personal Computer Memory Card International Association"—not that that's any more helpful!

Some initialisms have unique pronunciations, such as NAACP ("N double-A C-P": National Association for the Advancement of Colored People). On occasion, you'll run across an abbreviation that some people treat as an acronym and others treat as an initialism. One example is ASAP (as soon as possible), pronounced "A-S-A-P" by some and "A-sap" by others.

Before examining how to treat an abbreviation, it's best to determine if you need it in the first place.

When to Abbreviate

Abbreviations aren't appropriate for every situation. For example, words that you can safely abbreviate in headings or tables may need to be spelled out in general text. To decide whether to use an abbreviation, consider

- Whether your audience is familiar with the abbreviation—or can easily become so,

- Whether the abbreviation is conventional for the field or publication, and

- Whether the abbreviation will save space and effectively prevent repetition.

You can almost always make a good case for abbreviations in scientific and technical works. Using abbreviations in place of multisyllabic words can make pages much less overwhelming, besides saving valuable space.

In nonscientific, nontechnical works, it's usually best to abbreviate more frugally. Too many abbreviations in running text can make a page look choppy, slow the pace of reading, and hamper your communications.

Another place where it's usually best not to abbreviate is in foreign communications. English is tough enough for non-native speakers; don't make them decipher excess abbreviations.

Once you've decided to use an abbreviation, you next need to determine how you'll treat it.

Treatment of Abbreviations

This section examines how to capitalize, punctuate, and space abbreviations, and how to form plurals and possessives. The quick-reference charts provide more guidelines and examples.

Capitalization

Many abbreviations may be uppercase, lowercase, or a mixture of both. In special cases, they may even be in small caps, such as AD (*anno Domini*) and BC (before Christ) with a year (AD 1998). Many abbreviations are equally acceptable as either upper- or lowercase (for example, PR or pr for public relations).

In general, the case of an abbreviation should match that of the word or words it represents. Acronyms and initialisms, which usually appear in caps or small caps, are an exception. For agencies and organizations, for instance, most authorities favor all caps or small caps with no periods.

Acronyms that we've already absorbed into English as common nouns appear in lowercase. One such example is scuba (self-contained underwater breathing apparatus).

Occasionally, a difference in case (uppercase vs. lowercase) distinguishes one abbreviation from another (T for tablespoon, t for teaspoon).

Punctuation

Abbreviations may contain punctuation all of the time, some of the time, or none of the time. It's simply a matter of style.

Periods. The most often-used punctuation mark in abbreviations is the period. The current trend favors omitting periods whenever possible, particularly in measurements and rates. In fact, the American National Standards Institute recommends that periods be eliminated from all units of measure: hr (hour), MHz (megahertz), rpm (revolutions per minute), unless they are needed for clarity (sq. ft). Whether you normally use periods or not, don't eliminate them when readers could mistake an abbreviation for another word, such as in or long (as in inches and longitude). Now, didn't that throw you for a second?

Also make certain that initialisms which spell unrelated words, like MORON (Manager of Research on Nutrition), contain periods. If you're authorized to change poorly conceived titles, by all means, do so. I see no reason why this title couldn't be Manager of Nutritional Research and abbreviated as MNR. Bureaucrats sometimes lose sight of such details.

Abbreviations used as symbols, such as those for chemical elements (Ca for calcium, He for helium, and so on), rarely take periods. In such cases, context clarifies meaning. Note, however, that abbreviations for chemical elements require specific cases. Check a periodic table when in doubt.

When an abbreviation consists of two or more letters for a single word, such as RR (railroad), you can omit the periods.

Abbreviation conventions vary both with publication type and with geography. While some publishers set compass directions with periods (N. for north, N.W. for northwest), others set them without (N, NW). British and Continental usage omit the periods after Dr. (doctor), Mr. (mister), Ms. (neutral female title), and other courtesy titles. Some British abbreviations end at different places than their U.S. counterparts (*advert* vs. *ad* for advertisement, *maths* vs. *math* for mathematics).

Many style guides accept more than one usage. For instance, *The Chicago Manual of Style* endorses both I.Q. and IQ (intelligence quotient). Of course, within a single document, you should stick to just one style.

Ampersands, Hyphens & Slashes. Sometimes, an abbreviated word will contain an ampersand, a hyphen, or a slash. For example: P&L (profit and loss), R&D (research and development), S&H (shipping and handling), AFL-CIO (American Federation of Labor and Congress of Industrial Organizations), Op-Ed (opinion editorial or opposite editorial), T-R (transmit-receive), c/o (care of or in care of), l/c (lowercase), and w/v (weight per volume).

Contracted abbreviations may or may not contain apostrophes (pd. for paid, rec'd for received). Slashes are sometimes used in their place (w/ for with).

Abbreviated compound words or phrases may also contain hyphens (A-V for audiovisual). Ampersands or slashes may represent the word *and* (b&w for black-and-white, P/L for profit and loss), often equally as well (A/V for audiovisual).

Spacing

The spacing of abbreviations tends to vary even more than the punctuation. Let's look, for instance, at standards for spacing between initials in proper names. Some publishers set spaces between first and middle initials (W. E. B. Du Bois); others omit the spaces (W.E.B. Du Bois).

One argument against spacing between initials is the risk that they may get separated when they fall at the ends of lines. It's best to keep all related initials together. Computer programs often let you insert nonbreaking spaces to ensure that initials stay together; however, doing so consumes a lot of time. Check your software documentation for details on nonbreaking spaces.

Plurals & Possessives

Occasionally, you may need to make an abbreviation plural or possessive. Some publishers form plural abbreviations by adding an *s* but no apostrophe—unless it is needed to prevent confusion.

Others use an apostrophe plus an *s* every time. A few plural abbreviations can be formed by doubling letters, such as *MSS* or *mss* (manuscripts) or *pp.* (pages).

For plurals of multiple-letter abbreviations, some publishers add an apostrophe plus an *s* to abbreviations that contain periods (Ph.D.'s for Doctors of Philosophy) and an *s* alone to those that don't (CEOs for Chief Executive Officers). When setting such a standard, you may wish to determine whether you'll need possessive abbreviations, like VCR's (video cassette recorder's) instructions. If so, reserve the apostrophe for the possessive form.

Defining Abbreviations

One final, but by no means unimportant, point to address is the definition of the abbreviations you use. If readers are to understand your communications, they must understand the abbreviations that appear in them. This usually means defining all but the most basic and widely used abbreviations.

Common practice calls for defining an abbreviation the first time it appears, then using just the abbreviation in subsequent text. Some publishers spell out the word and place its abbreviation in parentheses. Example: self-addressed, stamped envelope (SASE). Others do the reverse. Example: SASE (self-addressed, stamped envelope). It's best to use one approach or the other as a standard throughout a single document.

Sometimes an abbreviation will be so basic and widely used that a definition would be distracting. Use your best judgment about the need for a definition. If you're writing for a foreign audience, err on the side of too many rather than too few definitions.

This chapter defines all abbreviations that appear within it—speaking of which, the abbreviated chapter title, S.O.S., is the international radio distress signal: save our ship.

How to Use Chapter 8's Quick-Reference Charts

The quick-reference charts for Chapter 8 contain six major divisions. The section labeled Abbreviation Guidelines provides general guidelines for all types of abbreviations. These guidelines appear in the left-hand column and are organized alphabetically by bold key words.

The center or right-hand column provides examples that illustrate each guideline. Brackets contain clarifying information. Figure 34 shows a sample segment from a quick-reference chart.

General Guidelines	Example
Spell out approximate **measurements and rates**.	I try to write at least six hours a day. *not* I try to write at least 6 hr a day.

Figure 34 - Sample Quick-Reference Chart Segment

The Abbreviation Guidelines and the Capitalization, Plural, and Possessive Abbreviations sections are organized like Figure 34, with one exception. Thin gray lines set off common, but conflicting, style standards when more than one standard might apply. In such cases, a column with a checkmark (✔) contains "write-on lines," on which you can record the options you prefer or rank your preferences by number.

The Abbreviation Formats and punctuation sections include an additional column, which displays oversized punctuation marks for easy reference. These marks supplement the index entries, which list each punctuation mark (or symbol) alphabetically. Figure 35 shows a sample segment.

Punctuating Abbreviations	Mark	Example	✔
Some writers insert hyphens in abbreviated **compounds**.	**-** *hyphen*	co-ed (co-educational) E-O-M (end-of-month) Y-T-D (year-to-date) [WITH HYPHENS]	—
• Others omit the hyphens.		coed EOM YTD [WITHOUT HYPHENS]	—

Figure 35 - Sample Quick-Reference Chart Segment

The Abbreviation Formats section lists guidelines for abbreviations that require multiple decisions, such as capitalization and punctuation or punctuation and spacing.

Once you become familiar with the layout of these charts and determine which options you prefer, you will find them quite useful. You can use a Word List/Style Sheet form to record additional guidelines (see the Appendix). Or, you can record them in a simple computerized style guide (see Chapter 1). For further information, see the glossary or explore the sources in the annotated bibliography.

The following abbreviations appear in this chapter's quick-reference charts:

AM	*ante meridiem* (before noon)	CST	Central Standard Time
CDT	Central Daylight Time	PM	*Post meridiem* (after noon)
cont.	continued		

Figure 36 - Abbreviation Key

Summary

This chapter has explained the different types of abbreviations:

- Basic abbreviations (which include clipped or truncated words, contracted words, hybridizations, and phonetic forms),

- Acronyms (groups of letters pronounced as words in their own right), and

- Initialisms (groups of letters pronounced individually).

This chapter has also addressed when to abbreviate words and offered two schemes for their definition. It has discussed the treatment of abbreviations (including capitalization, punctuation, and spacing, and how to form plural and possessive abbreviations) as well.

The quick-reference charts that follow present abbreviation guidelines and provide further examples.

Abbreviation Guidelines

GENERAL GUIDELINES	Example	✔
Most writers spell out **country names** in running text.	Style standards vary between Great Britain and the United States. [SPELL ALL COUNTRY NAMES]	—
• Some writers abbreviate U.S. and U.S.S.R. NOTE: Some omit periods for USSR.	Style standards vary between Great Britain and the U.S. [ABBREVIATE U.S. & U.S.S.R]	—
EXCEPTION: Abbreviate most country names used as adjectives. (See *country names, p. 165*.) (See *state names, p. 163*.)	U.S. style standards vary from Great Britain's. [ABBREVIATE ADJECTIVE FORM]	
Spell out **days of the week** in running text.	I'll fax the piece by Friday, March 28. *not* I'll fax the piece by Fri., March 28.	
CAUTION: Use ordinal endings when a day appears without a month. (See *days of the week, p. 171*.)	I'll fax the piece by the 28th.	
Define all abbreviations, as necessary, upon first use.	bklt (booklet) [ABBREVIATION] OSHA (Occupational Safety and Health Administration) [ACRONYM] CPU (central processing unit) [INITIALISM]	
• Some writers place the meaning first, followed by its abbreviation.	Oxford English Dictionary (OED) [MEANING FIRST]	—
• Others place the abbreviation first, followed by the meaning.	OED (Oxford English Dictionary) [ABBREVIATION FIRST]	—
NOTE: When the abbreviation is better known than its meaning, you can omit the meaning.	CD-ROM [ABBREVIATION BETTER KNOWN: COMPACT DISK–READ-ONLY MEMORY]	

General Guidelines *(continued)*	**Example**	✔
Common **Latin abbreviations** • Common terms can be abbreviated without a definition, particularly in scholarly writing. NOTE: Check a dictionary for the proper placement of periods.	cf. (*confer:* compare) e.g. (*exempli gratia:* for example) etc. (*et cetera:* and so forth) i.e. (*id est:* that is) P.S. (*postscriptum:* postscript) v. *or* vs. (*versus:* against)	
Spell out approximate **measurements and rates**. (See *measurements & rates, p. 166.*)	I try to write at least six hours a day. *not* I try to write at least 6 hr a day.	
Abbreviate **months** consistently. • Some writers spell out months with *five* or fewer letters.	Jan. Feb. March April May June —— July Aug. Sept. Oct. Nov. Dec. [SPELL OUT FIVE OR FEWER LETTERS]	
• Others spell out months with *four* or fewer letters.	Jan. Feb. Mar. Apr. May June —— July Aug. Sept. Oct. Nov. Dec. [SPELL OUT FOUR OR FEWER LETTERS]	
CAUTIONS: • Spell out months in running text, regardless of their length.	The May issue will be out in April. *not* The May issue will be out in Apr.	
• When the month appears with a specific date in running text, some writers abbreviate it.	The May issue will be out by —— Apr. 15. [ABBREVIATE SPECIFIC DATE]	
• Others spell it out. (See *days of the week, p. 171.*) (See *months, p. 173.*)	The May issue will be out by —— April 15. [SPELL OUT SPECIFIC DATE]	
Spell out **religious titles** that appear in direct quotes and/or without a person's full name. (See *courtesy & professional titles, p. 171.*) (See *religious titles, p. 168.*)	The reverend has made a number of positive changes. *not* The rev. has made a number of positive changes.	

General Guidelines *(continued)*	Example	PC	Traditional
Some writers set **state names** and the *District of Columbia* as two-letter postal code (PC) abbreviations with no periods.	Alabama	AL	Ala.
	Alaska	AK	Alaska
	Arizona	AZ	Ariz.
	Arkansas	AR	Ark.
• Others set them as traditional abbreviations with periods.	California	CA	Calif. *or* Cal.
	Colorado	CO	Colo.
	Connecticut	CT	Conn.
	Delaware	DE	Del.
EXCEPTIONS:	District of Columbia	DC	D.C.
	Florida	FL	Fla.
• Most writers spell out *Alaska, Hawaii, Iowa, Ohio,* and *Utah* in running text.	Georgia	GA	Ga.
	Hawaii	HI	Hawaii
	Idaho	ID	Idaho *or* Ida.
	Illinois	IL	Ill.
• Some also spell out *Idaho, Maine,* and *Texas.*	Indiana	IN	Ind.
	Iowa	IA	Iowa
	Kansas	KS	Kan. *or* Kans.
• Note the alternative abbreviations for *California, Kansas, Nebraska, New Mexico, North Dakota, Oregon, Pennsylvania, South Dakota,* and *Wisconsin.*	Kentucky	KY	Ky.
	Louisiana	LA	La.
	Maine	ME	Maine *or* Me.
	Maryland	MD	Md.
	Massachusetts	MA	Mass.
	Michigan	MI	Mich.
	Minnesota	MN	Minn.
NOTES:	Mississippi	MS	Miss.
	Missouri	MO	Mo.
– Spell out state names and the *District of Columbia* in running text, unless they appear with city names.	Montana	MT	Mont.
	Nebraska	NE	Neb. *or* Nebr.
	Nevada	NV	Nev.
	New Hampshire	NH	N.H.
	New Jersey	NJ	N.J.
– Circle your preferences on this page.	New Mexico	NM	N.M. *or* N. Mex.
	New York	NY	N.Y.
	North Carolina	NC	N.C.
	North Dakota	ND	N.D. *or* N. Dak.
	Ohio	OH	Ohio
	Oklahoma	OK	Okla.
	Oregon	OR	Ore. *or* Oreg.
	Pennsylvania	PA	Pa. *or* Penn.
	Rhode Island	RI	R.I.
	South Carolina	SC	S.C.
	South Dakota	SD	S.D. *or* S. Dak.
	Tennessee	TN	Tenn.
	Texas	TX	Texas *or* Tex.
	Utah	UT	Utah
	Vermont	VT	Vt.
	Virginia	VA	Va.
	Washington	WA	Wash.
	West Virginia	WV	W. Va.
	Wisconsin	WI	Wis. *or* Wisc.
	Wyoming	WY	Wyo.

General Guidelines *(continued)*	**Example**	✔
Abbreviate common **street names** when they appear with numbers, but spell them out otherwise. (See *country names, p. 161*.) (See *state names, p. 163*.) (See *street names, p. 167*.)	800 Adams Ave. (Avenue) 3900 Hwy. 183 (Highway) 1501 Fifth St. (Street) *but* The Austin Writers' League office is located on Fifth Street.	
Abbreviate as needed in **tables**, but define abbreviations as necessary in footnotes, legends, or running text.	ALIGN/INDENT (L R C J) Text (body)　　　　　J Chapter Number　　　R Chapter Title　　　　R L = left; R = right; C = center; J = justified	

Abbreviation Formats

FORMATS	Mark	Example	✔
Set most **acronyms and initialisms**, with no periods or spaces—especially agency and organization names. • Some writers use all caps.	• *period*	FYI (for your information) UPI (United Press International) ZIP (Zone Improvement Program) [UPPERCASE, NO PERIODS]	——
• Others use small caps. (See *acronyms, p. 168*.) (See *initialisms, p. 172*.)		FYI UPI ZIP [SMALL CAPS, NO PERIODS]	——
Set abbreviations containing **ampersands** (to represent *and*) with no space on either side.	**&** *ampersand*	Q&A (question-and-answer) U&lc (upper- and lowercase)	——
Set abbreviated **compass directions** in all caps. • Some writers use periods.	• *period*	N. (north) S. (south) E. (east) W. (west) N.W. (northwest) S.E. (southeast) [WITH PERIODS]	——
• Others omit the periods. (See *street names, p. 164*.) (See *street names, p. 167*.)		N S E W NW SE [NO PERIODS]	——
Some writers use periods and spaces in abbreviated **country names**.	• *period*	U. K. (United Kingdom) U. S. (United States) [WITH PERIODS & SPACE]	——
• Others use periods but no spaces.		U.K. U.S. [PERIODS, NO SPACE]	——
• Some writers omit both periods and spaces.		UK US USSR [NO PERIODS, NO SPACES]	——
• Others do so only for USSR. (See *country names, p. 161*.)		USSR [NO PERIODS, *USSR* ONLY]	——

Abbreviation Formats *(cont.)*	Mark	Example	✔
Abbreviated **eras** (AD and BC) can be set in any case.	• *period*	a.d. 1997 500 b.c. [LOWERCASE, WITH PERIODS]	——
NOTE: AD generally precedes the year while BC follows.		A.D. 1997 500 B.C. [SMALL CAPS, WITH PERIODS]	——
• Some writers use periods.		A.D. 1997 500 B.C. [UPPERCASE, WITH PERIODS]	——
• Others omit the periods.		AD 1997 500 BC [SMALL CAPS, NO PERIODS]	——
CAUTION: Avoid lowercase without periods.		AD 1997 500 BC [UPPERCASE, NO PERIODS]	——
People's **initials** • Some writers insert a space after each period.	• *period*	E. B. White [SPACE AFTER PERIODS]	——
• Others set initials with no space between.		E.B. White [NO SPACE AFTER PERIODS]	——
• Still others use a space between *two* initials, but no space between *three* or more.		E. B. White [SPACE WITH TWO INITIALS] W.E.B. Du Bois [NO SPACE WITH THREE INITIALS]	——
EXCEPTION: Omit periods from well-known initials. *(See Jr. & Sr., p. 172.)* *(See Chapter 11 for treatment of names in references.)*		JFK (John Fitzgerald Kennedy) LBJ (Lyndon Baines Johnson) MLK (Martin Luther King, Jr.)	
Omit periods from **measurements and rates** . . .	• *period*	c (cup) doz (dozen) lb (pound) [MEASUREMENTS] bps (bits/second) wpm (words/minute) [RATES]	
. . . unless they could be mistaken for another word.		in. (inch) *not* in long. (longitude) *not* long No. (number) *not* No	
NOTE: Singulars and plurals take the same form.		hr *not* hrs No. *not* Nos.	

Abbreviation Formats *(cont.)*	Mark	Example	✔
Match the case of abbreviated **street names** to that of the words they represent and end them with a period in running text.	● *period*	The fire began at 2187 George Washington Blvd. last night. (Boulevard)	
NOTE: Omit punctuation from envelopes and mailing labels to reduce delivery time. (See *compass directions, p. 165.*) (See *country names, p. 161.*) (See *state names, p. 163.*) (See *street names, p. 164.*)		ANYONE PO BOX 100 LUCKENBACH TX 78624	
Abbreviations for **time zones** can be set in any case. • Some writers use periods.	● *period*	c.s.t. c.d.t. [LOWERCASE, WITH PERIODS] C.S.T. C.D.T. [SMALL CAPS, WITH PERIODS] C.S.T. C.D.T. [UPPERCASE, WITH PERIODS]	___ ___ ___
• Others omit the periods. (See *times of day, p. 167.*)		cst cdt [LOWERCASE, NO PERIODS] CST CDT [SMALL CAPS, NO PERIODS] CST CDT [UPPERCASE, NO PERIODS]	___ ___ ___
Abbreviations for **times of day** (AM and PM) can be set in any case. • Some writers use periods.	● *period*	a.m. p.m. [LOWERCASE, WITH PERIODS] A.M. P.M. [SMALL CAPS, WITH PERIODS] A.M. P.M. [UPPERCASE, WITH PERIODS]	___ ___ ___
• Others omit the periods. (See *time zones, p. 167.*)		am pm [LOWERCASE, NO PERIODS] AM PM [SMALL CAPS, NO PERIODS] AM PM [UPPERCASE, NO PERIODS]	___ ___ ___

Capitalization of Abbreviations

CAPITALIZATION	Example
Most **acronyms** that have been absorbed as common nouns appear in lowercase. (See *acronyms & initialisms, p. 165*.) (See *initialisms, p. 172*.)	radar (radio detection and ranging) snafu (situation normal, all fouled up)
Match the case of **basic abbreviations** to that of the words they represent.	cont. (continued) ea. (each) mfg. (manufacturing)
EXCEPTION: Set most measurements and rates in lowercase with no periods.	5'2" (5 feet, 2 inches) 4 c (4 cups) 98.6° (98.6 degrees) 2400 dpi $50/hr
• Retain the initial cap when abbreviating proper nouns.	Eng. (English) Inc. (Incorporated)
• Retain capitalization used to distinguish one abbreviation from another. (See *British Usage, p. 173*.) (See *measurements & rates, p. 162*.) (See *measurements & rates, p. 166*.)	Cal (kilocalorie) v. cal (calorie) T (tablespoon) v. t (teaspoon)
Capitalize abbreviated **religious titles** that precede names.	Rev. Jesse Jackson (Reverend)
• Set those that follow or appear without a name in lowercase. (See *courtesy & professional titles, p. 171*.) (See *religious titles, p. 162*.)	Jesse Jackson, rev.

Plural Abbreviations

PLURALS	Singular	Plural	✔
Some writers add an *s* alone, whether the abbreviation contains periods . . .	P.E.	P.E.s [ADD *S* ALONE AFTER PERIOD]	——
. . . or not. NOTE: PE stands for *printer's error*; PEs stands for *printer's errors*.	PE	PEs [ADD *S* ALONE]	——
• Others add *'s* only for abbreviations containing periods and three letters or more.	M.F.A.	M.F.A.'s [ADD *'S* WITH PERIODS & THREE LETTERS OR MORE]	——
NOTE: MFA stands for *Master of Fine Arts*; MFA's (or MFAs) stands for *Masters of Fine Arts*.	MFA	MFAs [ADD *S* ALONE]	——
• Still others add *'s every time*. CAUTION: Avoid this choice if you also need to use possessive abbreviations.	MFA	MFA's [ADD *'S* EVERY TIME]	——
• A few plural abbreviations are formed by **doubling letters**.	l. (line) ms. (manuscript) p. (page)	ll. (lines) mss. (manuscripts) pp. (pages)	

POSSESSIVES	Singular/Plural	✔
Use an *'s* to form **singular** possessives, whether or not the abbreviation contains periods.	AA (singular) AA's (singular possessive) [ADD *'S*]	——
	A.A. (singular) A.A.'s (singular possessive) [ADD *'S*]	——
NOTE: AA stands for one *author's alteration*; AA's stands for one *author's (multiple) alterations.*	AA [AUTHOR'S ALTERATION] AA's [AUTHOR'S ALTERATIONS]	
Use an *s'* to form **plural** possessives, whether or not the abbreviation contains periods.	AAs' (plural possessive) [ADD S']	——
	A.A.s' (plural possessive) [ADD S']	——
NOTE: AAs' (or A.A.s') stands for two or more *authors' alterations.*	AAs' [AUTHORS' ALTERATIONS]	——
You can often change **plural possessives to singular** to prevent awkward wording.	These IRA terms aren't clear. *not* These IRAs' terms aren't clear.	——

Punctuation of Abbreviations

PUNCTUATION	Mark	Example	✔
Write **clipped or truncated words** pronounced as words in their own right with no periods. (See *British Usage, p. 173.*)	• *period*	info (information) logo (logotype) phone (telephone)	
Some writers insert hyphens in abbreviated **compounds**.	- *hyphen*	co-ed (co-educational) E-O-M (end-of-month) Y-T-D (year-to-date) [WITH HYPHENS]	——
• Others omit the hyphens.		coed EOM YTD [NO HYPHENS]	——
Abbreviate most **courtesy and professional titles**. • Most U.S. writers end the abbreviation with a period.	• *period*	Dr. (Doctor) Ms. (Neutral female title) Prof. (Professor) [U.S.]	——
• British and Continental style often omits the period. CAUTION: These titles have more specific meanings in British and Continental usage than in U.S. usage. (See *religious titles, p. 162.*)		Dr Ms Prof [BRITISH/CONTINENTAL]	——
Some writers insert periods after abbreviations for **days of the week**.	• *period*	Sun. Mon. Tues. Wed. Thurs. Fri. Sat. [LONG FORM]	——
• Others omit them. CAUTION: Do not mix long and short abbreviation forms. (See *days of the week, p. 161.*)		Su M Tu W Th F Sa [SHORT FORM]	——

Punctuating Abbreviations (continued)	**Mark**	**Example**	✔
Set most **initialisms** without any periods, particularly for agencies and organizations. (See *acronyms, p. 168.*) (See *acronyms & initialisms, p. 165.*)	• *period*	AP (Associated Press) FBI (Federal Bureau of Investigation)	
Some writers use a comma to set off the abbreviations *Jr.* **(junior)** and *Sr.* **(senior)** and may or may not end them with a period.	**,** *comma*	William Strunk, Jr. [U.S./WITH COMMA] William Strunk, Jr [BRITISH/CONTINENTAL/ WITH COMMA]	—— ——
• Others omit the comma. (See *courtesy & professional titles, p. 171.*) (See *Jr. & Sr., p. 172.*)		William Strunk Jr. [U.S./NO COMMA] William Strunk Jr [BRITISH/CONTINENTAL/NO COMMA]	—— ——
Most U.S. writers end the abbreviations *Jr.* **(junior) and** *Sr.* **(senior)** with a period.	• *period*	Martin Luther King, Jr. [U.S./WITH PERIOD AND COMMA] Martin Luther King Jr. [U.S./WITH PERIOD, NO COMMA]	—— ——
• Others omit the period. NOTE: British and Continental style often omit the period.		Martin Luther King, Jr [BRITISH/CONTINENTAL/ WITH COMMA, NO PERIOD]	——
(See *courtesy & professional titles, p. 171.*) (See *Jr. & Sr., p. 172.*)		Martin Luther King Jr [BRITISH/CONTINENTAL/ NO COMMA, NO PERIOD]	——
Some writers use periods in **lowercase or mixed-case abbreviations**.	• *period*	ed. (edited, edition, editor) Ph.D. (Doctor of Philosophy)	—— ——
• Others use no periods. (See *measurements & rates, p. 162.*) (See *measurements & rates, p. 166.*)		ed PhD	—— ——

Punctuating Abbreviations *(continued)*	**Mark**	**Example**	✔
End abbreviated **months** with periods.	• *period*	Jan. Feb. March April May June July Aug. Sept. Oct. Nov. Dec. [FIVE OR FEWER LETTERS]	——
(See *months*, p. 162.)		Jan. Feb. Mar. Apr. May June July Aug. Sept. Oct. Nov. Dec. [FOUR OR FEWER LETTERS]	——
Some writers use periods when two or more letters abbreviate a **single word**.	• *period*	e.k.g. (electrocardiogram) T.V. (television)	—— ——
• Others omit the periods.		ekg TV	——
Some writers use a **slash** to represent *and* or *per*, or to indicate a truncation. NOTE: Set the slash with no space on either side.	/ *slash*	I/O (input–output) [AND] n/30 (net in 30 days) [TRUNCATED] w/o (without) [TRUNCATED]	—— —— ——

BRITISH USAGE

Some British abbreviations end at different places than their U.S. counterparts. Check a dictionary whenever you're in doubt.

Numbers, Signs & Symbols

*Y*our primary goal for numerical styles should be to help readers comprehend numbers as quickly and easily as possible. In some instances, this may mean spelling out numbers; in others, it may mean using numerals.

When choosing between words and numerals, you may also wish to consider space constraints and esthetics. And, as always, consistency is a major concern.

This chapter discusses some basic numerical schemes and explores some typical guidelines for handling numbers. It also addresses the use of signs and symbols, including footnote and note symbols, and operational signs in numerical expressions.

Common Numerical Schemes

To simplify the way you manage numbers, it helps to settle on a basic approach. Publishers typically spell out most numbers below a preset cut-off point. Some publishers use a cut-off point of ten (typically newspapers and magazines). Others use a cut-off point of one hundred (typically publishers of books and journals). Still others use a cut-off point of twenty.

Notice that I said publishers spell out *most* numbers below their cut-off point; exceptions do exist. For instance, we usually express measurements as numerals. The quick-reference charts in this chapter address other exceptions.

Spelling Out Numbers vs. Using Numerals

How do you decide between words and numerals? Both have their advantages.

Because numerals stand out more, most people find them easier to read. Numerals convey a greater sense of accuracy and precision than words do. In addition, they save significant amounts of space.

Words, on the other hand, are more subtle and blend more easily into surrounding text. They therefore create a more formal look and are more esthetically pleasing. Many readers find a page full of words less overwhelming than a page full of numbers.

Choosing the Best Approach. As with any style decision, numerical standards should be set with the audience, medium, and message in mind. Beyond those factors, what counts most is consistency.

Numerical style differs less with geography than do most style matters. The most significant difference seems to be how numbers are punctuated. Some countries, for instance, use a comma for a decimal point in place of a period.

Like many other issues of style, numerical conventions also vary with the medium. If you're not sure which scheme best fits your situation, consider the trends shown in Figure 37.

Type of Publication	Generally Spell Out
Books—particularly humanistic & literary works	Numbers under 100
Newspapers, magazines, ads	Numbers under 10
Business & technical documents	Numbers under 10

Figure 37 - Standard Cut-Off Points for Spelling Out Numbers

Newspapers, magazines, and advertisements often use more numerals because space is limited. So do business and technical documents (including legal, scientific, and statistical works)—more to ease reading than to save space. Publishers of such materials usually favor a cut-off point of ten.

Books—particularly humanistic and literary works—tend to have more spelled-out numbers. Publishers of such materials usually favor a cut-off point of one hundred.

Typical Exceptions. With any numerical style, some numbers are always spelled out and some are always numerals. For example, when a number begins a sentence, you should always spell it out. (If it's a year, try to rephrase the sentence.)

Most publishers use numerals for dates, measurements, exact sums of money, rates, and times (December 31, 1999; 8 lbs; $3.69; $40/hr; 9AM). Many publishers use numerals for round numbers over 999,999 (3 million copies). They may also spell out centuries, decades, and percentages (except in tables or in technical copy). The quick-reference charts in this chapter outline other exceptions to standard cut-off points. Style manuals list additional guidelines (see the annotated bibliography).

Adjacent & Related Numbers. Once you've determined a cut-off point, decide what you'll do when closely related numbers above and below the cut-off point appear together. For instance, if your cut-off point is ten, what will you do if you wish to compare 9 and 112 in the same sentence and to still maintain consistency? In such a case, many publishers use the same style for both numbers. Some publishers use numerals for both (9 and 112); others spell them out (nine and one hundred twelve). Still others stick to their cut-off point (nine and 112) and sacrifice consistent structure.

For clarity's sake, spell out one of two adjacent numbers not separated by a comma. (For example: The editor waded through twenty 500-page manuscripts last month.)

When numbers appear in a series, either use all numerals or spell out every number in the series. (For example: The entries in the fiction contest included 39 mysteries, 88 romances, 7 westerns, 666 horror stories, and 2,001 science fiction manuscripts.)

Arabic, Roman & Ordinal Numbers

"Ordinary" or *cardinal numbers* express amounts and may be spelled out (one, two, three) or written as numerals (1, 2, 3). Numerals may be either *arabic* (1, 2, 3) or *roman numerals* (I, II, III or i, ii, iii). You will need to determine which of these forms to use, and when. Then you'll need to decide how to treat ordinals. *Ordinals* are numbers with suffixes such as *–nd, –rd, –st,* or *–th* that indicate their order (1st/first, 2nd/second, 3rd/third, etc.). The next few paragraphs discuss these choices in greater detail.

Arabic Numbers vs. Roman Numerals. Arabic numbers are easier for readers to interpret than roman numerals. In addition, arabic numbers are faster to type. Sometimes publishers use roman numerals for a more formal look. A common practice among book publishers is to use lowercase roman numerals for the *folios* (page numbers) on pages with *front matter* (prefaces, tables of contents, and so on) and arabic numbers for the remainder of the book.

If you use roman numerals, keep the following in mind:

- A repeated letter increases a roman numeral's value.
  (I = 1; III = 3)

- A smaller number that precedes a larger number reduces the larger number's value by that of the smaller number.
  (I = 1, V = 5; IV = 4)

- A smaller number that follows a larger number increases the larger number's value by that of the smaller number.
  (V = 5, I = 1; VI = 6).

- A bar over a roman numeral multiplies its value by one thousand.
  (V = 5; $\overline{V}$ = 5,000)

Figure 38 displays eight arabic numbers along with their roman numeral equivalents.

Arabic numbers	1	5	10	50	100	500	1,000	10,000
Roman numerals	I	V	X	L	C	D	M	$\overline{X}$

Figure 38 - Arabic Numbers & Roman Numeral Equivalents

Note that roman numerals can be written in either upper- or lowercase without changing their value, though lowercase roman numerals of fifty or more are rare.

Ordinal Numbers. Ordinal numbers most commonly appear in the names of churches; government, military, and political entities; lodges and unions; some streets (particularly those under a standard cut-off point); and so on.

We omit ordinal endings (*–nd, –rd, –st,* or *–th*) when dates appear as numerals, but we pronounce those endings in spoken form. In other words, we write *May 1,* but we say *May first.*

Sometimes numerals with ordinal endings appear in footnotes, reference lists, and tables. The quick-reference charts that begin on page 183 provide some examples.

Numerical Expressions

Most style problems in numerical expressions relate to physical formatting. Some standard formatting guidelines follow:

- Italicize all letters, but not numerals, that appear in an equation. For example:

$$E = mc^2$$

- Align division lines and operational signs (+, - , x, ÷, =, and so on) horizontally. For example:

$$\frac{2x^4 - 3x^2 - x + 3}{x + 1} = 3$$

- Set equations that won't fit on one line of text centered on separate lines. For example:

$$(x^2)^3 = x^{(2)(3)} = x^6$$
$$(x^3 y^5)^2 = x^{(3)(2)} xy^{(5)(2)} = x^6 y^{10}$$

- If an equation runs over to a second line, divide the equation at the left of an operational sign. (It's okay to break equations *within running text* on either side of an operational sign.) Then center the second and following lines. For example:

$$\sqrt{(x_1 - x_2)^2 + (y_1 - y_2)^2}$$

$$= \sqrt{0 + (7 - 3)^2} = \sqrt{16} = 4$$

Styles vary regarding the amount of space that's inserted before and after operational signs. See the entry for Footnotes and Notes, p. 183, in the quick-reference charts for more information.

This book shows only simple numerical expressions. If you need more in-depth information on the treatment of mathematical and statistical text, check a style guide such as *The Chicago Manual of Style, The New York Public Library Writer's Guide to Style and Usage,* the *Publication Manual of the American Psychological Association,* the U.S. Government Printing Office's *A Manual of Style,* or *Words Into Type.*

Guidelines for Signs & Symbols

Publishers of general works often limit the use of signs and symbols to figures and tables, footnotes, titles, equations, measurements, and similar forms. Signs and symbols are more readily accepted in business and technical documents than in humanistic and literary materials. The quick-reference charts at the end of this chapter illustrate guidelines for common signs and symbols.

In *Technical Writing: Structure, Standards, and Style*, Robert Bly and Gary Blake suggest these guidelines for signs and symbols:

- Use too few signs and symbols rather than too many.

- Define signs and symbols the first time they appear.

- Avoid duplicating signs and symbols unnecessarily.

- Make certain that the signs and symbols you use fit the grammatical structure of the sentence.

The quick-reference charts illustrate many common signs and symbols. Because footnotes and notes present special challenges, let's explore them a bit further.

Footnotes & Notes

In some cases, you may need symbols to help differentiate one footnote or note from another. Most publishers precede a footnote or note with a superscript letter, number, or symbol. Figure 39 provides some examples.

Arabic numbers	[1]Note	[2]Note	[3]Note	[4]Note	[5]Note	[6]Note
Lowercase letters	[a]Note	[b]Note	[c]Note	[d]Note	[e]Note	[f]Note
Symbols	[*]Note [**]Note	[†]Note [††]Note	[‡]Note [‡‡]Note	[§]Note [§§]Note	[‖]Note [‖‖]Note	[#]Note [##]Note

[*] (asterisk), [†] (dagger), [‡] (double dagger), [§] (section), [‖] (parallels), [#] (number or pound sign)

Figure 39 - Standard Footnote & Note Schemes

How to Use Chapter 9's Quick-Reference Charts

The quick-reference charts for Chapter 9 contain four sections:

1. Basic Guidelines

2. Spelling Out vs. Using Numerals

3. Punctuating Numbers

4. Signs & Symbols

The left-hand column of each chart lists widely accepted usage guidelines (organized alphabetically by bold key words) and notes common exceptions.

Occasionally, the left-hand column will refer to a usage note. These notes appear at the end of the chapter, after the quick-reference charts.

The center column shows examples that illustrate each guideline and presents various standards when more than one option might apply. Figure 40 shows a sample segment from a quick-reference chart.

Mostly Spell Out *(continued)*	**Examples**	✔
Numbers **ending sentences** • Some publishers spell out ages and dates that end sentences.	I published my first poem in nineteen-sixty. [SPELL OUT ENDING NUMBERS]	___
• Others use numerals.	I published my first poem in 1960. [USE NUMERALS FOR ENDING AGES & DATES]	___

Figure 40 - Sample Quick-Reference Chart Segment

Some of these charts contain customizing features. The columns with a checkmark (✔) contain "write-on lines," on which you can record the options you prefer or rank options when you find more than one acceptable.

The Punctuating Numbers, and Signs & Symbols sections include additional columns that display oversized punctuation marks or oversized symbols. These marks supplement the index entries, which are listed by the name of each mark or symbol.

Figure 41 shows a segment from a quick-reference chart.

Punctuating Numbers	Mark	Example	✔
Indicates a **decimal**	**.** *period*	pi=3.14159265 8.5% [U.S./BRITISH]	—
CAUTION: Many countries use a comma in place of a decimal point.	**,** *comma*	pi=3,14159265 8,5% [CONTINENTAL]	—

Figure 41 - Sample Quick-Reference Chart Segment

Once you become familiar with the layout of these charts and determine which options you prefer, you will find them quite handy. You can use a Word List/Style Sheet form to record further guidelines for numbers, signs, and symbols (see the Appendix).

The following abbreviations appear in this chapter's quick-reference charts:

C	Celsius
cont.	continued
F	Fahrenheit
GPO	U.S. Government Printing Office's *A Manual of Style*

Figure 42 - Abbreviation Key

Summary

This chapter has introduced common numerical schemes for using numerals versus spelling out numbers and has explained advantages and disadvantages of these schemes.

This chapter has also addressed the differences between arabic, roman, and ordinal numbers and has mentioned typical applications. In addition, it has discussed formatting guidelines for numerical expressions and guidelines for signs and symbols, including footnotes and notes. The quick-reference charts that follow provide additional guidelines and examples.

Numerical Guidelines

BASIC SCHEMES	Example	✔
Some writers spell out numbers **under ten** in running text.	Elsie has freelanced nearly eight years. She's used a computer for 14 years. [SPELL OUT NUMBERS UNDER TEN]	—
• Others spell out numbers **under twenty**.	Elsie has written on computers for about fourteen years. She's used a computer for 21 years. [SPELL OUT NUMBERS UNDER TWENTY]	—
• Still others spell out numbers **under one hundred**.	Elsie has been a writer for twenty-one years. She hopes to be at least 101 when she retires. [SPELL OUT NUMBERS UNDER ONE HUNDRED]	—
Some writers spell out the first of two **adjacent numbers** not separated by a comma.	Bob has written forty-two 30-minute video scripts. [SPELL OUT FIRST NUMBER]	—
• Others spell out the smallest.	Bob has written 42 thirty-minute video scripts. [SPELL OUT SMALLEST NUMBER]	—
Some writers spell out any number **adjacent to a date or measurement**. (See [1]*Usage Note, p. 202.*) (See [2]*Usage Note, p. 202.*)	Since 1990 eighteen new editors have joined us. Our old computer accommodates four 16MB RAM chips.	— —
Use one of these schemes for **footnotes and notes**: • Arabic numbers	1 2 3 4 5 6 7 8 9 10 11 12 [1]Usage notes follow the quick-reference charts. [ARABIC NUMBERS]	—
• Lowercase letters	a b c d e f h i j k l [a]Usage notes follow the quick-reference charts. [LOWERCASE LETTERS]	—
• Symbols	* † ‡ S ‖ # ** †† ‡‡ SS ‖‖ ## [*]Usage notes follow the quick-reference charts. [SYMBOLS]	—

Basic Schemes (continued)	**Example**	✔
Some writers use numerals for all **measurements**.	16 tons 500 miles 32°F	____
• Others spell some out measurements.	sixteen tons five hundred miles thirty-two degrees	____ ____ ____
In running text, some writers spell out **ordinals under ten**, and use numerals plus ordinal endings for higher numbers.	Most Americans celebrate the Fourth of July. [SPELL OUT ORDINALS UNDER TEN] Friday the 13th is a date many people dread. [ORDINAL ENDINGS TEN & OVER]	____ ____
• Some publishers use the **complete ordinal ending** (*nd* or *rd*).	*The Elements of Style* (3rd ed.) [USE COMPLETE ORDINAL ENDING]	____
• Others form 2nd and 3rd with a **numeral and *d* alone**.	*The Elements of Style* (3d ed.) [USE D ALONE WITH 2ND & 3RD]	____
Some writers spell out **related numbers** when some, but not all, numbers that appear together are normally spelled out.	Over the years, Peg published sixty-four short stories, one hundred three poems, seven novels, and five chapbooks. [SPELL OUT ALL NUMBERS]	____
• Others use all numerals.	Over the years, Peg published 64 short stories, 103 poems, 7 novels, and 5 chapbooks. [USE ALL NUMERALS]	____
Some publishers use **roman numerals** for special elements: • Certain dates	MCMXCVIII [1998]	____
• Folios in a book's front matter	Preface . . . . v Chapter 1 1	____

• Items in outlines	I. Style and Grammar
	    A. A Friendly Refresher
	    B. Common Problems
	II. Style and Mechanics
		____

• Literary titles (See *roman numerals, p. 185.*)	*Star Trek V: The Final Frontier*	____

Basic Schemes *(continued)*	**Example**	✔
Some publishers use **roman numerals** for special elements:		
• Model names		
	Apple *III* computer	⎯
• Personal names	Pope John Paul II	⎯
• Vehicle and vessel names	*Explorer I Sputnik I*	⎯
• Volume numbers	*Funk & Wagnalls Standard Desk Dictionary: Volume II, N–Z*	⎯

(See *celestial bodies, p. 143.*)
(See *celestial bodies, p. 144.*)
(See *item numbers, p. 191.*)
(See *roman numerals, p. 184.*)

Spelling Out vs. Using Numerals

MOSTLY SPELL OUT	Examples	✔
Special street **addresses**		
• Some writers spell out only the number *one.*	One Lago Vista Lane [SPELL OUT ONLY NUMBER ONE]	——
• Others spell out *one and ordinals under ten.*	1501 W. Fifth [SPELL OUT ORDINALS UNDER TEN]	——
• Still others spell out *ordinals under one hundred one.*	Forty-Second Street [SPELL OUT ORDINALS UNDER 101]	——
– Some writers capitalize the part after the hyphen.	Forty-Second Street [CAP]	——
– Others use lowercase.	Forty-second Street [LOWERCASE]	——
• Some writers spell out all *round numbers.* (See *addresses & ZIP codes, p. 189.*) (See [2]*Usage Note, p. 202.*)	Five Thousand Big Bucks Boulevard [SPELL OUT ROUND NUMBERS]	——
Ages in general text	My laser printer is ten years old. [SPELL OUT AGES]	——
• Some writers consider ages measurements and use numerals instead. (See *ages, p. 189.*) (See [1]*Usage Note, p. 202.*)	My laser printer is 10 years old. [USE NUMERALS]	——
Approximations or indefinite expressions	This piece will total seven or eight hundred words. [SPELL OUT APPROXIMATION]	——
• Some publishers use numerals when the words that precede them imply approximations. (See *exact amounts, p. 190.*) (See *monetary amounts, p. 192.*)	This piece totals roughly 750 words. [IMPLIED APPROXIMATION]	——

Mostly Spell Out *(continued)*	**Examples**	✔
Numbers **beginning sentences** (excluding listed items) TIP: Recast sentences that begin with dates. (See *ending sentences, p. 187.*)	Sixty publishers rejected that book; then it became a best-seller.	
Centuries and decades near the turn of a century	Desktop publishing first appeared in the nineteen eighties. [DECADES NEAR TURN OF CENTURY]	___
• Some writers spell out all centuries and decades.	Isaac Asimov is perhaps the most prolific twentieth-century writer. [ALL CENTURIES & DECADES]	___
• Others use numerals with ordinal endings for numbers above a standard cut-off point. (See *centuries, p. 144.*) (See *centuries & decades, p. 189.*) (See *ranges, p. 193.*)	Isaac Asimov is perhaps the most prolific 20th-century writer. [USE NUMERALS WITH ORDINAL ENDINGS]	___
Numbers (other than years) in **dialogue or direct quotes**	"I've revised this at least thirty-seven times," Carl complained.	___
EXCEPTION: Some publishers use numerals for complicated numbers that appear in dialogue or quotes.	"Seventy alien bodies are stored at site X86.321," Suzy exclaimed. [USE NUMERALS FOR COMPLICATED NUMBERS]	___
Numbers **ending sentences** • Some publishers spell out ages and dates that end sentences.	I published my first poem in nineteen-sixty. [SPELL OUT ENDING NUMBERS]	___
• Others use numerals. (See *beginning sentences, p. 187.*)	I published my first poem in 1960. [USE NUMERALS FOR ENDING AGES & DATES]	___
Numbers in **proper names** (See *centuries, p. 144.*) (See *centuries & decades, p. 187.*) (See *centuries & decades, p. 189.*)	Roaring Twenties	___

Mostly Spell Out (continued)	Examples	✔
Round numbers • Some writers spell out round numbers over 100.	The average manuscript page has two hundred fifty words. [SPELL OUT ROUND NUMBERS OVER 100]	—
• Others spell out round numbers over 1,000.	Sylvia's first book contained sixty thousand words. [SPELL OUT ROUND NUMBERS OVER 1,000]	—
TIP: Use short forms for numbers over 1,000.	Sylvia's first book contained fifteen hundred words. [SHORTEN LARGE NUMBERS OVER 1,000]	—
• Some writers spell out round numbers over 1,000,000.	Her book sold three million copies in its first year. [SPELL OUT ROUND NUMBERS OVER 1,000,000]	—
• Some writers spell out *million* **and** *billion* because readers may be less familiar with these amounts. CAUTION: One billion means one thousand million in the U.S., but one million million in some countries.	Her book sold 3 million copies in its first year. [SPELL OUT MILLIONS, BILLIONS]	—
• Some writers spell out all round numbers over a standard cut-off point when they can be written as one or two words. Compound numbers count as single words. (See [1]*Usage Note, p. 202.*) (See [2]*Usage Note, p. 202.*)	Sid's first advance totaled forty-five hundred dollars. [SPELL OUT ROUND NUMBERS OVER CUT-OFF POINT]	—
Years in formal contexts	two thousand AD	—
• Some writers prefer numerals.	AD 2000	—
• AD precedes a year written in numerals, but BC follows it.	Plato died in 347 BC	—
TIP: Recast sentences that begin with years. (See *beginning sentences, p. 187.*)	The year 1986 was difficult for me. *not* 1986 was a difficult year for me.	

MOSTLY USE NUMERALS Examples   ✔

For **addresses and ZIP codes** (See *addresses, p. 186*.) (See *ordinals under ten, p. 184*.)	1501 W. 5th, Austin, TX 78703	___
For **ages** in business and technical documents	The defendant is 23 years old. [YEARS, ROUNDED OFF]	___
(See *ages, p. 186*.)	The victim died at age 17 years, 4 months, and 5 days. [YEARS, WITH MONTHS & DAYS]	___
For **centuries and decades** • Some writers use numerals with ordinal endings for centuries.	Isaac Asimov is perhaps the most prolific writer of the 20th century. [USE NUMERALS]	___
• Others spell them out. (See *centuries & decades, p. 187*.) (See *ranges, p. 193*.) (See *years, p. 193*.)	Isaac Asimov is perhaps the most prolific writer of the twentieth century. [SPELL OUT]	___
For **dates**	December 31, 1999 [U.S.]	___
• The U.S. military and many foreign countries write the day first, then the month and year. They also omit any separating commas.	31 December 1999 [MILITARY/BRITISH]	___
• Some countries use lowercase roman numerals for months. CAUTION: To prevent confusion when dates will be read outside the U.S., avoid using all numerals.	31.xii.99 [CONTINENTAL]	___
• Some writers spell out the day, and/ or use the ordinal ending, when the day precedes the month. (See *beginning sentences, p. 187*.) (See *centuries & decades, p. 187*.) (See *ending sentences, p. 187*.) (See *ordinals under ten, p. 184*.) (See *years, p. 193*.)	The thirty-first of December 1999 [SPELL OUT DAYS WITH ORDINAL ENDINGS]	___

Mostly Use Numerals *(continued)*	**Examples**	✔
For **decimals**	pi=3.14159265 [U.S./BRITISH]	——
CAUTION: Many countries use a comma in place of a decimal point.	pi=3,14159265 [CONTINENTAL]	——
• Many publishers precede decimal fractions less than one with a zero. (See *decimal, p. 195.*)	0.99999 [LEADING ZERO]	——
For "**engineering numbers**" in business and technical works, with—		
• Figures and tables	Fig. 9.1 Table 3.4 [FIGURES & TABLES]	——
• Parts, chapters, sections, and subsections	II.4.3. This Agreement may not be assigned by either party without written consent. . . . [PARTS, CHAPTERS, SECTIONS, ETC.]	——
• Paragraphs and lines	1.3 Some style guides describe standards for physical formats (page layouts and type specifications). Others concentrate purely on content and mechanics. [PARAGRAPHS & LINES]	——
• Some publishers spell out such numbers.	Part Two, Section Four, Paragraph Three [SPELL OUT]	——
• Some publishers print such numbers and the words that introduce them in bold type.	**Fig. 9.1 Table 3.4** [BOLD] **II.4.3.** This Agreement . . . [BOLD]	—— ——
For **exact amounts** (See *approximations, p. 186.*) (See *monetary amounts, p. 192.*)	This piece totals 750 words. [EXACT AMOUNT]	——
For numbers **following spelled-out numbers** in business and legal documents	Payment is due within thirty (30) days of receipt.	——

Mostly Use Numerals *(continued)*	**Examples**	✔
For **fractions and mixed numbers** (whole numbers paired with fractions) in business and technical documents	1/4 3 1/4 [SPLIT]	___
	$\frac{1}{4}$ [STACKED]	___
NOTES:		___
• If no special fraction key is available, place a space between the whole number and the fraction.	3 1/4	
• Or, create a fraction character by superscripting the numerator and setting both it and the denominator to one third the size of the body.	$^1/_4$	___
CAUTION: Do not combine fractions with spelled-out numbers. (See *fraction, p. 195*.) (See *[1]Usage Note, p. 202*.)	$3\,^1/_4$ *or* three and one-fourth *not* three $^1/_4$ or three and $^1/_4$	___
For **item numbers** in lists and outlines • Some publishers use arabic numbers.	1. bold 2. italics 3. underlines [ARABIC]	___
• Others use roman numerals. (See *roman numerals, p. 185*.) (See *letter or number preceding a listed item, p. 73*.) (See *listed items, p. 196*.)	I. bold II. italics III. underlines [ROMAN]	___
For **measurements**, which may appear as symbols, abbreviations, or words, including—	3# [SYMBOLS] 3 lb [ABBREVIATIONS] 3 pounds [WORDS]	___ ___ ___
• Dimensions and distances	2" by 4" 500 miles	___
• Heights and weights	5'2" 210 lb	___
• Latitudes and longitudes	lat. 30°N16', long. 97°45' W	___
• Temperatures and so on	98.6° 32°F 100°C 360°	___

Mostly Use Numerals *(continued)*	Examples	✔
For **multiple measurements**, which should be as consistent as possible (See *ages, p. 186.*) (See *ages, p. 189.*) (See [1]*Usage Note, p. 202.*) (See [3]*Usage Note, p. 202.*)	Mix together: 3 c flour, 2 T honey, and 2 c milk. *not* Mix together: 14 oz flour, 2 T honey, and 2 c milk.	—
For monetary amounts		
• Some writers use symbols and numerals.	$50 [USE SYMBOLS & NUMERALS]	—
• Others prefer numerals and words.	50 dollars [USE NUMERALS & WORDS]	—
• Some writers spell out monetary amounts below a standard cut-off point.	This book costs about thirty dollars. [SPELL AMOUNTS UNDER CUT-OFF]	—
• Some writers spell out approximate amounts.	$3.89 [EXACT AMOUNTS] *but* about four dollars [APPROXIMATIONS]	—
• Some writers omit the zeroes (cents) from even amounts of money unless related numbers are uneven amounts. NOTE: *GPO* covers foreign currency extensively. (See *million & billion, p. 188.*) (See [1]*Usage Note, p. 202.*) (See [2]*Usage Note, p. 202.*)	$30 *not* $30.00 [OMIT ZEROES] *but* $3.89 + $5.00 = $8.89	—
For **percentages, proportions, and ratios** (See *proportion or ratio, p. 197.*) (See *score or vote, p. 198.*)	Authors generally pay their agents 10–15%. The ratio of points to picas is 12:1.	— —
• Some writers spell out the word *percent* in narrative.	Ana sells 80 percent of the articles she proposes.	—
• Others use the % symbol, particularly in scientific and technical copy.	We expect 80% of these cases to display marked improvement.	—

Mostly Use Numerals *(continued)*	**Examples**	✔
For **ranges**	Books commonly have 60–70 characters per line. [U.S. ONLY]	——
NOTE: Readers outside the U.S. may be more familiar with ranges expressed in from/to format.	Books commonly have from 60 to 70 characters per line. [INSIDE OR OUTSIDE OF U.S.]	——
CAUTIONS: • Do not truncate dates across different centuries.	1998–2001 *not* 1998–01	
• Do not truncate ranges with more than three consecutive zeroes. (See *centuries & decades, p. 187.*)	2000–2001 *not* 2000–01	
For **rates** (See *per, p. 197.*)	My printer prints 300 dots per inch and up to 6 pages a minute.	——
For **scores and votes** (See *proportion or ratio, p. 197.*)	The editors' team beat the designers' team 3 to 1.	——
For **serial numbers** (See [3]*Usage Note, p. 202.*)	Acct. # 081064061 Bulletin 179	——
For **telephone and fax numbers** (See *telephone or fax number, p. 198.*)	512-499-8914	——
For **times**	6:00 AM 11:15 PM	——
• Some publishers omit the zeroes from times that fall on the hour.	6 AM 11 PM *but not* 12 AM or 12 PM	——
CAUTION: For clarity, add the word *noon* or *midnight* to forms of 12:00. (See [1]*Usage Note, p. 202.*)	12 noon [OR MIDNIGHT] 12:00 noon [OR MIDNIGHT] 12 o'clock noon [OR MIDNIGHT]	——
• Some publishers spell out even, half, and quarter hours.	six o'clock one quarter after eleven	——
For **years** in most text	AD 2000 Plato died in 347 BC.	—— ——

Punctuating Numbers

PUNCTUATION	Mark	Example	✔
Separates **acts and scenes in plays**.	**:** *colon*	"Inherit the Wind" 2:1	
Separates the elements of street **addresses**.	**,** *comma*	1501 W. 5th, # E-2 Austin, TX 78703 U.S.A. [STACKED]	——
EXCEPTIONS: • Keep states and zip codes on the same line.		1501 W. 5th, # E-2, Austin, TX 78703, U.S.A. [RUN-IN]	——
• Avoid punctuating mailing addresses on envelopes. (See *addresses, p. 86*.)		1501 W 5TH # E2 AUSTIN TX 78703 USA [ENVELOPE ADDRESS]	——
Separates **biblical chapters and verses**.	**:** *colon*	Psalms 23:6	——
Joins **compound numbers** from 21 to 99, unless one or both parts already contain a hyphen.	**-** *hyphen*	forty-five 509-66-7248	—— ——
• Do not hyphenate hundreds, thousands, millions, and so on, but do hyphenate compound numbers under one hundred.		one hundred five thousand eighty-three million	—— —— ——
Separates the elements of **dates**.	**,** *comma*	April 2, 1918 [U.S.]	——
CAUTION: When dates will be read both inside and outside the U.S., avoid using hyphens.	**-** *hyphen*	4-2-18 (April 2, 1918) [U.S.]	——
(See *dates, p. 195*.)		2-4-18 (2 April 1918) [MILITARY/BRITISH/CONTINENTAL]	——

Punctuating Numbers *(cont.)*	Mark	Example	✔
Separates the elements of **dates**. • Some countries separate the day, month, and year with periods.	• *period*	2.*iv*.18 [CONTINENTAL]	——
CAUTION: When dates will be read both inside and outside the U.S., avoid using slashes.	/ *slash*	4/2/18 (April 2, 1918) [U.S.]	——
(See *dates, p. 194*.)		2/4/18 (2 April 1918) [MILITARY/BRITISH/ CONTINENTAL]	——
Indicates **decades** (only if the context clarifies the century or decade you're referring to).	ʼ *apostrophe*	Desktop publishing first appeared in the '80s. [CLOSED]	——
CAUTION: Although setting apostrophes within decades is still acceptable, there is a strong trend away from it.		Desktop publishing first appeared in the 80's. [OPEN]	——
Indicates a **decimal**.	• *period*	pi=3.14159265 8.5% [U.S./BRITISH]	——
CAUTION: Many countries use a comma in place of a decimal point. (See *decimals, p. 190*.)	, *comma*	pi=3,14159265 8,5% [CONTINENTAL]	——
Separates a numerator from a denominator in a **fraction** formed without a special key. • Do not substitute a hyphen in place of a slash in a fraction. (See *fractions & mixed numbers, p. 191*.)	/ *slash*	Two common paper sizes are 8 ½" x 11" and 8 ½" x 14". *not* Two common paper sizes are 8 1-2" x 11" and 8 1-2" x 14".	——
Separates **house and street numbers**, when both are expressed with numerals. (See *addresses, p. 86*.)	— *en dash* ($1/2$ *em dash*)	801–34th Street	——

Punctuating Numbers *(cont.)*	Mark	Example	✔
Separates **hundreds, thousands, millions**, and so on.	**,** *comma*	5,000 5,000,000	
NOTE: Omit such commas in—			
• addresses		1501 W. Fifth [ADDRESSES]	
• decimal fractions		.23456 [DECIMAL FRACTIONS]	
• page numbers		page 1001 [PAGE NUMBERS]	
• phone numbers		499-8914 [PHONE NUMBERS]	
• serial numbers		#0123158 [SERIAL NUMBERS]	
• years with fewer than five digits (See *decimals, p. 190*.) (See *decimal, p. 195*.)		2001 AD *but* 20,001 AD [YEARS WITH FEWER THAN FIVE DIGITS]	
Introduces **listed items**.	**( )** *parentheses*	Three character formats used for emphasis are **(1)** bold, **(2)** italics, and **(3)** underlines.	___
• Some writers omit opening parentheses and set only closing parentheses after letters or numbers introducing listed items.	**)** *single parenthesis*	Three character formats used for emphasis are 1**)** bold, 2**)** italics, and 3**)** underlines.	___
TIP: Set vertical lists with letters or numbers followed by periods and save parentheses for lists run in with text.	**.** *period*	Three character formats used for emphasis are 1**.** bold, 2**.** italics, and 3**.** underlines.	___
Joins the parts of a **measurement** or a **numerical modifier**. (See *measurements, p. 191*.) (See [1]*Usage Note, p. 202*.) (See [2]*Usage Note, p. 202*.)	**-** *hyphen*	I just got another six-figure contract! Submit all of your manuscripts on 20-lb bond.	___ ___

Punctuating Numbers *(cont.)*	Mark	Example	✔

Introduces items in an **outline**.	•
	 period
		I. Character Formats
		   A. Bold
		   B. Italics Problems
		   C. Underlines
			——

May replace the word *per*. CAUTION: Some publishers object to this form.	**/** *slash*	My printer prints 300 dots/inch and up to 6 pages/minute.	——
Separates the parts of a **proportion or ratio**. • Some writers use a colon.	• • *colon*	The ratio of points to picas is 12:1.	——
• Others use a slash.	**/** *slash*	The ratio of points to picas is 12/1.	——
Separates **ranges**. • Some publishers use an en dash. CAUTION: When submitting manuscripts to publishers, always use a hyphen.	**—** *en dash* *(¹/₂ em dash)*	A–Z 9–5 ages 5–8 Chapters 1–5 pages 3–9 Books commonly have 60–70 characters per line. [U.S. ONLY]	—— —— —— ——
• Others use a hyphen. CAUTIONS:	**-** *hyphen*	A-Z 9-5 ages 5-8 Chapters 1-5 pages 3-9 Books commonly have 60-70 characters per line. [U.S. ONLY]	—— —— —— ——
• Spell out *and*, *to*, or *through* if *between* or *from* precedes the range.		I try to write at least six hours a day, sometime between 9 AM and 11 PM.	
• Readers outside the U.S. may be more familiar a *from-to* format. (See *centuries & decades, p. 187*.) (See *centuries & decades, p. 189*.) (See *score or vote, p.198*.)		Books commonly have from 60 to 70 characters per line. [INSIDE/OUTSIDE U.S.]	——

Punctuating Numbers *(cont.)*	**Mark**	**Example**	✔
Indicates a **score or vote**. • Some writers use a colon.	**:** *colon*	The editors' team beat the designers' team 3:1.	___
• Others use an en dash.	**–** *en dash* (*¹/₂ em dash*)	The editors' team beat the designers' team 3–1.	___
• Still others use a hyphen.	**-** *hyphen*	The editors' team beat the designers' team 3-1.	___
NOTE: Some writers separate all scores and votes with the word *to*.		The editors' team beat the designers' team 3 *to* 1.	___
Separates numbers in a **telephone or fax number**. • Some writers use a hyphen.	**-** *hyphen*	512-499-8914	___
• Others use parentheses.	**( )** *parentheses*	**(512)** 499-8914	___
• Others use a slash.	**/** *slash*	512/499-8914	___
• Still others use a period.	**.** *period*	512.499.8914	___
Separates hours, minutes, seconds, and fractions of seconds in **times**.	**:** *colon*	3:32:08 PM [12-HOUR TIME]	___
• In *24-hour time*, no AM or PM follows.		15:32:08 [24-HOUR TIME: 32 MIN, 8 SEC AFTER 3 PM]	___
• *Military time* is 24-hour time with no colons.		1532 [MILITARY TIME: 32 MIN AFTER 3 PM]	___
Separates **unrelated numbers**.	**,** *comma*	Since 1990, 38 new editors have joined us.	___

Signs & Symbols

SIGNS & SYMBOLS	Mark	Example	✔
For adding numbers • Some publishers insert a space on each side of an operational sign.	**+** *plus sign*	2 + 2 = 4 [SPACED]	——
• Others omit the spaces.		2+2=4 [NO SPACE]	——
For the word *and* in • Abbreviations	**&** *ampersand*	B&W [BLACK AND WHITE]	
• Bibliographies and reference lists		Zinsser, William. *On Writing Well* (5th ed.). New York: Harper **&** Row, 1994.	
• Figures, tables, and lists		**Type of Publication** Books—particularly humanistic **&** literary works Newspapers, magazines, ads	
• Footnotes and notes		[2] British usage for both double **&** single quotation marks generally counters U.S. usage.	
• Headings		Footnotes **&** Notes Signs **&** Symbols [HEADINGS]	
• Literary titles		Funk **&** Wagnalls [ENCYCLOPEDIA] *U&lc* [MAGAZINE]	
• Names of organizations (only if the organization itself uses an ampersand) (See [4]*Usage Note, p. 202.*)		AT&T [TELECOMMUNICATIONS] Baker **&** Taylor [BOOK DISTRIBUTOR]	
For the word *at* in rates and e-mail addresses	**@** *at sign*	750 words @ .50/word StyMei@aol.com	

Style Meister: The Quick-Reference Custom Style Guide   **199**

Signs & Symbols *(cont.)*	Mark	Example	✔
To indicate **cents** (See [3]*Usage Note, p. 202.*)	¢ *cents sign*	By the time I got my first "real" paycheck, my net worth totaled a mere 4¢.	
To indicate **copyright** • Some publishers use the copyright symbol without the word *Copyright*.	© *copyright symbol*	©1998 by Juan Ho	——
• Others use both the symbol and the word.		© Copyright 1998 by Juan Ho	——
• Others use only the word.		Copyright 1998 by Juan Ho	——
For **degrees** • Some publishers repeat the symbol but not the F or C. • Others omit all but the last symbol.	° *degree sign*	60° to 80°F [CLOSED RANGES] 60°, 70°, or 80°F [CLOSED SERIES] 60 to 80°F [OPEN RANGES] 60, 70 or 80°F [OPEN SERIES]	—— —— —— ——
For **dividing numbers** • Some publishers insert a space on each side.	÷ *division sign*	4 ÷ 2 = 2 [SPACED]	——
• Others omit the spaces.		4÷2=2 [NO SPACE]	——
To indicate **dollars** (See [3]*Usage Note, p. 202.*)	$ *dollar sign*	$40 an hour	
For indicating **equals** • Some publishers insert a space on each side.	= *equals sign*	2 + 2 = 4 [SPACED]	——
• Others omit the spaces.		2+2=4 [NO SPACE]	——
For measurements in **feet** NOTE: Avoid apostrophes and "smart quotes" in place of foot marks and inch marks.	' *foot mark*	5'2" [FIVE FEET, TWO INCHES] *not* 5'2''	

Style Meister: The Quick-Reference Custom Style Guide

Signs & Symbols *(cont.)*	**Mark**	**Example**	✔
To join **fractional modifiers**	**-** *hyphen*	His book was two-thirds ghostwritten.	——
EXCEPTION: Set fractions used as nouns as two words.		The ghostwriter wrote two thirds of his book.	
For **greater than** • Some publishers insert a space on each side.	**>** *greater than sign*	9 > 6 [SPACED]	——
• Others omit the spaces.		9>6 [NO SPACE]	——
For measurements in **inches** NOTE: Avoid apostrophes in place of foot marks and "smart quotes" in place of inch marks. (See the tips on p. 271.)	**❚❚** *inch mark*	5'2" [FIVE FEET, TWO INCHES] *not* 5'2''	——
For **less than** • Some publishers insert a space on each side.	**<** *less than sign*	9 < 6 [SPACED]	——
• Others omit the spaces.		9<6 [NO SPACE]	——
For **multiplying numbers** • Some publishers insert a space on each side.	**✕** *multiplication sign*	6 ✕ 9 = 54 [SPACED]	——
• Others omit the spaces.		6✕9=54 [NO SPACE]	——
To indicate **numbers or pounds** (See [3]*Usage Note, p. 202.*)	**#** *number or pound sign*	Sharpen those #2 pencils. Submit your manuscripts on 20# bond.	

Signs & Symbols *(cont.)*	**Mark**	**Example**	✔
For the word *percent* CAUTIONS:	**%**		
• Use a percent sign only with a figure.	*percent sign*	Authors generally pay their agents 10–15**%**. [USE PERCENT SIGN]	
• Use the word *percent* when numbers are spelled out.		Authors generally pay their agents ten to fifteen percent. [SPELL OUT]	
• Do not use a percent sign in place of the word *percentage*.		A large percentage of Carol's manuscripts get accepted. *not* A large % of Carol's manuscripts get accepted.	
For subtracting numbers	**—**	12 – 4 = 8 [SPACED]	
• Some publishers insert a space on each side.	*minus sign*		——
• Others omit the spaces.		12–4 = 8 [NO SPACE]	——

USAGE NOTES

[1] Measurements, money, and times are generally set as numerals and are not necessarily treated the same as other numbers in the same sentence.

[2] Do not precede *hundreds, thousands, millions,* and so on with hyphens.

[3] Many publishers use ¢, #, and + signs only in lists, tables, equations, and certain business and technical documents.

[4] Use normal word spacing before and after an ampersand (&), unless matching a preexisting style. Do not precede an ampersand with a comma, except as called for in bibliographies and reference lists.

10

PC, or Not PC?

Bias-Free Language & Word Preference

This chapter examines bias-free or "politically correct" (PC) language and other word-preference issues. *Bias-free language* encompasses terms that relate to age, ethnicity, race, gender, marital status, sexual orientation, mental and physical characteristics, and socioeconomic factors.

Let me preface the information in this chapter by saying I am not promoting the use of bias-free language across the board. While I recommend it in the majority of situations to help reach the widest audience, it is not necessarily appropriate for all communications.

Biased language is sometimes warranted, for instance, in fiction and historical materials. If biased language helps portray a fictional character or historical figure, then by all means use it. Otherwise, lean toward bias-free language.

The Pros of Bias-Free Language

While proponents of bias-free language sometimes disagree about specifics, they generally have a unified intention: to treat all people as individuals and to decrease or eliminate prejudice and stereotypes. Most people dislike being labeled because most labels are demeaning and limiting. Even when people are relatively unbiased, their use of inappropriate or unnecessary labels can produce negative outcomes. For instance, medical workers' references to patients in terms of body parts and ailments ("Got a greenstick fracture of the left tibia in Room 3") counter the very concept of holistic treatment.

Many proponents of bias-free language stress the nuances of words. For example, mental health professionals often refer to clients with schizophrenia as *persons with schizophrenia* rather than *schizophrenics.* This, they say, helps destigmatize the label *schizophrenic* and helps offset the misconception that equates schizophrenia with split personalities.

The President's Committee on Employment of People with Disabilities offers some general guidelines that apply to other areas of bias-free language, as well as disabilities:

- Put the person before the disability (or label). For example, use *person with epilepsy* rather than *epileptic.*

- Avoid labels such as *afflicted, suffers from,* and *victim of.* For example, use *person with arthritis* rather than *victim of arthritis.*

- Avoid portraying people who have disabilities as either courageous and superhuman or poor and unfortunate. People with disabilities are just like everyone else. The same holds true for age, ethnicity, race, and so on.

- Avoid catchy expressions such as *handi-capable, physically challenged,* and *special.*

The annotated bibliography describes resources for more information on bias-free terms.

Two Keys to Bias-Free Usage

Accuracy & Appropriateness

The first key to bias-free usage is to determine whether a reference to age, gender, ethnic origin, race, marital status, sexual orientation, physical or mental characteristics, or socioeconomic factors is accurate and appropriate to the context. If not, then by all means eliminate that reference.

Current Terminology

If a reference is accurate and appropriate, the second key is to use current terminology. Because such terms tend to evolve rapidly, this can present a challenge. Over my lifetime the preferred term for black people living in the U.S. has evolved from *Negro* to *colored* to *black* to *Afro-American* to *African American*. Many people still prefer *black* (or *Black*) or even *person* (or *people*) *of color*. To stay current, keep attuned to trends in the media and be sensitive to preferences of the group itself.

While we're on the subject of race, I should mention that racial terms other than colors are proper nouns and thus are capitalized (*Asian, Hispanic, Native American*). Racial terms based on color may be either capitalized or lowercase (*black* or *Black*, *white* or *White*). It's simply a matter of style.

Some writers hyphenate compound racial terms only to indicate parentage of two different races or when the first part of the compound is a prefix rather than a complete word. *Asian-American*, would therefore be hyphenated only when a person has one Asian parent and one American parent—not if both parents are Americans of Asian descent. *Afro-American* is hyphenated because *Afro* is a prefix rather than a complete word.

The Cons of Bias-Free Language

Admittedly, proponents of bias-free language can and do go overboard at times. Bias-free language can be trendy and overly self-conscious. In the 70s, when delineating between *girls* and *women* was more in vogue, a friend called me about the birth of her second child. With some hesitation, she announced that she had had a little *woman*. I'd say that's going a bit overboard.

Most proponents of bias-free language aren't out to ban the use of certain words; they're simply encouraging people to use those words when they are appropriate and accurate. Because my friend did not give birth to a fully developed female, it's both accurate and appropriate to say she had a little *girl*.

Sometimes bias-free alternatives require you to think a bit harder, and sometimes their alternatives result in longer, more cumbersome forms. Whether such options warrant the extra space they require depends upon your circumstances and your values.

Some style guides recommend bias-free language only on a limited basis. *The Economist Style Guide*, for example, objects to *hearing-impaired* in place of *deaf*, and *disadvantaged* in place of *poor*. And it sees no problem with *crippled* in place of *disabled*, and *girls* for describing female teens. Nonetheless, it pays close attention to racial terms, cautioning for instance against using *red* in reference to Native Americans.

Critics sometimes find bias-free alternatives ridiculous or potentially confusing. For example, many take exception to the use of *chair* in place of *chairman*. People, they say, are not furnishings. Still, this usage is widely accepted and simply a matter of style.

While you may or may not agree with the intentions of bias-free language and the extent to which it influences our treatment of each other, you must still determine how to handle "PC" issues.

Now let's examine some other types of word preference.

Word Preference

Word-preference issues include the use of special terminology and value-laden words used or preferred by one culture, profession, organization, group, or individual. Word preference may also address wordiness.

Although word preferences are often subtle, they are quite powerful. Most often, they reflect the values of those who use them. With the growing emphasis on teamwork in the workplace, many organizations are using language to help transform perceptions of working relationships. For instance, calling supervisors *coaches* or *leaders* and supervisors' coworkers *associates* or *team members* connotes a shift away from more hierarchical working relationships.

Seemingly minor differences in word preference can also help shape public perception. In the 1980s, Apple Computer, Inc., very consciously adopted terminology that helped reinforce its image as a user-friendly company. They instructed users to *press* keys rather than *hit* them and to *run* commands rather than *execute* them.

Other issues of word preference you may need to address include the treatment of technical terms, jargon, and wordiness. The search-and-replace form in the appendix comes in handy for recording and managing such preferences. You can, for instance, search for all occurrences of *utilization* and *utilize* and replace them with *use* or search for *if this should prove to be the case* and replace it with *if, if so,* or *if this is the case.*

I encourage you to think carefully about both denotations and connotations of words and to update a word list for each project as word-preference issues arise.

How to Use Chapter 10's Quick-Reference Charts

The quick-reference charts for this chapter focus primarily on issues of gender because sexist language is still quite pervasive and is more frequently encountered than other forms of biased language. However, many of the alternatives presented in the charts apply to other issues of bias-free language as well.

The charts offer a variety of potential solutions to common problems of biased usage. Because more than one alternative may apply to the same situation, you may wish to explore several different alternatives before making a final choice. For instance, you might read all the suggested alternatives for pronouns at once so you can choose the best alternative for your situation.

The charts for Chapter 10 are organized by part of speech and then alphabetized by bold key words in the left-hand column. An exception to this scheme occurs in the Nouns section, where compounds appear by prefix, then root, then suffix rather than in alphabetical order. Figure 43 displays a sample chart.

NOUNS	Biased Usage	Bias-Free Alternative ✔	
Use parallel **courtesy titles** and avoid unnecessary references to marital status.	Faulkner, Fitzgerald, and *Miss* Porter are widely read authors.	*Mr.* Faulkner, *Mr.* Fitzgerald, and *Ms.* Porter are widely read authors.	—
		Faulkner, Fitzgerald, and Porter are widely read authors.	—

Figure 43 - Sample Quick-Reference Chart

The second column of the charts provides examples of biased usage. The third column provides alternatives. In blocks where no text appears, the text directly above that block applies.

In issues of word preference and bias-free language, *you* must define the limits. The best choices vary with the audience and the intent of each communication. You, or your coworkers or clients, must choose the words your readers are most likely to respond to. Use the "write-on" lines in the far-right column to record such preferences and limitations.

If you'd rather not think about parts of speech, scan for key-words in the far-left and center columns. For further information, explore the sources in the annotated bibliography.

The following abbreviation appears in this chapter's quick-reference charts:

cont.	continued

Figure 44 - Abbreviation Key

Summary

This chapter has addressed bias-free or "politically correct" language and word-preference issues. Bias-free language addresses age, ethnicity, race, gender, marital status, sexual orientation, mental and physical characteristics, and socioeconomic factors. The primary keys to bias-free usage are determining whether a label is accurate and appropriate to the context. In addition, bias-free language should consist of current terminology.

Word preference addresses special terminology and value-laden words used or preferred by one culture, profession, organization, group, or individual. Sometimes, it also addresses wordiness.

Bias-Free Usage

NOUNS	Biased Usage	Bias-Free Alternative	✔
Replace *boy* and *girl* with **man** and **woman** (or other appropriate nouns) when you're referring to adults.	The *boys* in the office hate to see you go.	The *men* in the office hate to see you go. *or* Your *coworkers* hate to see you go.	—— ——
NOTE: Use the write-on line to record a cut-off age (such as 12, 18, or 21) for using *man & woman* vs. *boy & girl*.	Kelly always wanted to be a career *girl*. This is Sally, one of the *girls* from the office.	Kelly always wanted to be a business *woman*. This is Sally, one of the *women* from the office.	——
Use genderless **compounds**. NOTE: Currently, *woman* is considered less biased than *lady*.	*lady*like *mother*ly	polite refined nurturing supportive	—— —— —— ——
	man hours *man*kind/*woman*kind *man*made *man*power	person hours human race humankind people hand-made human resources	—— —— —— —— —— ——
	one-*man* show one-ups*man*ship pen*man*ship sports*man*ship	one-person show solo competitiveness handwriting fair play	—— —— —— —— ——
	fore*fathers* chair*man* lay*man* middle*man* spokes*man*	ancestors chair chairperson moderator lay person contact go-between representative	—— —— —— —— —— —— —— ——

Nouns (continued)	**Biased Usage**	**Bias-Free Alternative**	✔
Use parallel **courtesy titles** and avoid unnecessary references to marital status.	Faulkner, Fitzgerald, and *Miss* Porter are widely read authors.	*Mr.* Faulkner, *Mr.* Fitzgerald, and *Ms.* Porter are widely read authors.	——
		Faulkner, Fitzgerald, and Porter are widely read authors.	——
Avoid terms of endearment such as *dear* and *honey*.	Would you type this for me, *dear*.	Would you *please* type this for me, *Chris*.	——
Replace **demeaning words and phrases**.	I'll **have** my *girl* fax the report to you.	I'll *ask* my *secretary* to fax the report to you.	——
	Could you help me move this table, *son*?	Could you help me move this table, *sir*?	——
Avoid **gratuitous modifiers**.	*lady* doctor *woman* judge	doctor judge	
	male nurse *male* teacher	nurse teacher	
	successful female advertising executive	advertising executive successful advertising executive	—— ——
Avoid **inappropriate or irrelevant metaphors**.	Barbara's a *good-looking broad*.	Barbara's a *talented writer*.	
CAUTION: Avoid non-parallel descriptions of women's appearance paired with men's accomplishments.	Zach's a gifted writer. Barbara's a *good-looking writer*.	Zach's a *gifted writer*. Barbara's a *gifted writer*.	
Avoid **inappropriate or irrelevant similes**.	Alison performs as well as *any man*.	Alison performs as well as *anyone*.	

Nouns *(continued)*	**Biased Usage**	**Bias-Free Alternative**	✔
Use genderless **job or role names**.	poet*ess*	poet	——
	steward*ess*	flight attendant	——
	meter *maid*	meter reader	——
	house*wife*	consumer	——
		homemaker	——
	police*woman*	officer	——
		police officer	——
	sales*lady*	sales rep	——
		salesperson	——
	working *mother*, working *woman*	employee	——
		parent	——
		worker	——
	council*man*	council member	——
	crafts*man*	artisan	——
		craftsperson	——
	mail*man*, post*man*	mail carrier	——
	police*man*	officer	——
		police officer	——
	watch*man*	guard	——
		security guard	——
	weather*man*	weather forecaster	——
	working *man*	employee	——
		worker	——
Replace **limiting words and phrases**.	*man* on the street	public	
	A *man's* got to do what a *man's* got to do.	A *person's* got to do what a *person's* got to do.	——
		You've got to do what *you've* got to do.	——

PRONOUNS	Biased Usage	Bias-Free Alternative	✔
Replace *he/she* with an *occupational title*.	*He* will deliver the galleys on Monday.	*The printer* will deliver the galleys on Monday.	—
Instead of *his/her*— • Use an *article*.	The successful writer must always keep *his* audience in mind.	The successful writer always keeps *a* specific audience in mind.	—
• Use *both genders, alternating* them throughout.		The successful writer must always keep *her* audience in mind. *then* Such a writer remains mindful of *his* purpose.	—
• Use *both genders, in her/his* order.		The successful writer always keeps *her or his* audience in mind.	—
• Use *both genders in his or her or his/her* order. CAUTION: Both options are awkward in text with frequent singular forms.		The successful writer always keeps *his or her* audience in mind. *or* The successful writer always keeps *his/her* audience in mind.	—
• Use a *plural form*.	The successful writer always remains mindful of *his* purpose.	Successful writers always remain mindful of *their* purpose.	—
• Use *second person*.	The successful writer must always keep *his* audience in mind.	When *you* write, always keep *your* audience in mind.	—
In some cases, you can use *its* instead of *his/her*—	That dog is nuts about *his* bone.	That dog is nuts about *its* bone.	—
CAUTION: Use this option only for animals and very young children of unknown sex.	A five-year-old child should know *his* address and phone number.	A five-year-old child should know *its* address and phone number.	—

Pronouns *(cont.)*	**Biased Usage**	**Bias-Free Alternative** ✔
Avoid **needless personification**.	Plug the connector back into *his* socket.	Plug the connector back into *its* socket.
Repeat nouns. CAUTION: This option sometimes leads to awkward wording.	If *he* makes lots of changes on typeset pages, a writer may have to pay "author's alteration" fees.	If *a writer* makes lots of changes on typeset pages, *that writer* may have to pay "author's alteration" fees. —
Avoid linking gender to certain **occupational titles**.	entrepreneur . . . *he* executive . . . *he* maid . . . *she* secretary . . . *she*	See the preceding alternatives for *he/she* and *his/her* or use an occupational title or function in place of the pronoun.
Avoid linking gender to certain **roles**.	All employees and their *wives* are invited to the picnic.	All employees and their *spouses/partners* are invited to the picnic.
Add **specific names** to justify gender-bound pronouns.	The editor expects *his* writers to pay attention to style.	The editor, *Alan White*, expects *his* writers to pay attention to style. —
Use forms of *they* as **singulars**. CAUTION: This option simplifies editing, but it is technically incorrect. Many editors accept this form; some disapprove.	Each employee should consider what this change means to *him*.	Each employee should consider what this change means to *them*. —

VERBS	Biased Usage	Bias-Free Alternative	✔
Replace *man* used as a verb.	We'll need three more people to *man* the book fair booth.	We'll need three more people to *staff* (or *cover* or *run*) the book fair booth.	——

11

This, That & the Other

Special Cases, Odds & Ends

This chapter discusses those stylistic details that seem to fit under no particular category: bibliographies and reference lists, dialogue and speech, jargon, trademarks, and distinctive treatments of words.

Bibliographies & Reference Lists

A *bibliography* lists all of the sources the author used to write an article or a book, whether or not the author cites those sources in the text. A *reference list* contains bibliographic information for all of the sources cited in the text.

APA & MLA Style

Two of the best-known styles for bibliographies and reference lists are APA and MLA. The *Publication Manual of the American Psychological Association* fully outlines APA style. The *MLA Handbook*, published by the Modern Language Association, outlines MLA style. APA and MLA style have a few parallels, but they also have several differences:

- The way in which authors' names appear
- The way in which coauthors' names appear
- The position and punctuation of the publication date

- The capitalization scheme for titles

- The treatment of edition numbers

Author Names. APA style lists last names first, followed by spaced first and (when applicable) middle initials. For example:

Morris, **W.,** & Morris, **M.** (1992). *Harper dictionary of contemporary usage.* New York: HarperCollins.

MLA style lists last name first for the first author, then first name first for any coauthors. In addition, MLA style spells out authors' first names.

While APA style joins coauthors' names with ampersands, MLA style spells out *and.* For example:

Morris, **William**, **and Mary** Morris. *Harper Dictionary of Contemporary Usage.* New York: HarperCollins, 1992.

If you don't know an author's first name, or if an author uses initials instead, you can omit the first name, even in MLA style. An MLA-style reference to *The Elements of Style* would therefore read as follows:

Strunk, **William, Jr.,** and **E. B.** White. *The Elements of Style.* 3rd ed. New York: Macmillan, 1979.

Publication Dates. In APA style, publication dates appear immediately after the author's name. The dates are enclosed in parentheses, which are followed by a period. For example:

Boston, B. **(1996).** *STET again!: More tricks of the trade for publications people: Selections from the Editorial Eye.* Alexandria, VA: EEI.

In MLA style, the publication date falls right after the publisher's name, at the end of the entry, and is set off with a comma:

Boston, Bruce. *STET Again!: More Tricks of the Trade for Publications People.* Alexandria, VA: EEI, **1996.**

Capitalization of Titles. APA style capitalizes only the first word of a publication's title and subtitle. For example:

Gross, G. (Ed.). (1993). **Editors** on editing: **What** writers *need to know about what editors do* (Rev. 3rd ed.). New York: Grove.

MLA style matches the capitalization of the complete title:

Gross, Gerald, ed. ***Editors on Editing: What Writers Need to Know About What Editors Do.*** Rev. 3rd ed. New York: Grove, 1993.

Edition Numbers. APA style encloses edition numbers in parentheses placed directly after the title (and followed by a period). For example:

Zinsser, W. (1994). *On writing well: An informal guide to writing nonfiction* **(5th ed.).** New York: HarperCollins.

MLA style places edition numbers directly after the title (which ends with a period) with no parentheses:

Zinsser, William. *On Writing Well: An Informal Guide to Writing Nonfiction*. **5th ed.** New York: HarperCollins, 1994.

The differences between APA and MLA style in citing other types of references vary even more. The quick-reference charts in this chapter illustrate both of these styles for basic book and periodical entries.

Choosing a Standard

In my experience, APA is a common standard for professional journals, and MLA is a common standard for academic style. However, these are only broad generalizations. Many professional fields have their own style standards. For instance, associations for engineering, linguistics, medicine, and other specialties often publish their own style guides.

Many publishers follow APA or MLA style. Some use a variation of one of these styles. For instance, I've worked with publishers who generally follow APA style but print the publication date without parentheses and/or move it to the end of the citation. I've also worked with publishers who follow either APA or MLA but use a different capitalization scheme for titles. The annotated bibliography in this book represents such a variation.

A Few Words of Advice

When writing for a particular publisher or publication, it's always wise to obtain and follow their guidelines. You usually have to send away for guidelines from book and consumer-magazine publishers; scholarly journals often print their guidelines in one or more issues a year. You can also study back issues to get a sense of the publisher's standards. I recommend thumbing through a minimum of three issues. It's best to tailor your style to each publication. If you find that too time-consuming, at least aim for a standard common in the field or the medium you're writing for.

If you use a computer and you plan to publish regularly in journals with different bibliographic standards, you might wish to set up a reference database. Bibliographic software programs, such as Bookends Pro and EndNote2 Plus, can make such information easier to manage.

As you analyze bibliographic style, note the differences in styles used for citations within text and those used for end notes and footnotes.

Organizing Bibliographies & Reference Lists

Most bibliographies and reference lists are alphabetized by the first author's surname, then by title for works with unspecified authors. However, you also need to consider how to alphabetize

- *M'*, *Mc*, and *Mac* prefixes,

- foreign names with particles,

- compound surnames,

- acronyms and initialisms, and

- numbers.

Then you'll need to decide how to organize multiple works by the same author—alphabetically by title or chronologically, by publication year.

Your approach to alphabetization may vary with the style guide you use.

Dialogue & Speech

The following are some basic rules for the treatment of dialogue and speech (direct quotes):

1. Separate dialogue from its tag line with a comma, but do not do so for speech when it would separate a subject from its predicate or when the speech is used as the object.

2. Capitalize the second part of a broken quote—whether dialogue or speech—only when it starts a new sentence.

3. Start each new speaker's speech on a new line.

4. When one person's speech spans more than a paragraph, use opening quotation marks before each paragraph but closing quotation marks only after the last.

5. Capitalize the first word of unspoken thoughts. Then either place them in double quotation marks or set them in italics or roman type. Like *Words into Type,* I favor italics for unspoken thoughts (*Did I mention this before?*).

6. Italicize unspoken thoughts that appear with spoken dialogue.

The quick-reference charts illustrate some of these guidelines.

Distinctive Treatment of Words

Another point of style that most works of nonfiction (and to a limited extent, fiction) must address is the distinctive treatment of words. This refers to the typographic styles and punctuation used to emphasize words, identify new terms, and handle special cases like computer key cap names and signage.

The quick-reference charts in this chapter illustrate several options. Chapters 12 and 13 contain further information about typography and design concerns.

Jargon

Because of the prevalence of jargon these days, this topic could easily get out of hand. Much like nonbiased language, jargon should be used only when it's accurate and appropriate. Your audience must understand and identify with the terms you use, even if you must sometimes acquaint them with new terms. Every profession and specialty has its own vocabulary, which is usually appropriate for communications within that profession. A good number of the words I add to word list/style sheets might be classified as jargon related to a particular field.

Jargon only becomes a problem when it gets unleashed on an unsuspecting public or is not defined as needed for the audience. For instance, you need not define *computerized tomography* or *magnetic resonance imaging* when writing for physicians, but when writing for the general public, you may need to explain these terms. Whenever you're in doubt, a good rule of thumb is to define new terms upon first use.

Also consider whether a word might be misinterpreted or taken out of context. I once prepared a handout with proofreading tips that directed students to *"scan* the page backwards to quickly locate errors." One woman found this confusing because we had just completed a discussion about production technology, and she'd assumed I was referring to an electronic scanner rather than to scanning with one's eyes.

Another type of jargon occurs when a word that is normally used as one part of speech is used as another part of speech. For instance, editors often become alarmed when writers use nouns as verbs. *Utilize* is perhaps the best known example of a "verbized" noun. Language purists object to such forms because they use words as the "wrong" part of speech. Other "objection-able" forms include *computerize, finalize,* and *prioritize.*

To these purists, I say Lighten up! English is an evolving lan-guage. As long as you communicate your message clearly and don't alienate your audience, most anything goes. The trick is knowing just how much your audience will buy. I'm not sug-gesting that anything goes, but I see no problem with such forms when no other word expresses your thoughts as well.

As with many style issues, some people are adamantly against "verbized" nouns, and others accept them readily. What's "right" is anyone's guess. The challenge is to determine where you or your organization wishes to draw the line, and then to stick to your decision consistently.

Trademarks

Trademarks are names, symbols, slogans, and other devices that businesses use to distinguish themselves and their products from the competition.

- An ® symbol indicates that a trademark has been registered with the U.S. Patent and Trademark Office.

- A ™ symbol indicates a manufacturer's intent to use a name as a trademark when the name is not yet registered with the federal office.

- An ᔆᴹ symbol identifies the source of a service, rather than a product, and is treated like a trademark symbol.

Just as writers must police their own copyrights, manufacturers must police their own trademarks. Although trademarks are protected under federal and state laws, the manufacturers themselves must confront those who misuse them.

Registering a trademark with the U.S. Patent and Trademark Office (and then using the ® symbol) offers minimal protection. But exclusive rights come only with extensive use. Manufacturers who can't keep the public from treating their trademarks generically can lose their trademark rights. If writers use trademarks as generic terms too frequently, manufacturers essentially lose their rights. The "genericides" of *Kleenex* and *Xerox* demonstrate the difficulty manufacturers confront.

Trademark owners therefore generally prefer that trademark symbols display each time their trademarks are used, but this practice consumes valuable time and space. Most writers therefore opt for another alternative.

Alternatives to Printing Trademark Symbols

Many writers avoid trademarks altogether and stick to generic nouns (such as *copy machine* or *photocopier* in place of *Xerox*) and generic verbs (such as *copy* or *photocopy* in place of *xerox*). Other writers take care to match the capitalization, punctuation, and spacing of trademark names (CorelDRAW!, WordPerfect) every time they appear.

To save space and streamline production, many publishers print a list of all trademarks that appear in a book on the copyright page or elsewhere in the book's front matter. (Macintosh® is a registered trademark of Apple Computer, Inc.; PostScript® is a registered trademark of Adobe Systems, Inc.; Style Meister™ is a trademark of Castle Communications; Windows™ is a trademark of Microsoft.) Then they omit the symbols in the remaining text.

The quick-reference charts that begin on page 225 present several alternative treatments for trademarks. No matter which option you use—

• Capitalize the first letter at the very minimum;

• Include a trademark's generic term at least once within each communication—preferably the first time the trademark appears; and

• Always check a trademark's spelling, no matter how familiar the term may seem. You may, for instance, be surprised to learn that the correction fluid most of us call "white out" is actually spelled *Wite-out* (a registered trademark of Bic Corporation).

The International Trademark Association and the U.S. Trademark Association ask writers to use trademarks as adjectives (as in *Day-Timer* time planner) and to also follow the guidelines listed in the Figure 45.

Do Not Use Trademarks As—	Replace—	With—
Generic nouns	Please hand me that *Post-it*.	Please hand me that *Post-it* note [or self-stick note].
Plurals	Some people think *Macintoshes* are superior to IBM-compatibles.	Some people think *Macintosh* computers are superior to IBM-compatibles.
Possessives	I love *Sharpie's* angled points.	I love the angled points of *Sharpie* felt-tip pens.
Verbs	Please *xerox* [or Xerox] this for me.	Please *copy* [or photocopy] this for me.

Figure 45 - Trademark Guidelines

Where to Turn for More Information

Because standard dictionaries list a minimal number of trademarks and new products enter the market each day, you may wish to confirm the capitalization, spacing, spelling, and special formatting of a trademark against the product packaging or against the manufacturer's ads.

You can get answers to trademark questions through the following resources:

- The International Trademark Association in New York (212) 768-9887, hotline: (212) 768-9886, 2–5 PM

- The U.S. Trademark Association in New York (212) 986-5880

- The Internet site: http://www.general.net/trademark/faq.htm

According to *The New York Public Library Writer's Guide to Style and Usage* (1994), capitalization is all that is necessary. Of course, you should always make certain that you spell trademarks right.

The quick-reference charts at the end of this chapter illustrate a number of schemes for dealing with trademarks.

How to Use Chapter 11's Quick-Reference Charts

The quick-reference charts for Chapter 11 contain four sections:

1. Bibliographies & Reference Lists

2. Dialogue & Speech

3. Distinctive Treatment of Words

4. Trademarks

The left-hand column of each chart lists widely accepted usage guidelines (organized alphabetically by bold key words) and notes common exceptions. Occasionally, the left-hand column will refer you to a usage note. These notes appear at the end of the chapter. The center column shows examples that illustrate each guideline and presents various standards when more than one option might apply.

Some of these charts contain customizing features. The columns with a checkmark (✔) contain "write-on lines," on which you can record the options you prefer or rank options when you find more than one acceptable.

The Distinctive Treatment of Words section includes an additional column that displays oversized punctuation marks. You can scan this center column to quickly find the guideline you seek.

Once you become familiar with the layout of these charts and determine which options you prefer, you will find them quite handy. You can use a Word List/Style Sheet form to record further guidelines (see Appendix).

The following abbreviations appear in this chapter's quick-reference charts:.

Ed(s).	Editor(s)
ed.	edition
F. M.	First initial. Middle initial.
No.	number
Rev.	revised

Figure 46 - Abbreviation Key

Summary

This chapter has addressed the odds and ends of style: bibliographies and reference lists (focusing on APA and MLA standards); dialogue and speech, including unspoken thoughts; jargon; and trademarks.

The quick-reference charts illustrate these points, and in addition, address the distinctive treatments of words (bold, italics, small caps).

Bibliographies & Reference Lists

CITATIONS	APA	✔	MLA	✔
A **book** written **by one author**	Last, F. M. **(year)**. *Book title*. Publisher's Location: Publisher.	—	Last, First M. *Book Title*. Publisher's Location: Publisher, year.	—
Examples:	O'Conner, P. T. (1996). *Woe Is I: The grammar-phobe's guide to better English in Plain English*. New York: Grosset/Putnam.		O'Conner, Patricia T. *Woe Is I: The Grammar-phobe's Guide to Better English in Plain English*. New York: Grosset/Putnam, 1996.	
A **book** written **by two or more authors**	Last, F. M., **&** Last, F. M. **(year)**. *Book title*. Publisher's Location: Publisher.	—	Last, First M., **and** First M. Last. *Book Title*. Publisher's Location: Publisher, year.	—
Examples:	Bly, R. W., & Blake, G. (1995). *The elements of technical writing*. New York: Macmillan.		Bly, Robert W., and Gary Blake. *The Elements of Technical Writing*. New York: Macmillan, 1995.	
A **book chapter** written **by one author**	Last, F. M. **(year)**. Chapter title. In F. M. Last **(Ed.)**, *Book title* **(page/pages)**. Publisher's Location: Publisher.	—	Last, First M. "Chapter Title." In *Book Title*. Ed. First M. Last. Publisher's Location: Publisher, year, page(s).	—
Examples:	Howard, G. (1993). Mistah Perkins—He dead: Publishing today. In G. Gross (Ed.), *Editors on editing: What writers should know about what editors do* (Rev. 3rd ed. pp. 56–72). New York: Grove.		Howard, Gerald. "Mistah Perkins—He Dead: Publishing Today." *Editors on Editing: What Writers Should Know About What Editors Do*. Rev. 3rd ed. Ed. Gerald Gross. New York: Grove, 1993, 56–72.	

Citations *(continued)*	APA	✔	MLA	✔
A **book chapter** written **by two or more authors**	Last, F. M., **&** Last, F. M. **(**year**)**. Title of chapter. In F. M. Last **(**Ed.**)**, *Book title* **(**page/pages**)**. Publisher's Location: Publisher.	—	Last, First M., **and** First M. Last. "Title of chapter." In *Book Title*. Ed. First M. Last. Publisher's Location: Publisher, year, page(s).	—
Examples:	Brindamour, J.L., & Lubow, J.M. (1993). An annotated bibliography of books on editing and publishing. In G. Gross (Ed.), *Editors on editing: What writers should know about what editors do* (Rev. 3rd ed.), 366–377. New York: Grove.		Brindamour, Jean-Louis, and Joseph M. Lubow. "An Annotated Bibliography of Books on Editing and Publishing." In *Editors on Editing: What Writers Should Know About What Editors Do* (Rev. 3rd ed.). Ed. Gerald Gross. New York: Grove, 1993, 366–377.	
A **journal article** written **by one author**	Last, F. M. **(**year**)**. Article title. *Journal title*, *volume number*, page(s).	—	Last, First M. "Article Title." *Journal Title*, Volume no. Issue no. **(**year**)**: page(s).	—
Examples:	Curtis, J. E. (1997). Considering a corporate style guide? *Intercom, 44,* 22–25.		Curtis, James E. Considering a Corporate Style Guide? *Intercom*, 44, No. 8 (1997), 22–25.	
A **newsletter article** written **by one author**	Last, F. M. **(**year, month/months**)**. Article title. *Newsletter Title*, *volume number*, page(s).	—	Last, First M. "Article Title." *Newsletter Title*, Volume no. Issue no. date, year: page(s).	—
Examples:	Hale, C. (1997. April/May). Going post@l. *Copy Editor, 8,* 1, 6–7.		Hale, Constance. "Going post@l." *Copy Editor.* 8, April/May 1997, 1+.	

Dialogue & Speech

ENCLOSE

	Mark	Example	✔
The **dialogue or speech of one person**, when it spans two or more paragraphs NOTE: Use opening quotation marks before each paragraph but closing only after the last.	**" "** *double quotation marks*	"My signature isn't worth very much right now. "But some day—maybe—it will increase in value!" —Tennessee Williams	
Some writers enclose **unspoken thoughts** in quotation marks, especially when it's clear they are unspoken.	**" "** *double quotation marks*	I don't know why I didn't say "That deadline's too soon."	—
• Others capitalize the first letter and italicize them.		I don't know why I didn't say *That deadline's too soon.*	—
• Still others capitalize the first letter but leave the type in roman.		I don't know why I didn't say That deadline's too soon.	—

SEPARATE

	Mark	Example
A bit of **dialogue from its tag line**	**,** *comma*	"I'd have been here sooner," Jay said, "but I got abducted by some aliens."
CAUTION: Never separate a subject from its predicate or object.		The mayor said this area is "growing by leaps and bounds." [NO COMMA AFTER *IS*]

Distinctive Treatment of Words

GUIDELINE	Mark	Example	✔
For emphasis in general text • Some writers use bold.		A **byline** is an author credit line. [BOLD]	——
• Others use italics. (See [1]*Usage Note, p. 230.*)		A *byline* is an author credit line. [ITALICS]	——
For key caps in computer documentation • Some writers use bold.		Press the **Enter** key. [BOLD]	——
• Others use small caps. (See [1]*Usage Note, p. 230.*)		Press the ENTER key. [SMALL CAPS]	——
For new terms (on first use) • Some writers use double quotation marks. (See *British Usage, p. 230.*)	**" "** *double quotation marks*	A "byline" is an author credit line above or below a title.	——
• Others use single quotation marks.	**' '** *single quotation marks*	A 'byline' is an author credit line above or below a title.	——
• Others use bold.		A **byline** is an author credit line. [BOLD]	——
• Still others use italics. (See [1]*Usage Note, p. 230.*)		A *byline* is an author credit line. [ITALICS]	——
For signage • Some writers use double quotation marks.	**" "** *double quotation marks*	"Beware of boa constrictor."	——
• Others use small caps. (See [1]*Usage Note, p. 230.*)		BEWARE OF BOA CONSTRICTOR. [SMALL CAPS]	——

GUIDELINES	Frequency	Example	✔
Include a ® or a ™ symbol.	Each time	Style Meister™	___
	First time only	Style Meister™ *then* Style Meister	___
Match **manufacturer's capitalization and spacing**.	Each time	CorelDRAW!	___
	First time only	CorelDRAW! *then* CorelDraw *or*	___
		CorelDRAW! *then* Corel Draw	___
Use **italic, bold, or color**.	Each time	**Quicken** records	___
	First time only	**Quicken** records *then* Quicken records	___
Use **all caps**.	Each time	SHARPIE pens	___
	First time only	SHARPIE pens *then* Sharpie pens	___
Enclose **initial caps in quotation marks**.	Each time	"Illustrator" files	___
	First time only	"Illustrator" files *then* Illustrator files	___

Trademark Guidelines

(continued)	Frequency	Example	✔
Follow the trademark name with the word *brand*.	Each time	Scotch Brand adhesive tape	——
	First time only	Scotch Brand adhesive tape *then* Scotch tape	——
Use **initial caps** only.	Each time	Smead file folders	——

BRITISH USAGE

British usage for both double and single quotation marks generally counters U.S. usage.

USAGE NOTE

Chapters 12 and 13 present more typographic information.

Points & Picas

The Basics of Physical Format

*N*ow let's talk about style in the physical sense—the way that printed images appear on the page. Consistent physical style or *format* enhances communications just as much as consistent content does. Consistent format functions much like a road sign: It offers visual clues that help readers navigate through a message. Well-chosen subheads signal what lies ahead.

When you treat text blocks, lists, and other printed elements consistently, your readers can better interpret structure and understand relationships. Certain easily recognized elements, like warning statements and caution statements, not only save aggravation, sometimes they save lives!

If you are submitting manuscripts for publication, this chapter will help you better communicate with the people who produce your *camera-ready copy* (the final master used for reproduction).

If you are setting your own type or producing camera-ready copy but you're new to print production, this chapter will introduce you to the basics.

If you already know the basics of print production, you may want to skip ahead to Chapter 13 for in-depth information about type specification and page design.

Physical specifications generally are of three basic types: Page (or Document) Format, Character Format, and Paragraph Format. Let's take a closer look at each type.

Page Format

You're probably familiar with basic page or document formatting. In school, your teachers may have demanded that left- and right-hand margins be X inches wide and that the first line of text start Y inches from the top. Page or document format includes measurements for trim size, margins, live area, and columns, plus other recurring elements. I'll explain each of these terms.

Trim Size, Margins & Live Area

Large print jobs are run on huge sheets of paper, which are cut down to the final page or *trim size.* You should know the trim size before you format anything. Four common trim sizes follow:

- $8\,^1/_2$" x 11" (letter size)
- $5\,^1/_2$" x $8\,^1/_2$" (one-half of a letter-size sheet, cut horizontally)
- $8\,^1/_2$"x 14" (legal size)
- 11" x 17" (ledger size)

The *live area* or "positive space" is the portion of the page where the printed image (text, art, and so on) appears. The white space or "negative space" is the portion with no image. This space includes the open areas between elements, plus the *margins*—the distance from the edge of the paper to where the printed image begins.

Columns & Column Gutters

The live area is often subdivided into vertical columns of type or art, like the columns of a newspaper. The white space between two columns on the same page is the *gutter.* On multiple-column pages, column widths may vary, but column gutters are usually the same. Some people also use the term *gutter* for the inside margin that runs along the spine between facing pages.

Recurring & Mirrored Elements

Printed pages often contain recurring elements, such as headers, footers, and folios. A *header* is a block or line of information, like a chapter title, that repeats at the top of several pages. The headers on this page and page 233 read as follows:

Chapter 12 - Points & Picas   *Page Format*

A *footer* is a line or block of text that repeats at the bottom of several pages. The footer on this page also contains the *folio* (page number).

In *two-page spreads* (left- and right-hand pages that face one another), some elements may print as mirror images. For instance, most publishers place folios on the outside edge of pages so readers can locate them easily. It's therefore common for a header or a folio to fall on the left-hand side of a *verso* (left-hand) page and the right-hand side of a *recto* (right-hand) page. In other words, some elements alternate position, so they'll always be on the outside or always be on the inside in relation to the spine. In Figure 47, the headers and footers are mirrored.

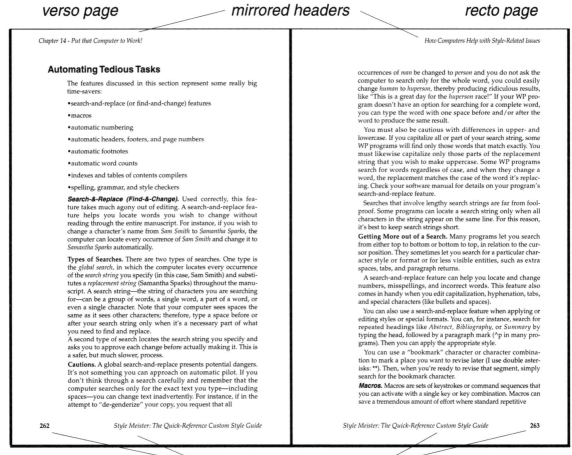

Figure 47 - Mirrored Elements on a Two-Page Spread

Most page-numbering schemes begin on a recto page to ensure that odd-numbered pages fall on the right and even-numbered pages fall on the left.

Character Format

Character formatting involves the type font, style, capitalization, size, and spacing.

Type Fonts & Styles

Much confusion surrounds the terms *font, type face, type family,* and *type style.* Even the authorities offer conflicting definitions. For this discussion, I'll adopt the approach taken by many computer software manufacturers: I'll use *font* in place of type face and *type style* to describe families and variations. The glossary contains more detailed definitions for these terms.

Fonts. A few common fonts include Bookman, Palatino, Times, Avant Garde, and Helvetica. Here's what they look like:

Bookman Palatino Times Avant Garde Helvetica

Type is broadly categorized as either serif or sans serif. *Serifs* are the small strokes at the ends of main letter strokes. *Sans serif* means simply "without serifs." Figure 48 illustrates the difference:

	Serif	**Sans Serif**
	Bookman	Avant Garde
serifs	Palatino	Helvetica
	Times	

Figure 48 - Serif vs. Sans Serif Type

Bookman, Palatino, and Times are all serif fonts. Avant Garde and Helvetica are sans serif fonts.

Style. Most fonts have a variety of styles, such as the following:

Times Bold   *Times Italic*   ***Times Bold Italic***

Helvetica Narrow   *Helvetica Oblique*

You can also style a plain font with variations such as **bold,** *italics,* underline, ALL CAPS, SMALL CAPS, and roman (plain) text. Some, but not all, systems offer specialty styles, like outline or shadow, but you should limit your use of fancy styles to decorative elements and display type—headings and such. <u>Double under-lines</u> and ~~strikethrough~~ styles come in handy when editing manu-scripts or marking them for a typesetter.

Roman. The generic term *roman* describes ordinary, vertically ori-ented type. The names of some roman fonts include the word *roman* (such as Times Roman), but the names of most roman fonts do not.

Bold. Bold type is heavy type that is often used for special terms or to emphasize a word, and for headings, captions, introductory letters in index entries, and so on.

Italic. In italic and *oblique* styles, the characters slant—usually to the right. Like bold letters, italics are often used for special terms or emphasis. The following elements often appear in italics: legal and legislative terms, mathematical and statistical unknowns, names of vehicles (ships, aircraft, spacecraft, trains), scientific names, stage directions in plays, and references to single letters.

Also, foreign words (other than proper names) that have not been absorbed into English are frequently italicized.

Literary titles sometimes appear in italics and sometimes appear in quotation marks. Common treatments for artistic and literary works appear in Figure 49.

Italicize	Use Quotation Marks
Books	Chapters
Long poems	Short poems
Magazines, newspapers	Short stories
Pamphlets, brochures	Songs, short compositions
Paintings	Operas, oratorios
Movies, TV series	Plays
Record albums	TV episodes

Figure 49 - Treatment of Literary Titles

As with most other style decisions, these guidelines are not uni-versally accepted. Some publications, particularly newspapers, don't use italics at all. They may use quotation marks in place of italics and use a different style for titles that would otherwise appear in quotation marks.

<u>Underline</u>. In the "old days," people used *underscored* (underlined) text primarily as a substitute for italics. But, with the dawn of desktop publishing, underlined text became passé. People who have the equipment generally use italics or other special formats instead (though underlined headings may be okay). When preparing camera-ready copy, feel free to use whatever special formats you need. Just try not to go overboard. Many publications use a maximum of three different styles per page.

Preparing a manuscript for publication is a different situation. Most publishers prefer to format materials on their own. For instance, many publishers ask you to underline words you want italicized rather than italicizing them on your own computer. Your editor, designer, and publisher will most likely determine the final character formats themselves.

This may be true even when you're submitting your manuscript electronically. When you supply a completely "clean" manuscript or file (free of any special character formats), it saves the publisher from reformatting your work to create the look the editor and designer prefer. Use only roman type and underlining (to indicate italics) unless your publisher requests otherwise. In the future, publishers might welcome special formats. Who knows? To be safe, always follow the publisher's guidelines.

Capitalization Schemes. Capitalization schemes include all caps, small caps, initial caps (capitalizing the first letter of a word), and dropped caps (setting an oversized letter for the first letter of a paragraph).

In a misguided attempt to make certain words look more important, many people tend to overcapitalize. *Up Style* caps, which are explained in Chapter 7, tend to be self-defeating. When you overuse caps, the words you most want to emphasize become obscured by the excess caps that surround them, and nothing gets emphasized effectively. The reader's visual clues for proper nouns and acronyms get bogged down in the mire.

In addition, capital letters are more difficult to read. We perceive words letter-group by letter-group, so the distinctive outlines of words set in lowercase letters help us recognize them faster than the same words set in all caps.

You can see this difference for yourself: Place a blank card or page over the two lines that follow this paragraph. Slide the card down to reveal the top half of the first line. (Align the card with the dashes at the beginning and end of the line.) Then reveal the top half of the second line. Notice how much faster you can decipher the bottom line (set mainly in lower-case letters) than the top line (set in all caps).

— USE ALL CAPS CONSCIOUSLY AND SPARINGLY! —

— Use all caps consciously and sparingly! —

I'm not saying never use all caps; under the right circumstances, all caps are quite effective.

You can use all caps to startle readers or snag their attention, or to create humor or emphasize a word. Humorist Dave Barry applies caps masterfully—and deliberately. Other perfectly legitimate applications of all caps include brief headlines, titles, logos, trademarks, and labels; text requiring an aura of dignity; simulated computer printouts; names of computer keys: DELETE, ENTER, RETURN, SHIFT; and so on. For many of these applications, small caps work equally well.

Small caps can be effective for acronyms; simulated newspaper headlines, telegrams, and cables; and the text of signs. (When you use small caps to represent quoted matter or the contents of a telegram or sign, omit the quotation marks.)

While we're talking about small caps, here's an important technical tip: In many word-processing programs, you must enter the characters you want to set in small caps as lowercase letters, then highlight them and apply the small caps style.

Conveying Meaning & Creating Emphasis

Varied fonts and styles can do more than merely jazz up a publication: They also convey meaning and hold reader interest. They can grab a reader's attention and guide that reader through your message. You can use them for esthetics, for emphasis, for graphic organizers, and for fun. You can introduce or emphasize words by setting them in bold, italics, or all caps, or by underlining them. Changing to a different font or increasing or decreasing the type size often works as well.

Varying line length or changing justification or position offers other possibilities. If more than one color is available, a different color can provide both emphasis and interest. When only one color is available, reversed type within a box may do.

Bold is often good for new terms and emphasis, when used in moderation. But too much bold is overwhelming, so sometimes you may need a different style. For instance, if you're writing a manual and you set direct instructions and warnings in bold, you may prefer italics or another style for emphasis and for new terms.

Italics may be a good choice if 1) you've ruled out bold, and 2) you don't already have much italicized copy (such as book, magazine, newspaper, movie, or painting titles). Italics tend to slow readers down; use them in moderation.

All caps, like italics, tend to slow readers down. And, like bold, they can be overwhelming. All caps also look disproportionately larger than surrounding copy, so you might try small caps instead. If space is a concern, avoid all caps.

You can sometimes use quotation marks for new terms. They are, however, less acceptable for emphasis. You might try quotation marks when

1. The words meet the guidelines described in Chapter 5 or in Figure 49, which appears on page 235,

2. You don't already have a great deal of copy in quotation marks, or

3. You want to limit the number of fonts or styles used.

Point Size & Leading

Type is measured in *points:* The higher the point size, the larger the type. There are 12 points to 1 *pica* and approximately 6 picas (72 points) to the inch. This figure is approximate because a point actually measures .013837 inch, but that approximation is close enough for most purposes.

The vertical space between lines is called *leading*. Pronounced "ledding," the term dates back to the days when printers used pieces of lead to separate lines of metal letters. Some people refer to leading as "line spacing."

Point size and leading are recorded as fractions, with the point size as numerator and the leading as denominator. The standard point sizes for books and similar materials range from 9 to 12 points, usually with 2 additional points of leading. Most text blocks in this book are set $^{12}/_{15}$: that is, 12-point type with 15-point leading.

Measuring Leading. You can easily measure the leading between one line and another with a standard pica scale. (A *pica scale* looks much like a see-through ruler.) Simply measure from one baseline to another. A *baseline* is an invisible line that characters sit on, excluding their *ascenders* (the very tops of lowercase letters) and *descenders* (their "tails"). Figure 50 illustrates these terms.

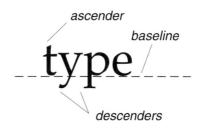

Figure 50 - Type on a Baseline

Chapter 13 discusses leading in more depth.

Measuring Point Sizes. For several reasons, determining a point size is a bit more difficult. Not all fonts measure the same—even at the same point size. Although measuring the height of an alphabet from ascender to descender will bring you close, the full point size may be slightly larger than the visible portion of a character.

And, to add to the confusion, U.S. and British points measure differently than points based on the metric system. But, unless you're working with a very intricate design, you need not worry about these differences.

What's more significant for most people is *x-height* (the height of a lowercase letter, excluding ascenders and descenders) as shown in Figure 51.

$$36\text{-pt.} \updownarrow x\text{-height} \updownarrow \mathbf{36\text{-pt.}}$$

Palatino   Helvetica

Figure 51 - Point Size and X-Height

A different x-height will make the characters in one font appear larger or smaller than those in another font in the same point size. Observe:

Avant Garde   Helvetica

The preceding words are both set in 12-point type—really!—but because Avant Garde has a larger x-height, it appears to be a larger point size.

Then how do you measure point size? Unless you're an expert, you pretty much have to guess. Type scales and viewing loupes can get you in the ballpark. Beyond that, you must rely on typesetters or computer software.

The variety of type on today's market is mind-boggling. Literally hundreds of fonts—both serif and sans serif—are available, and more pop up every year. A few serif fonts and a few sans serif fonts, in a variety of faces, are adequate for most people's needs. But it's nice to have a choice.

Now let's move on to paragraph formatting.

Paragraph Format

Paragraph formatting refers to one element's position in relation to other elements on the page. This involves *alignment* (horizontal spacing), *indentation,* and *tabs. Rules* (decorative lines) or *borders* (boxes), *screens* (shading), and colors are sometimes part of paragraph formatting as well. I'll limit this discussion to the basics: alignment, indentation, and tabs.

Alignment

Standard alignment choices include flush-left, flush-right, centered, and *justified* (perfectly even on both sides).

Indentation

Indentations are measured from the edge of the live area toward the center of the page. The indent for the first line of a paragraph often differs from the text that follows. Sometimes the first line is longer, and the remainder of the paragraph is indented. This results in a *hanging indent,* meaning the first line hangs out farther than the following lines. Hanging indents appear frequently in lists.

Figure 52 illustrates the difference between a paragraph set flush-left and a paragraph with a hanging indent.

Hanging Indent	No Hanging Indent
1. The first line of the paragraph has a smaller indent than the remaining lines (or has no indent at all).	1. Every line of the paragraph starts the same distance from the left-hand margin.
2. The number (or letter or bullet) preceding the first line "hangs" out into the left-hand margin.	2. The number "runs in" with the text, and the rest of the paragraph aligns flush left.

Figure 52 - Hanging Indent vs. No Hanging Indent

Tabs

If you're providing an electronic file to a publisher or you're producing camera-ready copy on a computer, it's usually best to set only one tab for each indentation, rather than a combination of tabs and/or spaces.

Summary

This chapter has explored the basics of page (document), character, and paragraph formatting and defined standard production and printing terms.

Page formatting involves setting measurements for trim size and margins, and columns and column gutters, and setting recurring and mirrored elements (headers, footers, and folios).

Character formatting involves choosing type fonts, styles, sizes, and leading, and addressing capitalization and spacing concerns.

Paragraph formatting involves alignment (left, right, centered, or justified), indentation, and tabs. Rules, borders, screens, and colors are sometimes involved as well.

Now that you're familiar with some print production lingo, it's time to explore the process in more depth. Chapter 13 presents some considerations for page design, type specification, and desktop publishing. If someone else is producing your final camera-ready master, Chapter 13 will give you insight into how they will produce it. Even if you never set a single character, this knowledge will help you communicate with those who produce your final pages. If you are producing your own publications, the information in Chapter 13 will help you plan your work and become better organized.

Production Pointers

Specifying Type & Desktop Publishing

The most effective communications treat equivalent elements exactly the same—even blocks of white space. In other words, they treat each chapter title the same, each equivalent heading the same, each list the same, and so on. Consistent physical formats not only help readers grasp the message, but also simplify life tremendously!

This chapter walks you through the basics of page design and type specification. It will help you prepare manuscripts for others to produce, or help you produce your own camera-ready copy. If you already have some production experience, this chapter contains tips that can help you become better organized and efficient.

The organization of this chapter follows the organization of the reproducible Format Specifications Chart contained in the appendix. This chart serves as a "graphic organizer" for physical specifications. Figure 53 provides a sample of a completed Format Specifications Chart.

Measurement Systems

Before you record any specifications, consider what type of measurement system (or systems) you'll use. The standard measurement system that most printers and publishers use is the point/pica scale. A few other scales are based on inches, centimeters, and millimeters. To simplify matters, I'll stick with points and picas for the examples in this chapter.

If you're producing your own camera-ready copy on a computer or specifying type for someone else to set, remember that the measurement systems in word-processing and page-layout software vary from program to program. Make certain your system is compatible with that of your typesetter or printer.

Sometimes you might wish to mix measurement systems. For instance, you might use inches for trim size and margins, and points and picas for everything else. That's fine, as long as you can keep the specifications straight.

To avoid confusion when you record specifications, always abbreviate the type of measurement you're using rather than using a number alone. You can indicate inches with a standard inch mark ("), centimeters with *cm*, and millimeters with *mm*. You can abbreviate points as *pt* and picas as *pi*.

You can also abbreviate combinations of points and picas with a single *p* nestled between two numbers (2p6). Picas fall to the left of the *p* and points to the right. The abbreviation 2p6 (2 picas, 6 points) equals 2.5 picas. (Remember, 12 points equal 1 pica.)

Page/Document Format

The following Page/Document specifications appear at the top of the Format Specifications Chart.

Trim Size, Margins & Live Area

First, determine the trim size. Some factors to consider include the way the audience will use the product, the length of the material, and the budget. At what distance will the reader view it? Does it need to be portable? Does it need larger pages to reduce the overall bulk? If your budget is tight, remember that standard trim sizes reduce printing costs. Once you know the trim size, you can determine the size of the live area.

Also consider whether the image will print horizontally, vertically, or as a combination of both (see Figure 53). If some pages print sideways, which way the reader will turn the page to view it? Must the page rotate to the left or the right?

If your final pages will be bound or three-hole drilled, leave an ample margin to accommodate the binding. All too often, such decisions are mere afterthoughts. But you don't want to do all that work and then have holes punched through your words! Plan at least .25 inch extra for three-hole drilled pages.

Format Specifications Chart

Project: _Style Meister: The Quick-Reference Custom Style Guide_   Last update: _12/31/97_

Page/Document   Bleed: _ Y _X_ N   Recto start: _X_ Y _ N
Trim Size: Width _33 pi_ Length _51 pi_   Folios: _1,2,3_
Live Area: Width _26 pi_ Length _44p6_   Mirror: _header/footer_
Maximum/minimum lines per column/page: _42/3 col._ _42/3 pg._
Margins: Top _2p6_ Bottom _4 pi_ Inside _3p6_ Outside _3p6_
Columns: Number _1_ Widths _26 pi_ Gutter _X_

| | | Character | | Paragraph | | | |
	Style						
Code	Description	Pt. Size / Leading	Font / Style (Rom. / Bold / Ital. / UL / Capitalization)	Align / Indent (L R C J / B)	# above ↑ # below ↓	Tabs (L R C D B / position / leader)	Rule / Border / Screen / Color
TX	Text (main body copy)	12/15	Palatino	-------	J	-------	-------
NW	New Word	12/15	Palatino Italic	-------	-------	-------	-------
EW	Emphasized Word	12/15	Palatino Bold	-------	-------	-------	-------
CN	Chapter Number	60/72	Brush Script	2 pi ↑	R	-------	30% gray
CT	Chapter/Article Title	36/36	Brush Script	1 pi ↑	R	-------	30% gray
H1	Subheads: 1st level (A) head	16/19	Palatino Bold	1 pi ↑ p6 ↓	C	-------	-------
H2	2nd level (B) head	14/17	Palatino Bold	p6↑ p3↓	L	-------	-------
H3	3rd level (C) head	12/15	Palatino Italic	p6↑	L run-in	-------	-------
RH	Header (running head)	9/12	Palatino Italic	1p6 ↓	L/R mirror	-------	-------
RF	Footer (running foot)	9/12	Palatino run-in folio	1p3 ↓	L/R mirror	C 13pi	-------
BL	Bulleted Lists • * □ ✓	12/15	Palatino p6↑ 1st, p6↓ last	p6↑ 1p↓	1 pi L/R. FL	1p6 L. hang 2p. 1st 2p	-------
NL/ AL	Numbered / 1. 1) (1) Alpha Lists a. a) (a)	12/15	Palatino p6↑ 1st, p6↓ last	p6↑ 1p↓	L 1. a., hang 1p6	1p R. 1p6 L. para. 1p6. 1st line –1p6	-------
Art							
FT	Figure title	12/15	Palatino Bold	1p ↑ p3↓	C	-------	Box tables
TH	Table head	11/13	Helvetica Bold	p6 ↑ p3↓	C 2 pi L/R	C, 3-col. 1p3 gutters	.5 rule-box
TT	Table text	11/13	Helvetica	p3 ↓	L 2 pi L/R	L: 2p6, 9p3, 16p	inset p6

Figure 53 - Sample Format Specifications Chart

You can record either the margins or the live area first. Once you know one, you'll know the other. If you already know your margin widths, record those first. If you want the live area to be a certain size but the margins are flexible, record the live area measurements first.

The Format Specifications Chart lists the margins as Top, Bottom, Inside, and Outside rather than Top, Bottom, Left, and Right. This is because the inside margin often differs on left- and right-hand pages.

Here's a further margin-related consideration: Pages generally have a better esthetic balance when the bottom margin is slightly larger than the top.

Some publishers set a minimum and maximum number of lines per page, which may vary with different types of pages. The top of the Format Specifications Chart includes a line for recording such numbers.

Columns & Column Gutters

If you know the approximate point size of your main text, you can use that amount to determine an appropriate column width. If you don't yet know the point size of your main text, you might move on to the Character Format section and record column specifications later. Point size and column width are interrelated, so you may need to adjust one or the other more than one time.

To determine column widths without the help of a designer, try one of the following guidelines (or try all four and choose the one you like best). Experiment until you achieve a look you like.

- Multiply the standard point size by two to two and one-half.

  If you're using 10-point type, a standard line or column width would measure 20 to 25 picas (10 pt × 2 = 20 pi; 10 pt × 2.5 = 25 pi).

  If you're using 12-point type, it would measure 24 to 30 picas (12 pt × 2 = 24 pi; 12 pt × 2.5 = 30 pi).

- Measure the width of one and one-half to two alphabet's worth of characters (39–52 characters) in the fonts and point sizes you're considering (39 characters = X picas) or (52 characters = X picas). This measurement may differ from one font to another. If you'll use a variety of fonts for major blocks of text, rule out this method.

- Measure the width of 45–75 characters per line: minimum (45 characters = X picas) or maximum (75 characters = X picas). Books commonly contain 60–70 characters per line.

- Set ten words of average length per line (5 characters per word = 50 characters) when using serif type.

   Set eight to nine average-length words per line when using sans serif type.

Any of these methods, or a combination, should help you achieve an acceptable look.

Recurring & Mirrored Elements

When setting page or document formats, also consider the following questions:

- Will chapters or sections always begin on a recto page?

- What page-numbering scheme will you use?

- Will pages have recurring elements, such as headers, footers, and folios?

- Will any recurring elements print as mirror images? If so, which elements?

Many page-numbering schemes begin on a recto page, so that odd-numbered pages fall on the right and even-numbered pages fall on the left. The Format Specifications Chart contains a Recto Start line on which you can record such intentions.

Many publications are numbered consecutively with arabic numbers (1, 2, 3) from beginning to end. Sometimes pages are numbered by section with "engineering numbers," particularly in scientific or technical works. In a publication with engineering numbers, the pages in Chapter 1 are numbered 1-1, 1-2, 1-3 (or 1.1, 1.2, 1.3), and the pages in Chapter 2 are numbered 2-1, 2-2, 2-3 (or 2.1, 2.2, 2.3), and so on. Illustrations, tables, and photographs also frequently have engineering numbers.

Publishers often number *front matter* (prefaces, forewords, tables of contents, and so on) separately, with lowercase roman numerals (i, ii, iii, iv), if numbers appear at all. Some publishers use *blind folios*—page numbers they count but don't print—for some front matter pages, such as title and copyright pages.

Traditionally, blank pages are completely blank; they don't even display a folio (although some organizations print a folio alone). Publishers often insert blank pages to ensure that each chapter starts on a recto page. To keep from confusing the printer or the reader, some publishers print statements like "This page intentionally blank" or "Page X is blank" on otherwise blank pages. (Of course, this makes such statements inaccurate, since the message appears on the page, but let's not nitpick.)

Use the Folios line on the Format Specifications Chart to record your page-numbering scheme. Use the Mirror line to record which elements, if any, are mirrored.

Electronic Style Sheets

Electronic style sheets are one of the most powerful, mind-blowing features available on a computer. Don't confuse electronic style sheets with word list/style sheets, like the ones I introduced in Chapter 1. Electronic style sheets record type specifications (paragraph and character formats) or *styles* rather than words. Most word-processing and page-layout programs now incorporate electronic style sheets.

People who use computers but don't know or don't use electronic style sheets format text "locally." To format an 18-point centered Helvetica Bold head with 20 points of leading without a style sheet might require as many as five steps. You'd 1) choose Helvetica, 2) choose Bold, 3) choose 18 point, 4) choose centered alignment, and 5) choose 20-point leading. Then you'd repeat those steps for every equivalent head. Such "local" formatting is not only labor intensive, but also often causes production problems down the line.

When you use an electronic style sheet, you set up a code, which is stored on a style sheet, just one time. Then when you wish to apply the same style to subsequent heads, you can do so in only one step!

Style Codes

When you use a style sheet, you set up the character and paragraph formats you want and assign each a code or tag. Codes that are easily associated with the elements they stand for (like BL for bulleted list, NL for numbered list, BQ for blocked quote, and so on) expedite the typesetting process. Make certain that each code is short and unique. Two-character codes are fairly standard. These codes can then be entered to apply both character and paragraph formatting with a keystroke or two. The Style column in the Format Specifications Chart contains several blank lines where you can record the codes and descriptions of individual styles.

If you are preparing a document that will eventually reside on the World Wide Web, using standard HTML codes whenever possible may ease the conversion to cyberspace. For further information, search for Hypertext Markup Language on the World Wide Web.

Style Descriptions

The Description column in Figure 53 lists some generic elements often included in printed materials. You may or may not need all of these elements, and you may need additional ones. You can duplicate the form in the appendix, customize it as needed, and use it for as many projects as you wish. *The Chicago Manual of Style* has a more complete list of elements included in various publications.

Note that Figure 53 lists multiple options for introducing listed items in bulleted and numbered/alpha lists. If your documents contain lists, you'll need to determine how to introduce the items in them.

As you work with style sheets, keep one thing in mind: Too many styles can present as many problems as no styles at all. It's easy to go overboard and create more than you need. Before you record a new style, make certain you haven't used the same specifications elsewhere.

Character Format

The Character Format portion of the Format Specifications Chart contains two columns: the Point Size/Leading column and the Font/Style column.

Point Size & Leading

Choosing an appropriate point size pretty much comes down to common sense. You must consider both your audience and the final product, while remaining conscious about the way it will be used.

Materials for the very young or the very old may require a larger point size. Readers' occupations might also influence point size. Lawyers and accountants, for instance, may tolerate smaller point sizes than sales clerks and construction workers would. You can set a paperback or pamphlet in smaller type than a reference manual to be used at a desk or on an overhead transparency, a poster, or a billboard.

Type Fonts & Styles

For many people, the desktop publishing revolution that began in the 1980s unleashed an unbridled eagerness to experiment with type fonts and styles. With all the possibilities, it's easy to get carried away. But overzealous application of fonts and styles can make a page look as if it's come straight from a type font catalog. This decreases the effectiveness of any communication (except, of course, a type font catalog).

One rule of thumb is to limit type variations to no more than three per page. Many designers recommend staying within just one type family, then achieving contrasts with italics, bolding, size variations, decorative elements, and so on. Every font has its own personality.

Choose a font that will reinforce your message and produce the response you're looking for.

Annual Report

Country Western Dance

Fairy Tale Time!

Handwritten notes

Candlelight Dinner

Typewritten Message

See what I mean?

Serif vs. Sans Serif Type

The first consideration in choosing type is whether serif or sans serif will be most effective. Popular opinion holds that serif type is easier to read. But what's easier to read is what's most familiar.

U.S. audiences often find serif type easier because that's what they're used to, but European audiences may prefer sans serif type because that's the norm over there.

Beyond those conventions, Figure 54 lists some other factors to consider.

Serif	Sans Serif
• Usually perceived as traditional, authoritative, and steady.	• Usually perceived as flexible, modern, and contemporary.
• More fonts are available to choose from.	• Requires more leading to compensate for lack of horizontal blending.
• Horizontal strokes help lead the eye along, but thin, delicate serifs may not reproduce well.	
• More lines can fit per page.	

Figure 54 - Serif vs. Sans Serif

Chapter 12 describes the type styles that appear under Character Format. The following section builds upon that information.

Roman Type

Roman type is plain text with no special style attributes. It is abbreviated on the Format Specifications Chart as *Rom*. When no other style is indicated, roman type is assumed.

Bold Type

Bold is frequently used for headings, captions, introductory letters in index entries, and special terms and emphasis. However, too much bold is overwhelming, so use it with care.

Italic Type

Because italic letters are more delicate and paler than surrounding roman type, they slow the reading process. Avoid long italic passages, and try using them primarily for subtle contrast. When the copy has many titles or other traditionally italicized elements, try to avoid italics for subheads and the like.

In addition to the applications outlined in Chapter 12, italics are often used for *jump lines* in publications (e.g., *continued on page 2*). They may also be used for cross-references in index lists (e.g., *see also*, oblique).

Underlining

Avoid underlining in camera-ready copy. Bold, italics, all caps, small caps, and quotation marks look more professional.

Capitalization

Be cautious about the use of caps. Excessive caps not only obscure a message, but they hog up lots of space. Words set in all caps take up as much as one and one-third the room that words in the same point size set primarily as lowercase letters take. Chapter 12 lists a number of appropriate uses for all caps and small caps. When small caps aren't available, some people set all caps at a lower point size. This may serve the purpose for many communications, but it is less desirable than true small caps. The slightly lighter strokes of a smaller point size may look too pale when compared to surrounding type.

Now let's explore the elements of paragraph formats.

Paragraph Format

Paragraph formatting includes alignment, space above and below, indentation, and tabs. Paragraph formatting may include rules, borders, screens, and colors as well.

Alignment

The first Paragraph format column in the Format Specifications Chart provides space for recording both alignment and indentation of various elements.

The alignment choices include L (left), R (right), C (centered), J (justified), and B (bottom). Each choice has its own advantages.

Left-aligned or *ragged-right* type conforms more naturally to the letter-groups our eyes are used to reading than other alignment styles. However, without hyphenation, ragged-right type can produce a very jagged look when set in narrow columns. Because wavy left-hand margins are much more difficult to follow, try to

Style Meister: The Quick-Reference Custom Style Guide

limit your use of right-aligned or *ragged-left* type to very short bits of information. You might, for instance, use ragged-left type for photo captions or to "run around" a piece of art.

You should generally limit centered type to display elements and copy produced for very formal occasions. While *justification* (aligning margins at both the left and right) produces a more formal look, it sometimes leaves awkward spaces between words or *rivers* (distracting lines of white space) flowing through a block of text. This problem is particularly pronounced in narrow columns.

One last consideration is whether columns and pages will "bottom align." Bottom alignment occurs when the last line in each column or on each page rests on the lowest point of the live area. You can bottom align text by adding extra leading above subheads and other elements where the extra space will be less noticeable.

Space Above & Below

Chapter 12's Character Format section states that the standard amount of leading between lines in most printed materials is usually two points more than the point size.

Sometimes, you'll want more or less leading above or below certain elements to tie them closer together or to set them apart from other elements on the page. Use the "# above ↑ /# below ↓" (Space Above/Below) column on the Format Specifications Chart to record such measurements.

You can measure leading either from the top of an element or from its baseline. Just make certain you stick to one method or the other. The *baseline* of a block of text refers to the imaginary line upon which characters sit, excluding their *descenders* or "tails." The baseline of a piece of art is the bottom of the art.

It's often hard to measure from the top of one text block to another because the lowercase ascenders may be uneven. It's usually easier to measure leading from baseline to baseline—from the baseline of the top block of text to the baseline of the text below it.

However, if the second element is a piece of art or a decorative element, it's easier to measure from the baseline of the first element to the top of the art that follows. See Figure 55.

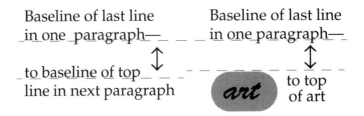

Figure 55 - Measuring Between Text & Art

Indentation

Some elements span the entire width of the live area. Others may indent from one or both sides. All lines of a paragraph may indent an equal amount, or the first line may have a hanging indent.

To create a hanging indent, consider how much space the hanging characters will consume and how much white space you want between them and the rest of the text. If setting a numbered list, you may need to "hang for ten." This means if the list contains a two-digit number, you'll set the indent for the bulk of the text far enough away from the margin to accommodate both digits.

Remember to consider the width of each number and the character format. An eight, for instance, is wider than a one, and bold text consumes more space than roman. Once you've determined how much room the hanging characters and the space after them require, set the paragraph indent. Then, for the first line only, subtract that amount. Figure 56 illustrates one typical paragraph format for a hanging indent.

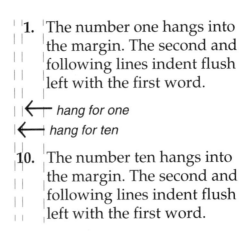

Figure 56 - Format for a Hanging Indent

Tabs

The third Paragraph format column in the Format Specifications Chart provides space for recording tabs. Standard tab choices include left-aligned, right-aligned, centered, decimal, and bar (vertical line) tabs. You can also specify *leaders*—characters that precede the tab, like a series of dots between a table-of-contents entry and its corresponding page number (Chapter 1 . . . . . . 1).

The Tabs column provides space for recording tab positions, alignments, and leaders.

Special Effects

One last consideration in paragraph formatting is whether you wish to add special effects: rules, borders, screens, color, or other decorative elements. You can handle these items either electronically (on a computer or a typesetting system) or mechanically (through pasteup or hand-drawn work). You can make special effects notations in the far-right column of the Format Specifications Chart.

Don't get discouraged if you can't come up with perfect specifications on your first try. Type tends to take a bit of "tweaking" to create just the right look. Like many other creative processes, page design is an evolutionary art. That's why I've included the Last Update line at the top of the chart.

Record the date each time you refine a specification, and make certain to keep all the players on your publication team informed. It also helps to provide coded sample pages to illustrate each specification. The process will get easier as you build on your experience.

Summary

This chapter explained each step of type specification, in relation to the Format Specifications Chart on page 245. The chapter covered page (document), character, and paragraph formats and offered tips and examples to help you choose what's most appropriate for your situation.

In addition, this chapter has introduced the concept of electronic style sheets, which are available in many word-processing and page-layout programs.

While Chapters 12 and 13 provide an introduction to physical formatting and design, these issues can get much more involved, particularly when computer setups differ. For further information, explore the Design & Production resources in the annotated bibliography.

Put That Computer to Work!

Automating Style Preferences

By now, you may be wondering how a computer might help you tackle style (unless you're one of those holdouts who abhors technology). If you're deeply attached to your typewriter, or if you have a computer but haven't fully mastered its capabilities, you have plenty of company. Many people experience at least a little "technophobia."

In this chapter, I'd like to gently nudge you toward technology or expand your grasp of what computers can do. Many people use computers as mere glorified typewriters, but that's akin to driving a jet cross-country without ever leaving the ground! Yes, computers are sometimes complex and frustrating. But if you have a bit of patience, they can greatly simplify your work.

How Computers Help with Style-Related Issues

Let us first clarify some terminology. The computers I'm talking about are personal or professional computers (PCs)—both names for microcomputers—rather than mainframes or larger versions. When people use the term *PC* they're usually talking about an IBM-compatible microcomputer as opposed to a Mac (Macintosh) microcomputer produced by Apple Computer, Inc.

A computer can help you deal with style in three ways:

1. By automating tedious but necessary tasks,

2. By changing the physical format of text, allowing you to do your own typesetting, and

3. By providing ways to organize and record style decisions.

Some of the features that help you record and organize text on a computer mimic those of a typewriter. Others go way beyond them. This chapter overviews some advantages—and limitations—of computers, concentrating on style-related features. Because computer hardware (machines) and software (the "brains" that run those machines) vary greatly, you may not have every feature I mention. If you're like most people, though, your computer probably has many more capabilities than you imagine—time-saving features you need only explore. I've used the most generic names I could think of for these features. Your software owner's manual may use other names, but the terms in this chapter should at least point you in the right direction.

Basic Word-Processing Features

Most people making the transition from typewriter to computer quickly become aware of three basic word-processing features. These are word wrap, automatic hyphenation, and commands that help you easily copy, insert, delete, and move text.

Word Wrap. Here's something many new computer users notice right away: Computers, unlike typewriters, don't make you press RETURN to move to the next line. When you reach the character limit for one line, the cursor (the insertion symbol) moves to the next line automatically. This feature is called *word wrap*. On a computer, you press RETURN only when you're ready to move on to a new paragraph or when you wish to force a line to end at a certain point. If you're making the transition from typewriter to computer, you'll therefore need to make this adjustment.

Automatic Hyphenation. Just as with automatic line endings, computers can provide automatic hyphenation. However, the hyphens may not always fall precisely where you desire. For that reason, some people simply turn off the automatic hyphenation option. See your software owner's manual to learn how.

When a hyphen doesn't fall where you wish it to, you can enter a regular *hard hyphen* where you want the line to break, regardless of its width, or an optional *soft hyphen* character that tells your computer the most acceptable places to break the word, if need be. When you enter a hard hyphen, the computer prints it like any other character. A soft hyphen, on the other hand, prints only when it falls within a word that breaks at the end of a line.

Soft hyphens are often preferable to hard hyphens because edits may cause line endings to change, forcing you to remove unwanted hard hyphens from words in mid-line. Don't worry about inserting soft hyphens at every point where a word might break, however. It's best to wait and deal with hyphenation when you're polishing your final draft. See your software owner's manual to learn how to insert soft or optional hyphens.

Copying, Inserting, Deleting & Moving Text. One of the greatest advantages of a computer is the ease with which you can copy, insert, delete, and move text. This makes revision considerably easier. Remember having to retype an entire page from scratch or backspace to erase every character that followed one lousy mistake? With a computer, you can complete these tasks with ease.

Most software programs let you manipulate text by selecting a command from a *menu* (a list of options or "commands" that displays on a computer screen) or by pressing a special key or key combination. If you make an error, UNDO, UNDELETE, and REVERT commands can often help you retrieve previous work.

Entering, Editing & Manipulating Text

This section discusses some additional features that help you enter, edit, and manipulate text:

- windows
- outlining
- tables

Windows. Cutting, pasting, and moving text becomes easier still with a feature called *windows*. A windows feature lets you split the image on your computer screen into two or more parts (horizontally or vertically) so you can view two or more images simultaneously. These images might be two or more parts of the same document, two or more documents created with the same software program, or two or more documents created with different programs.

Let me clarify that I'm using the term *windows* generically rather than referring to Microsoft's Windows software per se. Windows capabilities are built into Macintosh computers and can be added to PCs.

With a couple of open windows, you can move chunks of text from one file to another with ease. Some programs (for example, Microsoft Word) let you split a single file into two or more windows so you can view different portions of it at the same time.

I find windows particularly useful when I'm composing on my computer screen. For instance, I can split an article into three windows and view the introduction in one window, the main body in the second, and the reference list in the third. That sure beats "scrolling" up and down a computer screen or shuffling through endless piles of paper!

Outlining. Another useful feature is outlining. This lets you "collapse" a manuscript to an outline view or "expand" an outline with a press of a key so you can view the entire manuscript. The lines of your outline can become headings in your manuscript, or the headings in your manuscript can become the outline itself. Figure 57 illustrates document versus outline view.

document view   *outline view*

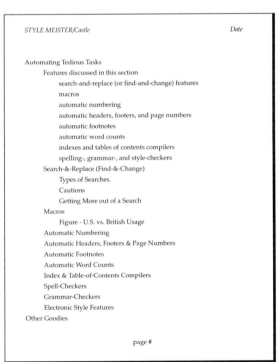

Figure 57 - Document vs. Outline View

For each block of text, you indicate the corresponding outline level, often with one keystroke. If you need to reorganize an outline, you can *promote* (indent) or *demote* (outdent) portions of the outline with just one keystroke or key combination. For example, in WordPerfect for DOS, you press TAB to promote text to the next level and TAB + SHIFT to demote it.

Some programs let you move whole chunks of an outline from one place to another while retaining your numbering sequence. Many word-processing programs have built-in outlining capabilities. If your program doesn't, stand-alone outlining software that can be used with most word-processing software is readily available. See your software owner's manual to learn how.

Tables. Many word-processing packages include a command that allows you to create tables without setting a single tab. Computer tables consist of horizontal rows and vertical columns of boxes called *cells*.

With a table command, you type text into columns that you can widen, narrow, or rearrange with ease. Many programs let you add borders and shading to individual table cells. The cells "stretch" or "shrink" vertically on the screen as you enter or delete text.

Figure 58 illustrates how a table looks on a computer screen.

Column Head	Column Head
This block of text is called a *cell*.	This block of text is called a *cell*.
All of the cells stacked on the left make up a *column*.	All of the cells stacked on the right make up a *column*.
Two or more cells set side by side make up a *row*.	Two or more cells set side by side make up a *row*.

Figure 58 - Sample Table Format

You can also convert plain text to a table or convert a table back to text with a keystroke or two.

A table's cell boundaries show up on the computer screen (usually as dotted lines), but they do not print on paper unless you apply borders to the cells.

Now let's see how a computer can automate otherwise tedious tasks.

Automating Tedious Tasks

The features discussed in this section represent some really big time-savers:

- search-and-replace (or find-and-change) features
- macros
- automatic numbering
- automatic headers, footers, and page numbers
- automatic footnotes
- automatic word counts
- indexes and tables of contents compilers
- spelling-, grammar- and style-checkers

Search-&-Replace (Find-&-Change). Used correctly, this feature takes much agony out of editing. A search-and-replace feature helps you locate words you wish to change without reading through the entire manuscript. For instance, if you wish to change a character's name from *Sam Smith* to *Samantha Sparks*, the computer can locate every occurrence of *Sam Smith* and change it to *Samantha Sparks* automatically.

Types of Searches. There are two types of searches. One type is the *global search*, in which the computer locates every occurrence of the *search string* you specify (in this case, Sam Smith) and substitutes a *replacement string* (Samantha Sparks) throughout the manuscript. A search string—the string of characters you are searching for—can be a group of words, a single word, a part of a word, or even a single character. Note that your computer sees spaces the same as it sees other characters; therefore, type a space before or after your search string only when it's a necessary part of what you need to find and replace.

A second type of search locates the search string you specify and asks you to approve each change before actually making it. This is a safer, but much slower, process.

Cautions. A global search-and-replace presents potential dangers. It's not something you can approach on automatic pilot. If you don't think through a search carefully and remember that the computer searches only for the exact text you type—including spaces—you can change text inadvertently. For instance, if in the attempt to "de-genderize" your copy, you request that all occurrences of *man* be changed to *person* and you do not ask the computer to search only for the whole word, you could easily change *human* to *huperson*, thereby producing ridiculous results, such as "This is a great day for the *huperson* race!" If your word-processing program doesn't have an option for searching for a complete word, you can type the word with one space before and/or after the word to produce the same result.

You must also be cautious with differences in upper- and lower-case. If you capitalize all or part of your search string, some word-processing programs will find only those words that match exactly. Likewise, capitalize only those parts of the replacement string that you wish to make uppercase. Some programs search for words regardless of case, and when they change a word, the replacement matches the case of the word it's replacing. Check your software manual for details on your program's search-and-replace feature.

Searches that involve lengthy search strings are far from fool-proof. Some programs can locate a search string only when all characters in the string appear on the same line. For this reason, it's best to keep search strings short.

Getting More out of a Search. Many programs let you search from either top to bottom or bottom to top, in relation to the cursor position. They sometimes let you search for a particular character style or format or for less visible entities, such as extra spaces, tabs, and paragraph returns.

A search-and-replace feature can help you locate and change numbers, misspellings, and incorrect words. This feature also comes in handy when you edit capitalization, hyphenation, tabs, and special characters (like bullets and spaces).

You can also use a search-and-replace feature when applying or editing styles or special formats. You can, for instance, search for repeated headings like *Abstract, Bibliography,* or *Summary* by typing the head, followed by a paragraph mark (^p in many programs). Then you can apply the appropriate style.

You can use a "bookmark" character or a character combination to mark a place you want to revise later. (I often use double asterisks: **). Then, when you're ready to revise that segment, simply search for the bookmark character.

Macros. Macros are sets of keystrokes or command sequences that you can activate with a single key or key combination. Macros can save a tremendous amount of effort where standard repetitive actions are required. For instance, a macro might let you insert a return address or a signature block in a letter, set up mailing labels, change a font, convert all caps to lowercase (or vice versa), print a file, or prepare a fax with a single keystroke.

Some word-processing programs come with a built-in macro feature. If yours doesn't, stand-alone macro programs (such as QuicKeys, PC Tools, or Norton Desktop's ScriptMaker) are readily available. Many software programs (for instance, WordPerfect) also let you customize special keys or key combinations for running macros. If you need to make the same series of changes to each chapter of a book, you can record a macro when editing one chapter and then apply that macro to each chapter that follows.

One use of a search-and-replace macro might be to change a series of "Americanized" words to their British equivalents. Figure 59 provides an example (with the U.S. usage on the left and the British usage on the right).

Search for	Replace with
organization	organisation
program	programme
labor	labour
maximize	maximise
elevator	lift
traveler	traveller

Figure 59 - U.S. vs. British Usage

For this search, you'd create a macro that searches the file for each word on the left and replaces it with the corresponding word on the right. Then you'd run the macro for every file you wish to "Britainize." The annotated bibliography cites several sources that address British usage.

I'd like to add a caution about macros: A single error in a macro has the potential for tremendous havoc! Always test a macro thoroughly on a backup copy of a file before you run it on the real thing.

Automatic Numbering. Have you ever typed a numbered list, and later inserted another point, which meant you had to retype the entire list? Not only does a computer make such insertions a breeze, but many programs will renumber the entire list for you.

It's usually as simple as selecting the list and then choosing a numbering command.

Automatic Headers, Footers & Page Numbers. With a computer, you can type the text of headers, footers, and page numbers just once and the computer will place them on each page automatically. Remember, a header is a line or block of information that repeats at the top of each page; a footer repeats at the bottom.

Some programs even allow different headers and footers for various sections, or for odd pages versus even. Some allow the first page of a section to have a different header or footer, or even none at all. Note that some word-processing programs center all page numbers at the top or the bottom of the page and allow no other options.

A less obvious use of a header or footer is its application as a "typesetter's slug." A *slug* includes information that helps identify a file, such as company, department, or customer name; typesetter or operator name; version or proof number; and file name. When you're working with multiple computer files, it's sometimes difficult to recall their exact names.

A slug can help you locate a file more quickly. Some programs update the date automatically each time you alter the file. They may even track the time. This can be important in fast-paced environments where several versions of the same file are produced in one day.

Automatic Footnotes. If you do scholarly work, be sure to check your options for footnote placement (bottom of page or end of section) and any limitations on footnote length. For instance, you may want to find out if the software allows different line spacing for footnotes versus text. Likewise, check whether the software will renumber all footnotes automatically when you make additions or deletions.

Automatic Word Counts. Many word-processing programs can produce automatic character, word, line, and paragraph counts for a selected block of text. Although these counts may not match those obtained with other methods exactly, they usually come pretty close.

Index & Table-of-Contents Compilers. Although you must still determine the content for indexes and tables of contents, your computer can do the drudge work. No more tedious renumbering if a last-minute edit causes page numbers to change! Most index and table-of-contents features in word-processing and page-layout programs rely on hidden codes embedded within regular text. With these features, you first decide what needs to appear in the index or table-of-contents, then you mark that information with a hidden code, like .i. for index or .c. for table of contents. You enter these codes by choosing a special command or pressing a key combination. (See your software manual for information about these commands and codes.) The program then compiles the information and records the page number where each entry appears. Slick, huh?

Speaking of hidden text, some people use this feature extensively to write notes to themselves or to their coworkers. For instance, when you're writing, you might list synonyms in hidden text until the right word strikes you. Or, when you're editing, you might mark a manuscript with notes like "recast to present tense," "rewrite for parallel structure," or "change to bulleted list." Notes written with hidden text do not appear in the printed version, and can be embedded almost anywhere within a document.

Spell-Checkers. Let me begin by saying always spell-check your work—even when it means multiple times in multiple drafts. But never rely on a spell-check alone.

Most spelling programs catch repeated words and even minor glitches in capitalization and punctuation. If you misspell a word you've used throughout a manuscript, most spelling programs can change every occurrence once you've typed in a single correction. Spell-checkers are available for different languages and for different professional needs, such as legal or medical words. Many programs let you build customized dictionaries for spell-checking individual projects.

Spell-checkers are a great invention, but they're far from flawless. Don't let them lull you into a false sense of security! Because computer memories have only so much space, computer programs have limitations. Some spell-checkers, for instance, will question the plural forms of words they recognize readily in singular. Few spell-checkers will notice if you omit a word or use the wrong word accidentally. For instance, they won't catch simple transpositions such as *form* for *from.* Despite those science fiction plots, computers can't read your mind—yet! They haven't a clue about context. Spell-checkers even let you add misspelled words to their dictionaries! So you must be very careful.

Overlooking a computer's limitations can lead to disaster. One of the worst situations I've run across was a "tiny" typo in a newsletter. A line in a paid advertisement should have read "*Rate* provided by [advertiser's name]," but it ran as "*Rape* provided by [advertiser's name]." Both words were spelled right; the spell-checker did its job just fine, but what a difference that one character made!

Grammar-Checkers. Grammar-checkers often include spell-checking programs. Several grammar-checkers are available for the Macintosh and for IBM compatibles (running either Windows or DOS). Grammatik, PowerEdit, RightWriter, Sensible Grammar, CorrecText, and Correct Grammar are the best known.

Most are available as stand-alone software; some come with word-processing programs, like Ami Pro, Display Write, Lotus WordPro, MacWrite, Microsoft Word, WinWord, WordPerfect, and WriteNow.

Although they are improving, grammar-checkers tend to run slowly; require massive amounts of memory; flag problems without suggesting how to fix them; and make numerous incorrect, repetitive, unusable suggestions. Some even limit the number of errors they will flag.

Grammar-checkers do provide some insight, but only if you're patient and know which suggestions to ignore. You cannot assume that the grammar-checker knows better than you do. If you follow every bit of advice it supplies, you're almost certain to produce some glaring errors.

Electronic Style Features. Some grammar-checkers allow you to customize styles to better meet your preferences. You may, for instance, choose among academic, business, fiction, informal, legal, and technical styles, and activate or deactivate individual grammar rules.

Other Goodies

Many other useful software programs and utilities can extend your computer's abilities—dictionaries and thesauruses; glossaries, libraries, and scrapbooks (temporary "homes" for text and graphics); and database programs for compiling reference lists and creating personalized form letters and such. Such programs and utilities may come with your word-processing or page-layout software, or are available as add-on packages.

Changing the Look of Text

The formatting features discussed in this section include alignment, tabs, spacing, fancy character formatting, and electronic style sheets for type specifications.

Alignment

Word-processing programs help you align paragraphs and columns. Some also let you manipulate art and decorative elements. Some software programs let you place rules above or below a paragraph or even let you box it in. With the help of a computer, hanging indents become a cinch.

Tabs

One of the most significant differences between typewriters and computers is the way they handle tabs. On a typewriter, people often use a combination of tabs and/or spaces to create columns or indent text. This method often results in wavy columns. With a computer, you can set tabs (or absolute tabs) precisely where you want them and align text at the left, right, or center, or on a decimal point.

Spacing

Computers offer tremendous flexibility for line spacing (or leading). You're not limited to just 1, $1\,^1/_2$, or 2 line spaces between paragraphs, as you are on a typewriter. A computer lets you add or subtract an exact amount of space above or below each line. Rather than type multiple paragraph returns to get more separation, just press RETURN once and specify a measurement.

Fancy Character Formatting

Have you ever had to space backwards on a typewriter to underline characters or type over them repeatedly to make the letters bold? Those days are over when you work on a computer. Simply highlight the text and select bold for the style. See Chapters 12 and 13 for more about character formats.

A computer lets you specify the look of an entire block of text all at once, whether that block consists of a single paragraph or is several pages long. Just highlight the text you wish to alter, enter a command, and presto—you're done! Likewise, superscript and subscript characters require no tedious platen manipulations to get just the right position. And special key combinations can generate accent and diacritical marks like these: é, ç, ô, è, ü, ñ, and so on.

Electronic Style Sheets

Many computerized word-processing, typesetting, and page-layout programs include electronic style sheets for formatting documents. (Some programs call style sheets "libraries" or "glossaries.") Alignment, spacing, and character formatting can all be recorded on these style sheets.

When you use an electronic style sheet, you highlight a block of text and type in a format code instead of entering every specification for every element on the page. The computer applies both the paragraph and character formatting to all coded text elements in one step and changes their appearance automatically. Electronic style sheets provide tremendous flexibility for changing a design. With a typewriter, a design change means retyping everything.

Fine-Tuning Type

Page-layout software (like PageMaker and QuarkXPress) provides a level of control that once was available only to typesetters. For instance, you can track and kern to improve the overall look of your text. *Tracking* adjusts the spacing throughout the range of characters or words you specify (by highlighting them). *Kerning* adjusts the spacing between adjacent letter pairs. Figures 60 and 61 illustrate tracking and kerning.

Tracking adjusts space within a block of text.
(Tight tracking)

Tracking adjusts space within a block of text.
(Normal—no tracking)

Tracking adjusts space within a block of text.
(Loose tracking)

Figure 60 - Tracking

AV PA TA VA   AV PA TA VA

Ta Te To Tu Ty   Ta Te To Tu Ty

(Unkerned type)   *(Kerned type)*

Figure 61 - Kerning

Producing Polished Output

Desktop-publishing technology has made it increasingly difficult to distinguish computer-printed text from typeset copy. The tips in this section apply to the production of camera-ready materials rather than manuscripts you submit to publishers.

To produce professional-looking camera-ready copy, follow traditional typesetting standards:

- Don't set hard hyphens at the ends of lines. If subsequent edits change line breaks, you'll have to remove those hyphens individually.

- Use real zeroes (0) in place of capital *O*'s and real ones (1) in place of lowercase *l*'s.

- Use real bullets (•) in place of asterisks or lowercase *o*'s. You can usually produce a bullet character by pressing a key combination such as OPTION + 8 on a Mac, or by pressing a function key or key combination on a PC.

- When a normally italicized element appears in a block of italic text, set that element as roman to make it stand out.

- Use just one space between sentences instead of two. I know this probably goes against what your typing teacher taught you; nevertheless, in computer-printed or typeset copy, one space works better than two.

  Here's why: Each character on a typewriter consumes the same amount of space. To obtain adequate visual separation between sentences, you must therefore use two spaces. In contrast, the characters on a computer are proportional. Therefore, each letter consumes only the amount of space it requires.

  Figure 62 illustrates the difference between monospaced (typewritten) and proportional (typeset) type.

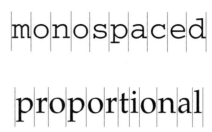

Figure 62 - Monospaced vs. Proportional Type

If you find it impossible to stop typing two spaces after ending a sentence, you can always search the entire document for two consecutive spaces and replace them with one just before you print it.

• Use em dashes—long dashes like these—in place of double or triple hyphens.

A common key combination used to produce an em dash is SHIFT + OPTION + - (hyphen).

• Use en dashes (dashes half as wide as em dashes) when you want a dash longer than a hyphen but shorter than an em dash. Publishers often use en dashes between ranges of dates or page numbers.

A common key combination used to produce an en dash is OPTION + - (hyphen).

• Use smart quotes (curly or slanted quotation marks) and apostrophes in place of vertical ones (" " not " "). Most word-processing and page-layout programs have an option for turning smart quotes on and off. (This option usually changes apostrophes at the same time.) See your software manual.

Like bullets, smart quotes are usually produced with key combinations such as OPTION + [and OPTION +] for double quotation marks, and SHIFT + OPTION + [and SHIFT + OPTION +] for apostrophes and single quotation marks.

Check both your hardware and software manuals for the specific combinations required to produce the preceding characters. Often these combinations are part of "universal key sets," meaning they will work with most any software program that is compatible with your computer.

If you need to use characters that aren't documented (as is often the case), contact the software manufacturer.

Some Limitations of Computers & Software

As wonderful as they are, computers are not foolproof; they're only tools. *You're* the one who must make those tough decisions. And you must work around computers' limitations.

Before revising anything on a computer, make a backup copy of your file. Save regularly and often: every 10–15 minutes if the job is complex or if you're on a "roll." Besides the possibility of human error, you may face technical problems from time to time. A power surge, a quick trip over a cord, or lack of room on your disk can make you lose hours and hours of work. So always, always, *always* back up your work!

Summary

This chapter has presented a number of style-related tips to help you get more out of a computer. It has discussed ways to enter, edit, and manipulate text; to automate tedious tasks; and to change the look of text.

We've looked at features that affect the way you enter, edit, and manipulate text, including word wrap, automatic hyphenation; copying/inserting/deleting/moving text; entering text in windows, outlines, and tables; and searching and replacing text.

We've also examined features that help you automate tedious tasks: automatic numbering; automatic headers, footers, and page numbers; automatic footnotes; automatic word counts; automatic index and table-of-contents compilers; and macros.

Finally, we've explored features that affect the look of text: alignment, tabs, spacing, and fancy character formatting.

This chapter has also discussed some of the limitations of computers and computer software.

This is the last "chapter." The appendix, annotated bibliography, glossary, and index follow. I hope you'll find this book indispensable as you create your own custom style guides!

Appendix

Customizing Tools

*S*ometimes, it's easier to edit on hard copy (paper), even if you make actual changes electronically. This appendix therefore provides several reproducible forms for your own use:

- the Format Specifications Chart
- the Search-and-Replace Form
- the Word List/Style Sheet

Furthermore, this appendix includes several pages for recording additional punctuation guidelines.

Chapter 12 introduces the Format Specifications Chart, and Chapter 13 discusses it in depth. Chapter 1 introduces the Search-and-Replace Form, and Chapter 14 explains it in depth. And, Chapter 1 addresses the Word List/Style Sheet form in depth.

Reproducing the Forms

While Castle Communications owns the copyright to these forms, you may make as many copies as you wish for your personal use. This does *not* include selling them to others, which is illegal.

If you do make copies, each reproduction must display this book's title. If you adapt the forms to another format, please include this credit line: "Adapted from *Style Meister: The Quick-Reference Custom Style Guide.*"

Format Specifications Chart   Project: _____   Last update: _____

Page/Document	Bleed: __ Y __ N	Maximum/minimum lines per column/page: _____	Recto start: __ Y __ N
Trim Size: Width ___ Length ___	Margins: Top ___ Bottom ___	Inside ___ Outside ___	Folios: ___
Live Area: Width ___ Length ___	Columns: Number ___	Widths ___ Gutter ___	Mirror: ___

		Character		Paragraph			
Style							
Code	Description	Pt. Size / Leading	Font / Style (Rom./Bold/Ital./UL/Capitalization)	Align / Indent (L R C J / B)	# above ↑ # below ↓	Tabs (L R C D B / position / leader)	Rule / Border / Screen / Color
	Text (main body copy)						
	New Word						
	Emphasized Word						
	Chapter Number						
	Chapter/Article Title						
	Subheads: 1st level (A) head						
	2nd level (B) head						
	3rd level (C) head						
	Header (running head)						
	Footer (running foot)						
	Bulleted Lists: • * ☐ ✓						
	Numbered / 1. 1) (1) Alpha Lists a. a) (a)						
Art							

Punctuation

JOB	Mark	Example	✔
	, *apostrophe*		—
	, *apostrophe*		—
	[ ] *brackets*		—
	[ ] *brackets*		—
	: *colon*		—
	: *colon*		—
	: *colon*		—

JOB	Mark	Example	✔
	, *comma*		—
	, *comma*		—
	, *comma*		—
	, *comma*		—
	, *comma*		—
	" " *double quotation marks*		—
	" " *double quotation marks*		—

JOB	Mark	Example	✔
	• • • *or* ● ● ● *ellipsis*		— —
	▬ *em dash* *(double dashes)*		—
	▬ *em dash* *(double dashes)*		—
	▬ *en dash* *(1/2 em dash)*		—
	▬ *en dash* *(1/2 em dash)*		—
	! *exclamation* *point*		—
	! *exclamation* *point*		—

JOB	Mark	Example	✔
	- *hyphen*		—
	- *hyphen*		—
	- *hyphen*		—
	- *hyphen*		—
	- *hyphen*		—
	( ) *parentheses*		—
	( ) *parentheses*		—

JOB	Mark	Example	✔
	• *period*		—
	• *period*		—
	? *question mark*		—
	; *semicolon*		—
	; *semicolon*		—
	' ' *single quotation marks*		—
	/ *slash*		—

Search-and-Replace Form

Project: _____   **Last Update:** _____

Search for	**Replace with**	✔

Word List/Style Sheet

Project: _____   **Last Update:** _____

A-B-C-D	*p.s.	pg.	Abbreviations Acronyms & Initialisms	*p.s.	pg.
E-F-G-H	*p.s.	pg.			
I-J-K-L	*p.s.	pg.	**Capitalization Style** __ Up __ Down **Contractions OK?** __ Yes __ No **Footnote Scheme**		

*p.s. = part of speech: m = modifier [adjective, adverb], n = noun, v = verb

Word List/Style Sheet

Project: _____   **Last Update:** _____

__M-N-O-P__	*p.s.	pg.	__Numbers__	*p.s.	pg.
			Spell most numbers below ___ 10 ___ 20 ___ 100		
__Q-R-S-T__	*p.s.	pg.	__Punctuation__		
			Basic scheme: ___ Closed ___ Open Serial commas? ___ Yes ___ No Space between initials? ___ Yes ___ No		
__U-V-W-X-Y-Z__	*p.s.	pg.	__Reference Style__		
			Alphabetize by: ___ date ___ letter ___ word		

*p.s. = part of speech: m = modifier [adjective, adverb], n = noun, v = verb

Annotated Bibliography

*T*his bibliography represents both some sources I recommend and those I used (or whose predecessors I used) to write this book. An asterisk precedes those titles I turned to repeatedly. Some of these sources are currently out of stock or out of print; however, you can usually obtain them through interlibrary loan or a book search service. For your convenience, I've grouped sources into the following alphabetical categories:

- "Bibles" of publication style—recognized and widely cited authorities

- British usage

- Design and production

- Editing guides

- Grammar guides

- Nonbiased language

- Writing guides

Where possible, I've indicated which books may be out of print, out of stock, or difficult to find as of the date this book went to print. This status can, of course, change at any time.

The "Bibles" of Publication Style

*American Psychological Association. *Publication Manual of the American Psychological Association* (APA) (4th ed.). Washington, DC: American Psychological Association, 1994. [POPULAR STANDARD FOR PROFESSIONAL JOURNALS]

*Copperud, Roy H. *American Usage and Style: The Consensus.* New York: Van Nostrand Reinhold, 1982. [ONE OF THE FEW STYLE GUIDES TO ADDRESS CONFLICTING USAGE; BASED ON RESPONSES OF AN EXPERT PANEL TO STYLE QUESTIONS; CURRENTLY OUT OF STOCK]

*Gibaldi, Joseph. The *MLA Handbook for Writers of Research Papers* (MLA) (4th ed.). New York: The Modern Language Association of America, 1995.

*Goldstein, Norm (Ed.). *The Associated Press Stylebook and Libel Manual* (AP) (6th ed.). Reading, MA: Addison-Wesley, 1996. [WIDELY USED STANDARD FOR NEWSPAPERS & CONSUMER MAGAZINES; REVISED & UPDATED 1998 EDITION AVAILABLE FROM PERSEUS PRESS]

Hale, Constance (Ed.). *Wired Style: Principles of English Usage in the Digital Age.* San Francisco: HardWired, 1997. [FOR TECHNICAL DOCUMENTATION; POPULAR STANDARD FOR ONLINE COMMUNICATION]

Microsoft Corporation. *The Microsoft Manual of Style for Technical Publications.* Redmond, WA: Microsoft Press, 1998. [POPULAR STANDARD FOR TECHNICAL DOCUMENTATION]

*Morris, William, & Morris, Mary. *Harper Dictionary of Contemporary Usage.* New York: HarperCollins, 1992. [SIMILAR TO COPPERUD; BASED ON RESPONSES OF AN EXPERT PANEL TO STYLE QUESTIONS; CURRENTLY OUT OF PRINT]

*Reader's Digest Association. *Success with Words: A Guide to the American Language.* Pleasantville, NY: The Reader's Digest Association, 1983. [NEARLY AS INDEPTH AS *CHICAGO*, BUT MORE READABLE FOR LAY AUDIENCE; INCLUDES SECTIONS ON BRITISH USAGE & DIALECTS OF ENGLISH, AS WELL AS OTHER LANGUAGES; CURRENTLY OUT OF PRINT]

Strunk, William, Jr., & White, E.B. *The Elements of Style* (3rd ed.). Boston: Allyn & Bacon, 1995. [WELL-KNOWN AUTHORITATIVE GUIDE; THIN, READABLE, BUT VERY PRESCRIPTIVE]

*Sutcliffe, Andrea J. (Ed.). *The New York Public Library Writer's Guide to Style and Usage.* New York: HarperCollins, 1994. [SIMILAR TO *CHICAGO*, BUT MORE READABLE FOR LAY AUDIENCES]

**United Press International (UPI) Stylebook: The Authoritative Handbook for Writers, Editors & News Directors.* (3rd ed.). Lincolnwood, IL: National Textbook Company, NTC Publishing Group, 1993. [A WIDELY USED STANDARD FOR NEWSPAPERS, CONSUMER MAGAZINES & BROADCAST MEDIA]

*U.S. Government Printing Office. *A Manual of Style* (GPO). Washington, DC: U.S. Government Printing Office, 1984. [AUTHORITATIVE GUIDE FOR GOVERNMENT PUBLICATIONS]

*University of Chicago Press. *The Chicago Manual of Style: The Essential Guide for Writers, Editors, and Publishers* (Chicago) (14th ed.). Chicago: The University of Chicago Press, 1993. [WELL-KNOWN, AUTHORITATIVE BOOK-PUBLISHING GUIDE]

*Warren, Thomas L. *Words Into Type* (WIT) (4th ed.). Englewood Cliffs, NJ: Prentice-Hall, 1992. [WELL-KNOWN, AUTHORITATIVE BOOK-PUBLISHING GUIDE]

British Usage

*Burchfield, R.W. *The New Fowler's Modern English Usage* (3rd ed.). Oxford: Clarendon Press, 1996.

*Butcher, Judith M. *Copy-Editing: The Cambridge Handbook for Authors, Editors & Indexers.* (3rd ed.). Cambridge, England: Cambridge University Press, 1992.

*Butler, Penny (Ed.). *The Economist Style Guide: The Essentials of Elegant Writing.* Reading, MA: Addison-Wesley, 1992. [CURRENTLY OUT OF STOCK; 1998 EDITION AVAILABLE FROM JOHN WILEY]

*Collier, David. *Collier's Rules for Desktop Design and Typography.* Wokingham, England: Addison-Wesley, 1991.

*De Vries, Mary A. *Internationally Yours: Writing and Communicating Successfully in Today's Global Marketplace.* Boston: Houghton Mifflin, 1994.

*Follett, Wilson. *Modern American Usage: A Guide.* New York: Hill & Wang, 1966. [REVISED EDITION PUBLISHED IN 1998]

Hart, Horace. *Hart's Rules for Compositors and Readers at the University Press, Oxford* (39th ed.). Oxford University Press, 1983. [CURRENTLY OUT OF STOCK]

*McArthur, Tom. *The Oxford Companion to the English Language.* New York: Oxford University Press, 1992.

*Moss, Norman. *British/American Language Dictionary: For More Effective Communication between Americans and Britons* (updated rev.). Lincolnwood, IL: National Textbook Company, 1991.

*Thompson, Della (Ed.). *The Concise Oxford Dictionary.* (9th ed.) Oxford: Clarendon Press, 1995.

*Tulloch, Sara. *The Oxford Dictionary of New Words.* Oxford: Oxford University Press, 1991.

Design & Production

Banks, Michael A., & Dibell, Ansen. *Word Processing Secrets for Writers.* Cincinnati: Writer's Digest, 1989. [CURRENTLY OUT OF PRINT]

Beach, Mark. *Getting It Printed* (rev. & updated ed.). Cincinnati, OH: North Light Books, F & W Publications, 1993.

Chicago Editorial Staff. *Chicago Guide to Preparing Electronic Manuscripts: For Authors & Publishers.* Chicago: The University of Chicago Press, 1987.

Craig, James. *Designing with Type: A Basic Course in Typography.* New York: Watson-Guptill, 1980.

Eckhardt, Robert C., Weibel, Robert, & Nace, Ted. *Desktop Publishing Secrets.* Berkeley, CA: Peachpit, 1992. [CURRENTLY OUT OF PRINT]

International Paper Staff. *Pocket Pal: A Graphic Arts Production Handbook* (17th ed.). Alexandria, VA: Printing Industries of America, 1997.

Parker, Roger C. *Looking Good in Print: A Guide to Basic Design for Desktop Publishing* (3rd ed.). Chapel Hill, NC: Ventana Press, 1993.

*White, Jan V. *Editing by Design: A Guide to Effective Word and Picture Communication for Editors and Designers.* New Providence, NJ: R.R. Bowker, 1982. [CURRENTLY OUT OF STOCK]

*White, Jan V. *Graphic Design for the Electronic Age: The Manual for Traditional and Desktop Publishing.* New York: Watson-Guptill, 1988.

*Williams, Robin. *The Mac is Not a Typewriter: A Style Manual for Creating Professional-level Type on Your Macintosh.* Berkeley, CA: Peachpit Press, 1990.

Williams, Robin. *The PC is Not a Typewriter: A Style Manual for Creating Professional-level Type on Your Personal Computer.* Berkeley, CA: Peachpit Press, 1992.

Editing Guides

Berner, R. Thomas. *The Process of Editing.* Boston: Allyn & Bacon, 1991. [CURRENTLY OUT OF STOCK]

*Boston, Bruce (Ed.). *STET!: Tricks of the Trade for Writers and Editors.* Alexandria, VA: EEI, 1986. [CURRENTLY OUT OF PRINT]

Boston, Bruce. *STET Again!: More Tricks of the Trade for Publications People: Selections from the Editorial Eye.* Alexandria, VA: EEI, 1996.

*Cook, Claire Kehrwald. *Line by Line: How to Improve Your Own Writing*. Boston: Houghton Mifflin, 1986.

Gross, Gerald (Ed.). *Editors on Editing: What Writers Should Know about What Editors Do* (rev. 3rd ed.). New York: Grove, 1993.

*Judd, Karen. *Copyediting: A Practical Guide* (2nd ed.). Menlo Park, CA: Crisp Publications, 1992.

*Lauchman, Richard. *Plain Style: Techniques for Simple, Concise, Emphatic Business Writing*. New York: AMACOM, 1993.

*Lindsell, Sheryl L. *Proofreading & Editing for Word Processors*. New York: Arco Publishing, 1985. [CURRENTLY OUT OF PRINT]

*O'Neill, Carol L., & Ruder, Avima. *The Complete Guide to Editorial Freelancing*. New York: Dodd, Mead & Company, 1974. [CURRENTLY OUT OF PRINT]

*Ross-Larson, Bruce. *Edit Yourself: A Manual for Everyone Who Works with Words*. Norton, 1985.

Stoughton, Mary. *Substance & Style: Instruction & Practice in Copyediting* (rev. ed.). Alexandria, VA: Editorial Experts, 1996.

Turabian, Kate L., Grossman, John, & Bennett, Alice. *A Manual for Writers of Term Papers, Theses, and Dissertations* (6th rev. ed.). Chicago: University of Chicago Press, 1996.

Grammar Guides

*Baugh, L. Sue. *Essentials of English Grammar: A Practical Guide to the Mastery of English* (2nd ed.). Lincolnwood, IL: National Textbook Company, 1994.

Booher, Dianna Daniels. *Good Grief, Good Grammar*. New York: Crest, 1989.

*Callihan, E.L. *Grammar for Journalists* (rev. ed.). Radnor, PA: Chilton Book Co., 1969. [CURRENTLY OUT OF PRINT]

Diamond, Harriet, & Dutwin, Phyllis. *English the Easy Way*. Woodbury, NY: Barron's Educational Series, 1996.

Floren, Joe. *Enough About Grammar: What Really Matters and What Really Doesn't* (2nd ed.). Wheaton, IL: Twain, 1992. [CURRENTLY OUT OF PRINT]

Gordon, Karen Elizabeth. *The Transitive Vampire: A Handbook of Grammar for the Innocent, the Eager, and the Doomed*. New York: Times Books, Random House, 1984.

Gordon, Karen Elizabeth. *The Well-Tempered Sentence: A Punctuation Handbook for the Innocent, the Eager, and the Doomed.* New Haven, CT: Ticknor & Fields,1983.

Montgomery, Michael, & Stratton, John. *The Writer's Hotline Handbook: A Guide to Good Usage and Effective Writing.* New York: New American Library, Dutton, 1981.

*O'Conner, Patricia T. *Woe Is I: The Grammarphobe's Guide to Better English in Plain English.* New York: Grosset/Putnam, G.P. Putnam's Sons, 1996.

Osborn, Patricia. *How Grammar Works: A Self-Teaching Guide.* New York: John Wiley & Sons, 1989.

*Pinckert, Robert C. *Pinckert's Practical Grammar: A Lively, Unintimidating Guide to Usage, Punctuation, and Style.* Cincinnati, OH: Writer's Digest Books, 1991. [CURRENTLY OUT OF PRINT]

*Safire, William. *Fumblerules: A Lighthearted Guide to Grammar and Good Usage.* New York: Dell Publishers Company, 1991. [CURRENTLY OUT OF PRINT]

*Shertzer, Margaret D. *The Elements of Grammar.* New York: Collier Books, Macmillan, 1996.

*Stilman, Anne. *Grammatically Correct: The Writer's Essential Guide to Punctuation, Spelling, Style, Usage and Grammar.* Cincinnati: Writer's Digest Books, 1997.

Non-Biased Language

*Dukes, Marilyn, & Poineau, Debbie. *Fact Sheet on Bias-Free Communication.* East Lansing, MI: Michigan State University, 1985.

*Goodwill Industries International. *People With Disabilities Terminology Guide.* [Brochure: Publication #5032.10]. Bethesda, MD: Goodwill Industries International, 1994.

*Maggio, Rosalie. *The Dictionary of Bias-Free Usage.* Phoenix, AZ: Oryx Press, 1991.

*Miller, Casey, & Swift, Kate. *The Handbook of Nonsexist Writing* (2nd ed.). New York: HarperCollins, 1992. [CURRENTLY OUT OF PRINT]

*Project on the Status and Education of Women. *Guide to Nonsexist Language.* Washington, DC: Association of American Colleges, 1986.

*Sorrels, Bobbye D. *The Nonsexist Communicator: Solving the Problems of Gender and Awkwardness in Modern English.* Englewood Cliffs, NJ: Prentice-Hall, 1983. [CURRENTLY OUT OF STOCK]

*South-Western Publishing Company. *Guidelines: Fair and Balanced Treatment of Minorities and Women.* [Booklet]. Cincinnati, OH: South-Western Publishing Company, 1976.

Writing Guides

*Alvarez, Joseph A. *The Elements of Technical Writing.* New York: Harcourt Brace Jovanovich, Inc., 1980. [CURRENTLY OUT OF PRINT]

Bates, Jefferson D. *Writing with Precision: How to Write So That You Cannot Possibly Be Misunderstood* (6th ed.). Lakewood, CO: Acropolis Books, 1993. [CURRENTLY OUT OF PRINT]

Bernstein, Theodore M. *The Careful Writer: A Modern Guide to English Usage.* New York: Atheneum, 1984. [CURRENTLY OUT OF STOCK]

*Bly, Robert W., & Blake, Gary. *The Elements of Technical Writing.* New York: Macmillan, 1995.

*Brusaw, Charles T., Alred, Gerald J., & Oliu, Walter E. *The Business Writer's Handbook* (5th ed.). New York: St. Martin's Press, 1997.

*Frank, Darlene. *Silicon English: Business Writing Tools for the Computer Age.* San Rafael, CA: Royall Press (P.O. Box 9022, San Rafael, CA 94912), 1985.

Hall, Donald, & Birkerts, Sven. *Writing Well* (9th ed.). White Plains, NY: Longman Publishing Group, 1997.

Hoover, Hardy. *Essentials for the Scientific and Technical Writer.* New York: Dover Publications, 1981.

*Ivers, Mitchell. *The Random House Guide to Good Writing.* New York: Random House, Ballantine Books, 1993.

Johnson, Edward D. *The Handbook of Good English* (rev. updated ed.). New York: Washington Square Press, Pocket Books, 1994.

*Pitrowski, Maryann V. *Re: Writing.* New York: HarperCollins, 1989.

*Venolia, Jan. *Rewrite Right!: How to Revise Your Way to Better Writing.* Berkeley, CA: Ten Speed Press, 1987.

*Venolia, Jan. *Write Right!: A Desktop Digest of Punctuation, Grammar and Style* (3rd ed.). Berkeley, CA: Ten Speed Press, 1995.

*Vrooman, Alan H. *Good Writing: An Informal Manual of Style.* New York: The Trustees of The Phillips Exeter Academy, 1967. [CURRENTLY OUT OF PRINT]

Weiss, Edmond H. *The Writing System for Engineers and Scientists.* Englewood Cliffs, NJ: Prentice-Hall, 1982. [CURRENTLY OUT OF PRINT]

Wiener, Harvey S., & Bazerman, Charles. *Writing Skills Handbook.* Boston: Houghton Mifflin, 1979.

Zinsser, William. *On Writing Well: An Informal Guide to Writing Non-fiction* (6th ed.). New York: HarperCollins, 1998.

Other Resources

Barnhart, Robert K. *The Barnhart Abbreviations Dictionary.* New York: John Wiley & Sons, 1995.

The Freelancer. [EXCELLENT BIMONTHLY NEWSLETTER OF THE EDITORIAL FREE-LANCERS ASSOCIATION; 71 WEST 23RD ST., STE. 1910, NEW YORK, NY 10010; 212/929-5400; HTTP://WWW.THE-EFA.ORG]

*Grover, Robert O. (Ed.). *U.S. News & World Report Stylebook: A Usage Guide for Writers and Editors* (8th ed.). Washington, DC: U.S. News & World Report, 1997.

*International Trademark Association. *Trademark Checklist.* New York: International Trademark Association, 1994.

*Polking, Kirk (Ed.). *Writer's Encyclopedia.* Cincinnati, OH: Writer's Digest Books, 1983.

*Protomastro, Mary Beth (Ed.). *Copy Editor: Language News for the Publishing Professional.* [EXCELLENT BIMONTHLY NEWSLETTER; P.O. BOX 604, ANSONIA STATION, NEW YORK, NY 10023-0604; 212/995-0112; HTTP://WWW.COPYEDITOR.COM]

*Sabin, William A. *The Gregg Reference Manual* (8th ed.). New York: Glencoe, McGraw-Hill, 1996.

*Shaw, Harry. *Dictionary of Problem Words and Expressions* (rev. ed.). New York: Pocket Books, Simon & Schuster, 1991.

*Stroman, J, & Wilson, K. *Administrative Assistant's and Secretary's Handbook.* New York: AMACOM, 1995.

*U.S. Trademark Association. *Trademarks: The Official Media Guide.* New York: U.S. Trademark Association, 1990.

Webster's New World Speller-Divider (2nd ed.) Old Tappan, NJ: Macmillan, 1992.

Glossary

abbreviation–a shortened form of a word or phrase used in place of its complete form. Three types of abbreviations include 1) basic abbreviations (clipped or truncated words, contracted words, hybridizations, and phonetic forms), 2) acronyms, and 3) initialisms.

absolute phrase–a phrase that modifies an entire sentence

abstract noun–a common noun that names an idea or quality that can't be perceived with the senses

acronym–an abbreviation consisting of the first letter or letters of the main parts of a compound word, usually excluding articles and prepositions. Acronyms are pronounced as words in their own right.

adjective–a word that compares, describes, emphasizes, or limits a noun or pronoun. Adjectives may be classified as comparisons, or descriptive, limiting, or predicate adjectives.

adverb–a word that affirms, compares, describes, introduces, joins, or negates a verb, adjective, or another adverb. Adverbs may be classified as affirmative or negative adverbs, comparisons, conjunctive or linking adverbs, expletives, or simple adverbs.

agreement–matching the case, gender, number, person, and tense of a subject and verb or a pronoun and its antecedent

antecedent–the noun to which a pronoun refers

arabic number–an "ordinary" number (1, 2, 3)

ascender–the upward stroke of a lowercase letter. Ascenders extend above the x-height or body of a letter (as in *b, d, f, h, k, l,* or *t*).

baseline–the imaginary line upon which characters sit, excluding their descenders

bold–heavy type used for emphasis

bullets–large dots, squares, or other symbols used to introduce items in a list

callouts–labels identifying individual areas or elements in a piece of art, or sequential numbers or letters assigned to items in a list

camera-ready copy (CRC)–the final master used for reproduction

cardinal number–the written form of a number (one, two, three)

case–the form of a pronoun that identifies it as the subject, object, or possessor. These forms are classified as the subjective (or nominative), objective, and possessive case.

clause–a group of words containing both a subject and a predicate. A clause may or may not form a complete thought.

closed punctuation–the punctuation scheme that favors more discretionary marks; sometimes called *formal, heavy,* or *traditional punctuation*

collective noun–a noun that names a group or collection of persons, places, things, ideas, or qualities

comma splice–a comma that incorrectly joins two independent clauses where a conjunction or semicolon should appear

common noun–a generic classification for a person, place, thing, idea, or quality. Three types of common nouns are abstract, concrete, and collective nouns.

complex sentences–a sentence containing two or more independent clauses

compound sentence–a sentence containing at least one dependent clause

compound-complex sentence–a sentence containing at least two independent clauses and at least one dependent clause

compound word–a combination of two or more words that express a single idea. Compounds may be hyphenated, solid (or closed), or split (or open).

concrete noun–a common noun that names an unspecified person, place, or thing that we can sense

Style Meister: The Quick-Reference Custom Style Guide

conjunction–a word that joins two or more words, phrases, clauses, or sentences, and reveals their relationship. Conjunctions may be classified as coordinate or subordinate conjunctions.

conjunctive adverb–an adverb that acts like a subordinate conjunction to join two clauses. Some examples include *also, anyhow, consequently,* and *however.*

contraction–a word in which an apostrophe represents a missing character or characters

coordinate conjunction–a word that joins two words or groups of words. Coordinate conjunctions may be correlative (*either–or, if–then, neither–nor*) or simple (*and, or, nor, but, yet, for*).

copy–*from an editing perspective:* text and headings; *from a production perspective:* anything that prints on the final page

demonstrative pronoun–a word that substitutes for the name or classification of a specific person, place, or thing (this, that, these, those)

dependent clause–a clause that does not form a complete thought on its own

descender–the downward stroke or "tail" of a lowercase letter that extends below the baseline (as in *g, j, p, q,* or *y*)

diacritical marks–accent marks (é, ç, ô, è, ü, ñ, and so on) that denote phonetic distinctions in many languages

direct object–a noun or pronoun that identifies the recipient or target of the action that the verb describes

distributive pronoun–an indefinite singular pronoun used to single out an individual or a pair from a group (each, either, neither)

down style capitalization–the capitalization scheme that favors lowercase letters whenever possible

em–a measurement equal to the width of a capital *M* in a given typeset point size

em dash–a long dash (indicated by a double dash in a manuscript). An em dash measures the width of one em.

en–a measurement one-half as wide as an em dash

en dash–a dash measuring the width of one en. En dashes are frequently used to separate ranges.

expletive–a word that fills a void but adds no meaning. Some examples include *it* and *there.*

first person–a pronoun that identifies the speaker. Examples include the singular forms, *I* (subjective), *me* (objective), and *my/mine* (possessive), and the plural forms, *we* (subjective), *us* (objective), and *our/ours* (possessive).

folio–a printed page number

font–all of the characters of one particular type family or style in the same point size

footer *or* **trailer**–copy that repeats at the bottom of each page

format–the physical appearance of a page and whatever appears on it

front matter *or* **preliminaries**–portions of a book that precede the main body. Examples include the title page; table of contents; lists of illustrations, tables, and abbreviations; foreword; and preface.

galley–a proof copy of the typeset text before it is divided and laid out into page proofs

gender–masculine or feminine; may reflect role expectations

gerund–a verbal form that ends in *–ing* and is used as a noun

gutter–the white space or margins on the inside edges of a two-page spread, or the space between columns

hard hyphen–a hyphen character that prints no matter where it falls in a line

header *or* **running head**–a block or line of information, such as a book or chapter title, that repeats at the tops of several pages in a document

homonym–a word that sounds like another word but has a different meaning

indefinite pronoun–a word that implies an antecedent, but does not specify one. Some examples include *any, anyone, each, either, every, everyone, everything, nobody, nothing, one, some,* and *someone.*

independent *or* **main clause**–a clause that forms a complete thought on its own

indirect object–answers the question, *To whom* or *To what*

infinitive–a verbal form preceded by the word *to* and used as an adjective, adverb, or noun

initial cap–a capitalized first letter in a word in which the other letters appear in lowercase

initialism–an abbreviation constructed like an acronym but pronounced as individual letters

intensive–a reflexive pronoun that emphasizes its subject

interjection–an exclamation or a word that expresses an emotion. Interjections may be classified as simple interjections (alas, oh) and compound or phrasal interjections (oh my).

interrogative pronoun–a pronoun used to introduce a question (who, which, what). These same words used in sentences other than questions are called relative pronouns.

intransitive verb–a verb that produces a clear meaning without a direct object

ISBN (International Standard Book Number)–the unique number assigned to each new book or new edition

italics–type with slanted letters (*italics*), indicated by underlines in a manuscript

justified–"squared up" or vertically aligned type

kern–the adjustment of letter spacing between adjacent letters to improve the optical spacing and overall look of the type

leader–a character, such as a series of dots, that precedes a tab

leading *or* **line spacing**–vertical spacing between lines of type; measured from baseline to baseline

linking verb *or* **auxiliary verb** *or* **helping verb**–a word that helps complete a verb and link the subject to its complement. Examples include forms of *be* and *do,* and forms that express mood, sensing, or tense.

live area–the portion of the page where the printed image appears

macro–a computerized sequence of keystrokes and/or commands. Once you've recorded a macro, you can activate it by pressing a single key or a key combination.

margin–the distance from the edge of the paper to where the printed image begins

menu–a list of commands a computer user can select from

modifier–an adjective or adverb or a clause or phrase that acts like one to affirm, compare, describe, emphasize, introduce, join, limit, or negate another word, clause, or phrase

mood–imperative (commanding or requesting), indicative (stating), interrogative (questioning), subjunctive (supposing)

nonrestrictive clause–a clause that presents additional information that's not necessary to complete the meaning of the sentence. Nonrestrictive clauses often start with *which.*

noun–a word that names or classifies a person, place, thing, idea, or quality. Nouns can be classified as common or proper nouns.

noun phrase–a group of words that acts like a noun

number–singular (one) or plural (more than one)

object–the part of a sentence that completes the sense of the predicate; that which the subject acts upon

objective case–the case used when the pronoun is the object. Use *me* (singular)/*us* (plural) for first person, *you* for second person, and *him, her, it, whom, whomever* (singular)/*them* (plural) for third.

open punctuation–the punctuation scheme that uses fewer discretionary marks; sometimes called *conversational, formal,* or *light* punctuation

ordinal–a number with a suffix that indicates its order (1st/first, 2nd/second, 3rd/third, and so on)

orphan–a single word or part of a word that falls at the top of a typeset page but ends the last paragraph on the preceding page

page proof–a proof copy that comes after the galley, when the text has been laid out into individual pages

participial phrase–a phrase in which the verb has a participial ending (*–d, –ed, –en, –ing, –n, –t*)

participle–a verbal form that ends in *–ing* (for present) or in *–d, –ed, –en, –n,* or *–t* (for past) and is used as an adjective

perfect tense–the verb tense that conveys that actions were, are, or will be completed (perfected). The perfect form combines a linking verb with a past participle. The past perfect uses *had.* The present perfect uses *has/have.* The future perfect uses *shall have/ will have.*

perfect progressive tense–the verb tense that combines the perfect and progressive tenses. The past perfect progressive form combines *had been* with a gerund form. The present perfect progressive form combines *has been/have been* with a gerund form. The future perfect progressive form combines *will have been* with a gerund form.

person–first (I, we), second (you), third (he, she, it, them)

personal pronoun–a word that substitutes for someone's name (I/me, you, he/him, she/her, it, we, they/them)

phrase–a group of related words that lacks either a subject or a predicate

pica–a standard measurement equal to 12 points. There are about six picas to an inch.

plural–a subject that relates to more than one person, place, thing, idea, or quality

point–a standard measurement for type size. One point equals .013837 inch. There are approximately 72 points in an inch.

possessive–the form of a noun or pronoun that reveals who or what possesses or owns something

possessive pronoun–a pronoun that identifies the possessor without using a proper name. Use *my/mine* (singular) and *our/ours* (plural) for first person, *your/yours* for second person, and *his, her, hers, its, whose* (singular) and *their/theirs* (plural) for third person.

predicate–the part of a sentence that completes what's being said about the subject. The predicate may consist of a verb or verb phrase and may also include modifiers and/or the object of the sentence.

preposition–a word that positions or shows the relationship between a noun and another word. Prepositions may be classified as simple and compound (or phrasal) prepositions.

prepositional phrase–a phrase that begins with a preposition

pronoun–a word that substitutes for a noun. Pronouns may be classified as demonstrative, indefinite, interrogative, personal, reciprocal, reflexive, or relative.

proper noun–a word that names a specific person, place, thing, idea, or quality

ragged–unjustified or unaligned type. Ragged-right type aligns at the left but not on the right; ragged-left type aligns on the right, but not on left.

reciprocal pronoun–a pronoun that combines *other* or *another* with an indefinite pronoun (each other, one another)

recto–right-hand page

reflexive pronoun–a personal pronoun that "reflects" its subject. Reflexive pronouns end in *-self* or *-selves* (myself, yourself, himself, herself, itself, ourselves, yourselves, themselves)

relative pronoun–a word that links a clause back to its antecedent. Some examples are *who, which,* and *that.*

restrictive clause–a clause that defines or restricts the word that precedes it. Restrictive clauses often start with *that.*

river–a distracting line of white space that flows vertically through a block of text

roman–plain, upright type

roman numeral–a number formed with a letter or combination of letters (I, II, III or i, ii, iii)

run-in head–a heading that appears on the same line as the text that follows it

run-on sentence–a sentence in which two or more independent clauses are joined without a conjunctive adverb or an appropriate punctuation mark

running head (see *header*)

sans serif–type without serifs

second person–a pronoun that identifies the person or thing spoken to. Examples include the forms, *you* (subjective/objective), *your/yours* (possessive). In the second person, both singular and plural forms are the same.

sentence fragment–a group of words that lacks either a subject or a predicate, or possibly both

serial comma–the comma before the conjunction that precedes the last item in a series of three or more items

serif–a small stroke at the end of a main letter stroke, ascender, or descender

sidebar–information that supplements a feature story; often boxed or screened or set in a contrasting font for visual separation

simple sentence–a group of words containing both a subject and a predicate and forming a complete thought

simple tense–the unembellished tense that relates a verb to the past, present, or future

singular–a subject that relates to one person, place, thing, idea, or quality

slug–a block of type containing typesetting information, such as company, operator, customer and/or job name; version number; date type was set or revised; and filename

small caps–capital letters whose vertical measurement equals the x-height of the lowercase letters in the same font

smart quotes–curly or slanted quotation marks, considered more professional than the straight quotation marks (") generally reserved to symbolize inches. When you use smart quotes, use smart (curly or slanted) apostrophes (') as well. Reserve straight apostrophes (') to symbolize feet.

soft hyphen–a hyphen that appears on a computer screen but does not print on the page unless it falls at the end of a line; sometimes called a *discretionary hyphen*

subjective *or* **nominative case**–the case used when the pronoun is the subject. Use *I* (singular)/*we* (plural) for first person, *you* for second person, and *he, she, it, who, whoever* (singular)/*them* (plural) for third person.

subordinate conjunction–a conjunction that joins and relates two or more words or groups of words, or reveals their relation-ship (*after, although, because, if, since, that, unless, where,* and so on)

tabs–indents of fixed widths from the left-hand margin; entered with the TAB key on a keyboard

tense–the form of a verb that relates to time. A verb's tense may be past, present, or future, each of which may be classified as simple, perfect, progressive, or perfect progressive.

third person–a pronoun that identifies the person or thing spo-ken of. Examples include the singular forms, *he/she/it/who/who-ever* (subjective), *him/her/it/whom/whomever* (objective), and *his/*

her/hers/its/whose, and the plural forms, *they* (subjective), *them* (objective), and *their/theirs* (possessive).

track–the adjustment of letter spacing throughout a specified range of characters or words to improve the optical spacing and overall look of the type

transitive verb–a verb that requires a direct object to complete its meaning

trim size–final page size

two-page spread–a set of left- and right-hand pages that face one another

type family *or* **type style**–variations of the same type style (bold, light, condensed, bold condensed, italic, oblique, etc.)

underscore–underline

up style capitalization–the capitalization scheme that favors initial caps for most "important" words

verb–a word that expresses an action or a state of being, and often relates it to the past, present, or future. Verbs can be classified as linking, transitive, and intransitive verbs.

verb phrase–a group of words that acts like a verb

verbal–a word that has a verb for a root and is used as another part of speech. Verbals may be classified as gerunds, infinitives, participles.

verso–left-hand page

white space–blank space, margins, or open areas on a page

widow–a single word or part of a word that appears alone on the last line of the last paragraph on a typeset page

word division–hyphenation at the end of a line used to indicate that a word continues from one line to another

word wrap–a word-processing feature that moves the text automatically from one line to the next without a return character at the end of each line

x-height–the height of a lowercase letter, excluding ascenders and descenders

Punctuation Marks & Signs & Symbols

& (ampersand)
′ (apostrophe)
@ (at sign)
[ ] (brackets)
¢ (cents sign)
: (colon)
, (comma)
© (copyright)
$ (dollar sign)

" " (double quotation marks)

. . . (ellipsis)
— (em dash)
– (en dash)
= (equals sign)
! (exclamation point)
′ (foot mark)
> (greater than sign)
- (hyphen)
″ (inch mark)
< (less than sign)
– (minus sign)
× (multiplication sign)
(number or pound)
( ) (parentheses)
% (percent)
. (period)
+ (plus sign)
? (question mark)
® (registered trade mark)
; (semicolon)
' ' (single quotation marks)
/ (slash)
(See *punctuation marks, signs & symbols,*
trademarks.)

A

a vs. *an* 61
abbreviating
    compass directions 165
    country names 161, 165
    days of the week 161
    eras 166
    initials 166
    measurements & rates 162, 166
    months 162
    religious titles 162, 168
    state names 163
    street names 164, 167
    time zones 167
    times of day 167
abbreviations
    acronyms 154, 168–169
    ampersands in 165
    basic 153–154, 168
    British 156–157, 172–173
    capitalizing 140, 155–156, 168
    defining for readers 158, 161
    format of 165–167
    in tables 164
    initialisms 154, 165
    Latin 162
    plural forms of 157–158, 169
    possessive forms of 157–158, 170
    punctuating 86, 156–157, 171–173
    recording styles for 12
    spacing of 157
    types of
    (See *abbreviations–basic, acronyms,*
     initialisms.)
    when to use 155
absolute phrases 19
acronyms 154, 168–169
addresses on envelopes 137

Feedback Form

Style Meister™: The Quick-Reference Custom Style Guide
(print edition, second printing)

In what ways was *Style Meister* most helpful to you?

What suggestions do you have for the next edition?

How did you hear about *Style Meister*?

___ Please send me information about the electronic edition of *Style Meister.*

___ Please add me to your mailing list.

Name _____

Company _____

Address _____

City _____ State _____ ZIP _____

Phone _____ Fax _____

E-mail _____

Castle Communications
P.O. Box 200255-358
Austin, Texas 78720